NV

Theodore Dwigh
American Anti-S

ALSO BY OWEN W. MUELDER

*The Underground Railroad in
Western Illinois* (McFarland, 2008)

Theodore Dwight Weld and the American Anti-Slavery Society

OWEN W. MUELDER

McFarland & Company, Inc., Publishers
Jefferson, North Carolina, and London

LIBRARY OF CONGRESS CATALOGUING-IN-PUBLICATION DATA

Muelder, Owen W., 1941–
    Theodore Dwight Weld and the American
Anti-Slavery Society / Owen W. Muelder.
      p.   cm.
    Includes bibliographical references and index.

    ISBN 978-0-7864-6396-1
    softcover : 50# alkaline paper ∞

    1. Weld, Theodore Dwight, 1803–1895. 2. Abolitionists —
United States — Biography. 3. Social reformers — United
States — Biography. 4. American Anti-Slavery Society —
History. 5. Antislavery movements — United States —
History —19th century. I. Title.
E449.W46M84 2011
326.092 — dc23
[B]   2011031200

BRITISH LIBRARY CATALOGUING DATA ARE AVAILABLE

Front cover: Wood engraving of Theodore Dwight Weld, 1885
(Library of Congress); cover design by David K. Landis (Shake It
Loose Graphics)

Manufactured in the United States of America

McFarland & Company, Inc., Publishers
  Box 611, Jefferson, North Carolina 28640
  www.mcfarlandpub.com

To John L. Myers

Table of Contents

They alone and single-handed fought the opening battles of a great war, which, although overshadowed and obscured by later and more dramatic events, were none-the-less gallantly waged and nobly won. It is customary to speak of our Civil War as a four years' conflict. It was really a thirty years' war, beginning when the pioneer Abolitionists entered the field and declared for a life-and-death struggle.
— John F. Hume, *Abolitionists*

Acknowledgments

Many individuals have generously given me their time in the course of the research and preparation for this book. Rodney O. Davis and Douglas L. Wilson, co-directors of the Knox College Lincoln Studies Center, offered many valuable suggestions and worthy criticism. Then president of Knox College, Roger L. Taylor, and the college's academic dean, Lawrence B. Breitborde, were supportive on several fronts. As always, librarians at Knox College were particularly helpful to me in numerous ways. These people include Jeff Douglas, Chief Librarian; Sharon R. Clayton, Associate Librarian; Jason L. Connell, Public Service Assistant Librarian; Anne Giffey, Assistant Librarian for Public Service; Mary Jo McAndrew, Senior Archives Assistant; Irene Ponce, Reader Service Technician; Carly Robison, Curator of Manuscripts and Archives; Laurie Sauer, Information Technologies Librarian; Heather Barrow Stafford, Assistant Librarian for Instructional Services; Kay Vandermullen, Special Collections Supervisor; and Student Librarian Sarah Miller. Knox College administrators, Peter Bailey and Vicki Romano, gave generously of their time as well. In addition, Knox College computer student technician Maxwell V. Galloway-Carson was very helpful.

I very much appreciate the encouragement given to me by Fergus M. Bordewich, who believes that a thorough examination of who comprised "Weld's Seventy" has never before been sufficiently addressed. I would also like to thank the founders and administrators of the National Abolition Hall of Fame. I am grateful to the Oberlin College Library Archives Department and archivists at the University of Michigan's Clement Library. I wish to thank Ron August, Jr., for sharing Weld family documents and materials.

I am most especially indebted to Emeritus Professor of History, State University of New York, Plattsburgh, John L. Myers. His comprehensive scholarship on the American Anti-Slavery Society agency system between 1833 and 1838 is unsurpassed. His willingness to elucidate different puzzles about certain members of the "Seventy" was invaluable. It was because I became familiar with his research that I was inspired to write this book.

I must call special attention to Nicole E. Henniger, my undergraduate student secretary, whose efforts were most beneficial. The contributions of my student secretary and research assistant, Laura Jorgenson, provided indispensable help to me in innumerable ways. Finally, and most importantly, I am indebted to my wife, Susan Hall Muelder, whose experience as an editor and journalist gave me help as a proofreader, wordsmith, and literary stylist.

Preface

One of the most important eras in our nation's history began at the end of the 1820s and extended throughout the 1830s as the United States witnessed the emergence of a remarkably well-organized effort to bring about the end of slavery in the nation. This was accomplished, to a great extent, by the formation of anti-slavery societies — nationally, regionally, and locally. During this time, men and women, both black and white, worked together in the first integrated social movement in American history. In this book I will address various aspects of the anti-slavery movement during this period, but will focus particular attention on the efforts of employed abolitionist agents.

American historians who have studied the history of the anti-slavery movement in our country during the nineteenth century have never been able to verify with absolute certainty the individuals who were recruited and hired by Theodore Dwight Weld in the mid–1830s to work as agents for the American Anti-Slavery Society. This group of people has come to be known as the "Seventy" or "Weld's Seventy." This book has been written primarily in an effort to report who the people were that comprised Weld's band. However, in order to appreciate the work these people did and the kinds of activities they were engaged in, the reader needs to have a basic understanding of the history of the abolitionist movement in America before 1840 and also become familiar with the workings of the American Anti-Slavery Society.

Chapters 1 and 2 will give the reader a general understanding of why the American Anti-Slavery Society was established and also examine the society's leadership, goals, and operation until it split apart in 1840. In addition, these chapters will address other important aspects of the abolitionist movement during the 1830s and discuss in detail the remarkably important contributions that Theodore Dwight Weld and his band of agents made to the anti-slavery crusade at that time.

Chapter 3 is a compilation of the people who I believe comprised Weld's group of agents. Members of Weld's Seventy are identified, along with information indicating where the agents came from, in what regions of the nation they carried out their work, and, in many cases, what became of these agents in their later lives. The third chapter also mentions individuals who some historians believe were members of Weld's band about whom questions remain regarding their inclusion in the listing of the Seventy. The reader will discover that it is probable that we will never know with absolute confidence who all of the people were in Weld's band and why I believe I have established a list of men and women who are the most likely abolitionists to have belonged to the Seventy.

Chapter 4 includes written accounts about slavery put down by some members of the Seventy that demonstrate the kinds of stories they almost certainly must have told while delivering their lectures and Chapter 5 discusses members of the Seventy who were actively involved with the operation of the Underground Railroad.

The appendices includes songs, poems, letters, reminiscences and tributes having to do with the anti-slavery movement in the 1830s, as well as two founding documents of the Society.

Introduction

When the framers of our country's constitution were hammering out various compromises between the Northern and Southern colonies in order to launch our nation, both regions realized that the United States would not be established unless slavery was allowed to continue to exist. Historian Howard Zinn succinctly described what happened at the Constitutional Convention in regard to the settlement of the economic wishes of the colonies:

> The Constitution was a compromise between slaveholding interests of the South and moneyed interests of the North. For the purpose of uniting the thirteen states into one great market for commerce, the northern delegates wanted laws regulating interstate commerce, and urged that such laws require only a majority of Congress to pass. The South agreed to this, in return for allowing the trade in slaves to continue for twenty years before being outlawed.[1]

The new American Republic, a federal union, freed southern states from being interfered with by the national government regarding the institution of human bondage and set the stage for slavery's expansion westward. Consequently, for the next several decades of our nation's history, anti-slavery advocates had to face the fact that the emancipation of slaves in the United States would be an extremely difficult thing to accomplish. With the 1793 patenting of the cotton gin by Eli Whitney (a machine actually conceived and made to function properly by Catherine Greene), cotton became the most important product in the nation. Thereafter, cotton's cultivation and production, expanded by the gain in potential cotton acreage from the Louisiana Purchase, and achieved by means of slave labor, became the basis of America's expanding economic wealth. This made the task of those trying to abolish human bondage even more difficult. By 1830, the number of slaves in America had climbed to approximately 2,000,000, from just under 700,000 in 1790. As this was happening, enormous amounts of Southern capital were invested in slave labor. Between 1830 and the beginning of the Civil War, the enslaved in the United States ranked as the second most valuable capital investment, outstripped only by land.[2]

In the last three decades of the eighteenth century, anti-slavery organizations were formed in several colonies and states. In 1794, the representatives of anti-slavery organizations from seven states met in Philadelphia where they agreed to appeal to state legislatures to abolish slavery and they also called for an immediate end to the slave trade. During this early era of the anti-slavery movement, including the first few decades of the nineteenth century, there were also several individuals whose courageous abolitionist efforts were significant. This group of early anti-slavery advocates included George Bourne, Elizabeth Chandler, James Forten, Benjamin Franklin, Isaac Hopper, Benjamin Lundy, Lucretia Mott, Charles Osborn, Thomas Paine, David Rice, Benjamin Rush, and David Walker.

In the late 1820s, the slavery issue exploded upon the national scene. This occurred when Congress passed the Tariff Law of 1828, which Southerners called the "Tariff of Abominations." New Englanders, unhappy with British wool being "dumped" on U.S. markets, managed to get this legislation passed with the help of Western congressmen. Southerners were sure that their agricultural products would face increased taxes in foreign ports when their goods were sent abroad. The tariff legislation represented the core concern Southern planters had during the Constitutional Convention when they registered their fears of a strong central government regulating commerce in ways that might ultimately be unfavorable to their interests. Southern congressmen also complained that a disproportionate amount of income from tariffs was spent on Northern internal improvements.

South Carolinians, led by John C. Calhoun, threatened secession; but President Jackson let it be known he would use federal troops to block such action. In 1832, South Carolina announced in its Ordinance of Nullification that the Tariff Act was "null, void, and no law, not binding upon this state." Jackson said it was impossible to believe that a state could remain in the Union but only abide by laws it defined as constitutional. Calhoun was so displeased with Jackson and his Northern adversaries that he resigned as vice-president on December 28, 1832. Earlier that month, President Jackson dispatched seven small ships and a man of war to Charleston harbor with orders to be ready for engagement. But in 1833, Henry Clay stepped forward with a compromise plan proposing that duties on certain goods remain high, but others should be gradually reduced. Clay's plan was agreed to, and this controversy simmered down; but the shadow of the slavery issue still loomed.

At about the same time, as Congress was struggling to settle its dispute over the Tariff of 1828, the anti-slavery movement in the United States developed a new approach. In the past, anti-slavery organizations tried to induce people to act harmoniously; but in the 1830s, a group of dedicated men and women decided to orchestrate their attack on the institution of slavery in a way and to a degree that had never happened before in the United States. As their efforts took shape in the 1830s, their fellow countrymen came to realize that these abolitionists were conducting their crusade with righteous militance.

Lewis Tappan, one of the most dedicated members of this new abolitionist clan, admitted that some of these crusaders were occasionally "indiscrete, and sometimes rash, both in language and measure," but "considering the opposition they met and the false statements uttered respecting their principles and measures, rarely has any reform been conducted with more discretion."[3] They utilized strategies of mass media mailing campaigns (journals, newspapers, pamphlets, etc.) and bypassed normally deferred to individuals and institutions of authority. Because of the intensified efforts by Northern abolitionists, there was, not surprisingly, a fierce outcry from Southerners. In 1836, South Carolina Congressman James H. Hammond, on the floor of the House of Representatives, proposed the option of murdering abolitionists:

> And I warn the abolitionists, ignorant, infatuated, barbarians as they are, that if chance shall throw any of them into our hands, he may expect a felon's death. No human law, no human influence, can arrest his fate... death and desolation pronounce his doom.[4]

One characteristic these new kinds of abolitionists exhibited from the beginning, despite facing real adversity, was an unshakable confidence that they would ultimately succeed. Many abolitionists were called radicals, fanatics, and extremists, but as these upholders of equal rights for enslaved people moved ahead with their efforts in the mid '30s and into the 1840s and 1850s, the overwhelming majority of them steadfastly resisted any appeals for violence. In 1852, abolitionist Wendell Phelps said, "On that point [violent tactics], I am willing to wait. I can be patient...the cause of three millions of slaves...must proceed slowly, and like every other change in public sentiment, we must wait patiently for it."[5]

Looking back now, we can see that what abolitionists started in the 1830s marked the beginning of the end of slavery in North America. No greater praise for the extent to which abolitionists understood and foresaw the importance of what the denial of equal rights meant to American society has been expressed than this observation by historian James M. McPherson:

> Although slavery was finally abolished, the abolitionist's racial equalitarianism was ahead of its time. Not until the twentieth century was the validity of the abolitionist argument confirmed. The history of our own time has demonstrated that the abolitionists had perhaps a deeper understanding of the racial problem than any other men of their time — and many of ours.[6]

In the 1830s, one specific group of remarkable anti-slavery men and women were associated with the American Anti-Slavery Society. By late 1836, this band of people came to be called the Seventy; its leader was Theodore Dwight Weld. Most of these crusaders were young to middle aged. The attribute that best characterizes all of these people was their shared virtue of courage. Over the course of the last two hundred years, few Americans have been willing, on a daily basis, to defend an unpopular idea knowing full well that the consequences would be facing vicious verbal insults and frequent attempts to physically bring them to their knees. Yet, this was an understood given for membership in the "Seventy." These abolitionist orators repeatedly left their home states and regularly ventured into hostile and unfamiliar cities and rural hamlets. There were no lines of support in place to give them aid other than that received from local anti-slavery comrades. The policy of police and law-enforcement officers was more often than not refusal to respond to the violence perpetrated against them. Nevertheless, in the face of all these obstacles, these abolitionists persevered. They believed that their mission was to complete the unfulfilled goals made by America's leaders during the Revolutionary War — namely to establish a society where liberty and freedom would be granted to all individuals, including the enslaved.[7]

British aristocrat Frederick Marryat in *A Diary in America*, an account of his traveling throughout North America in 1837 and 1838, took particular note of the growing influence of abolitionism in the United States by the end of the decade. He also foresaw the overwhelming impact that abolitionists would have on the nation's future:

> Examining into the question of emancipation in America, the first inquiry will be how far this consummation is likely to be effected by means of the abolitionists...It appears...that slavery can only be abolished by the slave state itself in which it exists; and it is not very probable that any class of people will voluntarily make themselves beggars by surrendering up their whole property to satisfy the clamour of a part. That this [abolitionist] party is strong, and is daily becoming stronger, is very true...There is one point to which I have not yet adverted, which is, whether the question of emancipation is likely to produce a separation between the northern and southern states? The only reply that can be given is that it entirely depends upon whether the abolition party can be held in check by the federal government. That the federal government will do its utmost there can be no doubt, but the federal government is not so powerful as many of the societies formed in America, and especially the Abolition Society, which every day adds to its members...In England people have no idea of the fanaticism displayed and excitement created in these societies, which are a peculiar feature in the states, and arising from the nature of their institutions. Their strength and perseverance are such that they bear down all before them, and, regardless of all consequences, they may eventually control the government.[8]

By 1840, these abolitionist crusaders had managed to expose many regions of the North to understanding what the poisonous damage of slavery meant to America. They had also forced the controversial topic of human bondage to be openly discussed and debated. It would take another twenty-five years before the enslaved were free, but the work of these people had created the momentum that ultimately led to emancipation.

Chapter 1

The Abolitionist Movement in the 1830s

And the Establishment of the American Anti-Slavery Society

As the anti-slavery movement began to cohere and move into its crusading era in the 1830s, it witnessed the emergence of numerous anti-slavery societies including a national body. In 1831 in New York City, a small collection of individuals started to put together teachings of moral idealism and philosophical concepts that had their roots in theology and the Enlightenment. The men who initially organized this effort were Lewis Tappan,[1] George Bourne,[2] Joshua Levitt,[3] Simeon Jocelyn,[4] William Goodell,[5] and Theodore Dwight Weld. For two years they designed and planned a national anti-slavery organization.[6] In December of 1833, at the urging of William Lloyd Garrison, the American Anti-Slavery Society (AASS) was officially established in Philadelphia. This organization's national offices, however, were located in New York City.[7]

William Lloyd Garrison, a native of Massachusetts, was the son of a heavy drinking father who abandoned the family when William was a boy. The young Garrison grew up poor, was raised by his mother and foster parents, and had a limited formal education. He learned typesetting, and after serving as an apprentice, he became a writer and editor for his hometown newspaper the *Newburyport Herald*. By 1825, he had become a reform-oriented journalist. Garrison met Quaker anti-slavery advocate Benjamin Lundy in 1828, and thereafter embraced the cause of the slave. Garrison worked with Lundy on the latter's *Genius of Universal Emancipation* and helped redesign the journal's layout. Lundy, one of the early giants of the anti-slavery crusade, published his *Genius* off and on from 1821 until his death in Illinois in 1839.

Lundy's periodical was published for a time in Baltimore, and while working with him there, Garrison was once jailed for seven weeks. He had been accused of committing libel when he wrote a "scathing" attack on Francis Todd, describing Todd as the owner of a slave trading vessel.[8] The *Genius* supported gradual emancipation, but by the early 1830s, Garrison had adopted the concept of immediate emancipation, which ended his relationship with Lundy.[9]

Sixty-two individuals attended the organizational meeting of the American Anti-Slavery Society, and two-thirds of its delegates were Congregationalists, Presbyterians, and Quakers. Theodore Weld was invited to the meeting, but he was unable to make the long trip back East from Ohio; however, he replied that my "heart is with you."[10] The gathering included four women, the most notable among them being Lucretia Mott,[11] who was invited to address the assemblage.[12] Three African Americans were in attendance — James G. Barbadoes, James McCrummill, and Robert Purvis.[13] The new national organization welcomed four black auxiliary societies into its membership by 1834. However, blacks were never fully admitted to the highest level of partnership or decision making in the AASS.[14] The majority of the delegates at the Philadelphia meeting were merchants, clergymen, students, and educators, but there were no statesmen. The participants met in a building that belonged to a black benevolent organization,[15] and a guard was posted at the front door to keep protesters from breaking up the proceeding. On one occasion during the gathering, the hostile crowd, loitering outside the building, grew so ugly the delegates decided not to adjourn for lunch.

Beriah Green, then president of the biracial Oneida Institute in New York, was made chair of the meeting when the delegates gathered together on the morning of the first session. It was Green who wisely reminded the delegates towards the end of the convention that the very establishment of the AASS meant a "storm and tempest will rise" and each member should "prepare for the worst."[16] Garrison was selected to draft the document that would represent the framework of what the new society stood for, and

Arthur Tappan (*The Life of Arthur Tappan* by Lewis Tappan, Cambridge, Hurd and Houghton, 1871).

he worked through the night before he finished the Declaration of Sentiments. The attendees discussed Garrison's draft the next day, but some alterations were made to his wording before the declaration was adopted; the most notable changes were suggested by Samuel J. May and John Greenleaf Whittier.

The heart of this document was a call for the immediate emancipation of slaves with specific emphasis on not reimbursing slaveholders for giving up their human property. The proceedings also included the drafting of a constitution, the announcement of support for a new petition campaign against slavery in the District of Columbia, a statement favoring a commitment to buying products made from free labor,[17] an agreement to formally establish affiliate groups, and an expression of the society's wish to preserve an alliance with abolitionists in Great Britain.[18] Lewis Tappan's brother, Arthur, was selected as the society's first president.[19]

The constitution of the American Anti-Slavery Society laid down these objectives:

> The object of this Society is the entire abolition of slavery in the United States. While it admits that each State in which slavery exists, has, by the Constitution of the United States, the exclusive right to *legislate* in regard to its abolition in said State, it shall aim to convince all our fellow-citizens, by arguments addressed to their understandings and consciences, that slaveholding is a heinous crime in the sight of God, and that the duty, safety, and best interests of all concerned, require its *immediate abandonment*, without expatriation. The Society will also endeavor, in a constitutional way, to influence Congress to put an end to the domestic slave trade, and to abolish slavery in all those portions of our common country which come under its control, especially in the District of Columbia — and likewise to prevent the extension of it to any State that may be hereafter admitted to the Union.
>
> The Society shall aim to elevate the character and condition of people of color, by encouraging their intellectual, moral, and religious improvement, and by removing public prejudice, that thus they may, according to their intellectual and moral worth, share an equality with the whites, of civil and religious privileges; but this Society will never, in any way, countenance the oppressed in vindicating their rights by resorting to physical force.[20]

The founders of the AASS were careful to disassociate themselves from endorsing physical violence in order to achieve their goals. They understood that any suggestion of physical coercion might send a signal to the enslaved that they would be justified in staging slave revolts. Nat Turner's murderous slave rebellion in Virginia in 1831 sent waves of fear through every slave state, but it also caused anxiety in the minds of many Northerners. Turner and a group of slaves who joined him had moved across the Virginia countryside murdering whites until their insurrection was put down by the state militia.

The American Anti-Slavery Society's campaign would be restricted to a war of words. Conversely, as the majority of abolitionists denounced violence, numerous anti-abolitionists often resorted to assault, battery, and even murder. Garrison was dragged through the streets of Boston by ruffians in 1835; and in the spring of 1836, Weld's ally, Dr. David Nelson, who had tried to establish a school in Missouri, was mobbed and forced to flee into Illinois. In 1837, American Anti-Slavery Society agent Jonathan Blanchard was stoned on the streets of Harrisburg, Pennsylvania; and that same year, Elijah P. Lovejoy,[21] an abolitionist newspaperman in Alton, Illinois, across the Mississippi River from St. Louis, was shot to death. Lovejoy's murder gave the anti-slavery movement a martyr and prompted John Greenleaf Whittier[22] to remark, "The cause is progressing ... I want no better evidence of it than the rabid violence of our enemies."[23]

Even when anti-abolitionists only limited their behavior to noisy interruptions of public speeches delivered by anti-slavery lecturers, their conduct often angered people in the audience who simply wanted to hear what these speakers had to say. Abolitionists deliberately drew attention to these kinds of unruly disruptions, showing that proslavery troublemakers were defying the principles of free speech and assembly. Many Northerners who decided to listen to an anti-slavery lecture or simply wanted to attend a meeting of individuals discussing the possible organization of a local anti-slavery society, resented the attempt of individuals who were denying them the opportunity to hear an open discussion of the subject. Indeed, attacks upon abolitionist speakers did, under some circumstances, rally support from people who were outraged at the way these crusaders were treated. Mob violence was overwhelmingly conducted at the very time that abolitionists were in the midst of trying to organize local auxiliaries.[24] Although some groups of rabid attackers formed spontaneously, more often than not, most mobs were organized beforehand. Spur-of-the-moment attackers were more likely composed of lower-class citizens whose actions were usually unpremeditated.[25]

The men who established the American Anti-Slavery Society were devout Christians who lent support to various other benevolent reform movements. Most abolitionists keenly recognized that clergymen were of critical importance to shaping public opinion. They believed that "ministers are the hinges of [a] community."[26] Abolitionists frequently raised concerns about slavery in the United States with ministers and church elders with whom they were familiar. They asked pastors to insert prayers for slaves into their Sunday services and to call attention to upcoming anti-slavery meetings. Abolitionists also made sure they were represented at church conferences and conventions. Advocates for emancipation sometimes used churches as meeting places, and their attacks against human bondage usually had a theological basis with a theme emphasizing the sin of slavery.[27] When the anti-slavery movement was crystallizing in the 1830s, it was, according to historian Robert Fogel, "a crusade in several senses." Fogel described its intensity thus:

> It was a militant and uncompromising war against slavery; it was a holy war, inspired by the deep religious convictions of its leaders... It was a crusade also in the sense that revivalist campaigns were crusades. The abolitionists wanted to save the souls of free people, the souls of their hearers, by bringing them to the realization that slavery was the vilest of all American sins, which corrupted not only the slaveholders but all those who countenanced the continuation of slavery, no matter how innocent their reason for doing so. Using all the methods of revivalism developed during the Second Great Awakening, the leaders of the new abolitionist movement sought to save Christians who failed to realize that no matter how pious they were in other respects, their immortal souls were stained and jeopardized by their complicity with slavery. They sought to reach especially the masses of Northerners who accepted the legitimacy of slavery or were indifferent to it, and to convert them, in the religious sense.[28]

Most of the men who sustained the abolitionist cause in the 1830s did not use elaborately constructed arguments or complicated philosophical ideas, but instead tried to effectively persuade listeners by means of evangelical techniques.[29]

Historian John R. McKivigan has tabulated the religious affiliations of the AASS leadership. Congregationalists and Presbyterians constituted almost half of the national society's officials between 1833 and 1840. Quakers, who played a significant role in the American Anti-Slavery Society during its establishment in 1833, saw their influence gradually decline. Quakers constituted nearly one-fifth of all AASS officials when the organization was founded, but that percentage dropped to only one-eighth by the end of the decade. The decline of Quakers within the AASS leadership can be partially explained by the fact that by the late 1830s many of that faith had drifted away from those abolitionists whose tactics and language seemed too extreme, intemperate, and rash.[30] During the first seven years of the national organization's existence, not a single Roman Catholic or Lutheran was an official of the AASS.[31] The Roman Catholic Church took a proslavery position in the South and a neutral stance in the North. But the Irish Catholic press throughout the North was critical of abolitionists and warned its readers that their efforts would bring down the Union.[32] Catholic and Episcopalian bishops did not allow their priests to take part in abolitionist activities.[33]

Before the AASS was founded, four denominations had joined in 1826 to establish the American Home Missionary Society (AHMS) to help create congregations on the frontier. This society, made up of Congregationalists, Presbyterians, Dutch Reformed, and Associate Reformed Churches, provided financial support for these denominations in Western settlements. By 1837, there were 146 missionary agents working for the American Home Missionary Society in Ohio, Michigan, Indiana, Illinois, and Wisconsin.[34] Despite the fact that the AHMS assumed a neutral or "noninterference" policy on the slavery question, many of the society's northern agents were abolitionists. Lewis Tappan was a very generous supporter of the American Home Missionary Society. In the 1830s, several ministers connected to the AHMS sent strongly worded requests to the society's directors urging them to change their neutral position on slavery; and in the 1840s, the society did cease to appoint slaveholding missionaries.[35] In 1857, the American Home Missionary Society officially adopted an anti-slavery stance.

It should be recognized, however, that strong ties existed between powerful economic forces and numerous organized religions throughout the United States that rejected the work of abolitionists. In fact, the overwhelming majority of religious leaders were not moved to join the anti-slavery crusade. Cotton was already "King" in America by the 1830s, and those who advocated anti-slavery principles were threatening the growth of the wealth cotton generated in the nation. Slavery directly and indirectly created enormous profits to both Southern planters and the owners of textile mills and shipping companies in the North. New York City functioned as the broker of cotton throughout the world. Therefore, there were large numbers of wealthy people in New England, New York, and New Jersey who did not want to see slaves emancipated. Slavery was one of the basic building blocks of New England's economic structure.

Beyond its wealthy merchants, other classes of Northeastern society benefited from the existence of human bondage in the South, like tanners, coopers, sailmakers, ropemakers, textile mill workers, sailors, craftsmen of ivory products, and insurers. Ships from Northern cities transported cotton to numerous European ports, but they also carried manufactured goods from New England to the South. These imports represented many times the dollar value of goods the North exported to Europe.[36] Wealthy Southerners lavishly spent money in the North. They sent their children to Northern schools, their wives shopped in Northern stores, men gambled at Northern racetracks, and families slept in the best hotels.[37]

Religious denominations, particularly Baptists, Methodists, Anglicans, Lutherans, and some Presbyterians and Congregationalists were not eager to denounce supporters of slavery who attended their churches and gave Southern and Northern clergymen their financial support. Ministers in all parts of the country were afraid that condemnation of slavery would drive some of their parishioners from their houses of worship. The lack of enthusiasm for anti-slavery advocacy by the majority of America's clergy was one of the greatest disappointments to abolitionists.[38]

Weld and the abolitionist Grimke sisters, Angelina and Sarah, accused pastors who showed weakness on the slavery question of "truckling subserviency to power ... and clinging with mendicant sycophancy to the skirts of wealth and influence."[39] Nonetheless, according to historian Gilbert H. Barnes, "from the beginning, the movement had been inextricably bound up with churches." Indeed, Barnes believed that religion was at the heart of the crusade:

> The churches were its forums and the homes of its local organizations; from the churches it drew its justifying inspiration. It was an aspect of the churches, non-sectarian in organization but evangelical in character — a part of the benevolent empire. Everywhere in the organization clergymen were in control. Even in Garrison's own New England Anti-Slavery Society, clergymen composed nearly two thirds of the delegates in a typical session of 1835. In every aspect, the agitation was "a moral movement — a religious movement" drawing its life from the churches.[40]

The reforming "pioneer abolitionists" of the 1830s assumed that everything that involved humankind was part of "the province of Christianity," and therefore, as agents of God, they were required to abolish slavery.[41]

The second, third, and fourth decades of the 1800s witnessed sweeping changes in the character of the United States. The nation's wealth increased rapidly, as did its population, due to gradual immigration of Europeans that was spurred by the devastation and unemployment left in the wake of the Napoleonic Wars. Americans also experienced a decline in mortality rates and an increase in birth rates.[42] But the new American republic also experienced a remarkable expansion of its democratic and political institutions that included several social reforms. Abolitionism was most certainly one of these reform movements; but others included efforts to expand educational opportunities, the women's rights movement, establishment of peace societies, improving the rights of sailors on the high seas, and attempts to improve conditions in prisons and insane asylums.

Another major reform effort for social change was the temperance movement that helped establish a model for political activism in the United States. Most temperance advocates believed that habitual drinking fostered drunkenness that in turn increased the likelihood of crime and poverty. Others pointed out that drinking stymied rational behavior, frequently led to violence against women and children, often destroyed families, and represented the ultimate expression of a craving for self-gratification. Temperance proponents called for total abstinence from the consumption of alcoholic beverages, and they believed that by doing so, individuals demonstrated sound morals and self-control. By 1810, 2 percent of all Americans' income was spent on liquor.[43] John Adams drank hard cider each morning and James Madison usually consumed a pint of whiskey every day.[44] Between 1790 and 1820, the "consumption of distilled spirits was climbing rapidly ... rising from two and a half gallons per person per year in 1790 to almost five gallons in 1820 ... an amount [that] nearly [triples] today's consumption."[45] Many people distilled their own alcoholic beverages at home.

Thousands of anti-slavery advocates attached themselves to the temperance movement[46] but in the South support for the movement was much more moderate "because of its connection to abolitionism."[47] Frederick Marryat, an English traveler to the United States in the late 1830s, wrote this about America's staggering addiction to liquor. They drank, he said, to "close a bargain ... they quarrel in their drink, and they make up with drink. They drink because it is hot; they drink because it is cold.... They drink early in the morning, they leave off at night; they commence it early in life, and they continue it until they soon drop into the grave."[48] Numerous issues of the anti-slavery publication, *Friend of Man*, had one or more notices announcing Temperance meetings or stories supporting the principles of Temperance. But at the forefront of the temperance movement and all other social change organizations was the ferment associated with the religious revivalism of the Second Great Awakening. Evangelical religion began to sweep across America in the early 1800s, but this crusade vastly expanded in the early 1820s.

All of these reform movements employed similar means of conversion. Among the methods these organizations used and improved upon were:

1. The establishment of a national organization or society with a clearly stated and understood object of purpose and enumerated goals.

2. The creation of an executive committee, with a president, officers, corresponding secretary, and an agency committee that directed the work of employed agents, who were sent into the field with instructions to enlist members and organize state and local auxiliaries.

3. The conducting of an annual national anniversary meeting in order to renew acquaintances, share ideas, review goals, and announce new programs.

4. The establishment of an ongoing fundraising body in order to sustain the Society's finances for projects, publications, salaries, and other needs.

5. The maintenance of a publication program for the printing of pamphlets, tracts, almanacs, newspapers, and journals for widespread distribution.

6. The encouragement of agents sent into communities to sustain their conversion efforts for lengthy periods of time that would often last for days and sometimes weeks until success was achieved.[49]

It was not by chance that the American Anti-Slavery Society was established in 1833, for that same year England acted to abolish slavery throughout the British Empire, though this was, in fact, accomplished gradually.[50] This action had an immediate and profound effect on the United States, for it forced the American press and public at large to recognize that the "slavery issue" was not going to disappear. John Quincy Adams believed that emancipation throughout the Empire could, "prove an earthquake on this [American] continent."[51]

An additional result of England making slavery illegal was the collapse of the American Colonization Society (ACS), which had been established in 1816. The ACS had promoted the idea that by raising money and receiving grants from the federal government, slaves could be purchased, freed, and resettled in Africa. Some Southerners supported the American Colonization Society movement because it gave them a way to get rid of free blacks living in their states. Many Americans in all parts of the country genuinely believed then that blacks and whites would never be able to find a way of living together in an integrated society. But the American Colonization Society's impractical ideas were doomed to failure from the beginning. The precepts of the ACS were never popular with free blacks. Historian Ira Berlin points out that after the Revolutionary War, African Americans increasingly felt that America was their home. "This sense of place was represented in every aspect of African life. The region between the Atlantic and the Alleghenies had become home."[52] The Colonization Society's plans barely got off the ground, and only managed to send fewer than 4,000 immigrants to Liberia "during its first twenty years of activity."[53]

One of the fundamental differences between colonizationists and radical abolitionists was their vision for the future of America's social structure. The abolitionists foresaw a new America, where, in time, blacks and whites would live comfortably with each other. Most abolitionists bitterly decried the American Colonization Society's efforts as shallow and little more than salve for a guilty conscience. Garrison said in 1832, "I look upon the overthrow of the Colonization Society as the overthrow of slavery itself—they both stand or fall together."[54] In the spring of 1833, Arthur Tappan, who only months later would be presiding as the head of the American Anti-Slavery Society, wrote a letter to Lewis Laine explaining that even though he had once been "one of [the colonizationists] warmest friends," he now believed that the ACS "had its origins in the single motive to get rid of free colored people" and "the Society will be regarded in its true character, and be deserted by every one, who wishes to see a speedy end put to slavery in this land of boasted freedom."[55]

Before the founding of the American Anti-Slavery Society, the New England Anti-Slavery Society (NEASS) was established in 1832 in Boston. William L. Garrison, who began publishing his vehemently anti-slavery newspaper *The Liberator* in 1831, was the driving force behind the creation of the New England Anti-Slavery Society. The notorious reputation of *The Liberator* was largely spread by its anti-abolitionist detractors. In the South, Garrison came to be the most despised individual associated with the abolitionist campaign. His wife Helen, a dedicated abolitionist crusader herself, lived in fear that she would someday learn that Garrison had been kidnapped and taken to Georgia.[56]

One of Garrison's ablest allies in helping to establish the NEASS was Samuel J. May, a Harvard graduate and Unitarian minister. In the course of his career, May filled ministerial posts in Connecticut, Massachusetts, and New York. He later served as vice-president of the AASS, was for a time one of the national society's agents, and was actively involved with the Underground Railroad. May once recalled delivering a speech on a Sunday night when he heard "hideous outcries — yells and screeches [from the crowd] ... I persisted in speaking for a few minutes ... but presently, a heavy stone broke through one of the blinds, scattered a pane of glass, and fell upon the head of a lady sitting near the center of the hall. She uttered a shriek and fell bleeding upon the floor."[57] May was a leading figure in the abolitionist movement for decades who steadfastly advocated pacifism.

William Lloyd Garrison (*The Anti-Slavery Crusade* by Jesse Macy, New Haven, Yale University Press, 1920).

The NEASS selected Quaker businessman Arnold Buffun as its first president. Buffun — a man of decided intellect, a sheepherder, inventor, and land speculator — was one of the first men put into the field as an anti-slavery agent. According to the first annual report of the NEASS, there were, in addition to the New England Anti-Slavery Society, only three other organizations like itself to be found anywhere in the nation. However, just one year later, twelve were established in Massachusetts, seven in Maine, six in Vermont and Ohio, five in New York, four in Connecticut, two in Pennsylvania, and one each in New Hampshire and Illinois.[58] The New England Anti-Slavery Society exerted much of its energy towards defeating the efforts of the American Colonization Society. The society also addressed the issue of segregated schools and attempted to help young blacks procure apprenticeships in the skilled trades. The New England Society had a modest beginning, but its membership gradually grew, and in 1835, the organization changed its name to the Massachusetts Anti-Slavery Society.[59] A good number of the New England Anti-Slavery Society's members eventually became deeply involved with the efforts of the American Anti-Slavery Society.

Women's anti-slavery organizations were also established throughout the 1830s. From Maine to Ohio, these female anti-slavery societies sponsored lectures, raised money, and circulated abolitionist literature. The first such society was formed by women in Salem, Massachusetts, in 1832. This organization was composed of black women, and their Constitution stated in part:

> We, the undersigned, females of color, of the commonwealth of Massachusetts being duly convinced of the importance of union and morality, have associated ourselves together for our mutual improvement, and to promote the welfare of our color, as far as consistent with the means of this Society, therefore we adopt the following resolutions.
>
> Resolved, That this Society be supported by voluntary contributions, a part to be appropriated for the purchasing of books, &c.: the other to be reserved until a sufficient sum be accumulated, which shall then be deposited in a bank for the relief of the needy.
>
> Resolved, That the meetings of this Society shall commence and conclude with prayer and singing. Any member who wishes to speak, is allowed the privilege: when any member speaks, there shall be no interruption.[60]

The women's societies in Boston, Philadelphia, and New York were particularly active, and the Boston and Pennsylvania female anti-slavery societies included black women. All of these organizations sponsored sewing bees and fairs, and the funds they brought in were given to state anti-slavery societies and the American Anti-Slavery Society. While the AASS was being formally organized in December of 1833, there were six female anti-slavery societies already in existence. The men's national society very much encouraged women to form additional female societies.[61] In Ohio, nine female anti-slavery societies were organized by the end of 1836.[62]

Women abolitionists faced mob violence just as their male counterparts did. In 1835, women attending a Boston FASS meeting had to endure verbal insults and thrown objects, and at another gathering of female abolitionists in Concord, Massachusetts, women needed to dodge "stones, rotten eggs, and other missiles."[63]

In 1837, many of these local societies helped establish the National Convention of Anti-Slavery Women. These women held their first meeting in New York City from May 9 to May 12. Approximately 10 percent of the women in attendance were black. There were no men present at this assemblage of women, who met in a church on the corner of Houston and Thompson Street. Some two hundred women from nine states elected Bostonian

Mary Anne Parker as the president of the new national women's anti-slavery organization.[64] Sarah Grimke was selected as one of six vice-presidents and Angelina Grimke was made one of four secretaries.[65] The convention passed a resolution introduced by Angelina calling for women to utilize "her pen, her purse, her influence, and her example to overthrow the horrible system of American slavery."[66] One of their primary successes was planning and organizing anti-slavery petition campaigns.

In May of 1838, the newly built Pennsylvania Hall was dedicated to hold office space and a meeting place for abolitionists. John Greenleaf Whittier was asked to read a poem as part of the official dedication ceremonies. When the women's national society held its second annual meeting at the hall a few days later, a mob broke into the building in the midst of the organization's deliberations. Angelina Grimke was one of the speakers when the rioting occurred. In order to protect black delegates, white women exited the hall with their African American sisters arm in arm while enduring angry insults and thrown rocks. The next day the riotous mob returned to Pennsylvania Hall and burned the structure to the ground. However, the women's abolitionist efforts persisted. In 1838, the number of women's auxiliary societies in Massachusetts had increased steadily; and in February of that year, Angelina Grimke wrote, "We abolitionist women are turning the world upside down."[67]

By the end of the decade, remarkably effective women crusaders for the abolitionist cause emerged. Throughout the 1840s and 1850s, the voice of anti-slavery women, particularly in the Middle West, had a tremendous impact on abolitionism in the nation. Among these women were Maria Weston Chapman, Lydia Maria Child, Betsy Mix Cowles, Laura Smith Haviland, Sarah Mapps Douglass, Lucretia Mott, Abby Kelley Foster, Elizabeth Cady Stanton, Maria Miller Stewart, Lucy Wright, and the Grimke sisters, Angelina and Sarah.

The official organ of the American Anti-Slavery Society was their newspaper, the *Emancipator*. When the AASS selected Joshua Leavitt to edit the *Emancipator* in 1837, its quality improved substantially. Leavitt was an imposing, confident, and forthright individual who associated himself with a wide variety of social reforms. He skillfully selected articles that combined educating its readers with persuasively constructed arguments against slavery. The paper cost its subscribers two dollars a year.

The American Anti-Slavery Society also had other publications, the most important of which were the monthly journal, *Human Rights*, and a children's magazine, *The Slave's Friend*.[68] The society's leadership realized that the indoctrination of the nation's youth was crucial, so the national society encouraged schools to have their anti-slavery literature on their library shelves. In 1837, AASS agent Henry C. Wright wrote, "It has long been a settled truth with me, that if we would regenerate and save this world, we must direct our efforts to children."[69] *The Slave's Friend* included songs and abolitionist poems, and the publication encouraged its young readers to gather contributions for the anti-slavery cause.

In 1836, the national society started publishing the *American Anti-Slavery Almanac*, which used pictures to illustrate the suffering of slaves. Local societies were told by the AASS executive committee to sell the almanacs for six cents each, but the branch auxiliaries were given permission to give leftover copies away free. In the mid–30s, the AASS started publishing the *American Anti-Slavery Examiner*. This publication, issued irregularly, was a series of monographs. All of these publications were made possible by the use of new steam-powered presses that drastically cut the expenses of printing.

The abolitionists were fortunate to have several talented journalists in their midst. Charles B. Bell, James G. Birney, Samuel Cornish, William L. Garrison, Joseph Horace Kimball, Joshua Levitt, Elijah P. Lovejoy, Benjamin Lundy, David Ruggles, and Henry B. Stanton were among the most notable. Abolitionists, anti-abolitionists, and even people who were neutral or relatively disinterested in the slavery issue were interested in reading about runaway slaves, attacks on abolitionist speakers, and stories about the slaves' lives. Newspapers helped mold the public opinion of all social classes, and by the 1830s, they had become the lifeblood of the republic. These journals informed people about court hearings and anti-slavery meetings, and they gave their readers the opportunity to express their own opinions by submitting letters to the editor. Newspapers were usually sold for six cents; and in 1833, the first penny newspapers (penny press) appeared. The public's desire for news was so great that it was not uncommon for a person to read more than one newspaper each day from cover to cover. Garrison said that they were "scattered over the land like raindrops," and gave voice to freedom's cause.[70]

The AASS received financial support solicited from various groups, state and local anti-slavery societies, and small contributors. These modest funds were collected from auxiliary societies from across the country and sent to the national society's office in New York City. Approximately 15 percent of the American Anti-Slavery Society's contributions came from African Americans.[71] Wealthy abolitionists were also an incredibly important source of significant revenues. The two most important financial subscribers were Arthur and Lewis Tappan. Before the national society was a year old, Arthur Tappan had donated $2,750 to the AASS.[72]

Wealthy New York philanthropist and abolitionist Gerrit Smith was another very generous supporter of the national society. Smith decided to join the American Anti-Slavery Society in 1835 because he had observed abolitionists in New York being mobbed in Utica as they attempted to organize a state anti-slavery society. Smith was elected president of the New York Anti-Slavery Society in 1836 and was a trustee of the anti-slavery Oneida Institute in upstate New York. The AASS was also aided by work gratuitously carried out by numerous men and women across the North. The society's agents, for instance, were usually given free room and board in the communities where they lectured.[73]

The AASS targeted Independence Day as a perfect date to solicit funds. The national society passed a resolution on May 28, 1834, calling on all auxiliaries to "hold public meetings on each Fourth of July; that meetings of the friends of the cause be held throughout our country on that day, and that we earnestly request that collections be then taken up in aid of the funds of the American Anti-Slavery Society."[74]

The American Anti-Slavery Society was organized prematurely by men who were not quite ready to launch a national society in 1833; but that year saw William L. Garrison return to the United States from England, where he was hailed as America's leading abolitionist.[75] Garrison, something of a free-lance agitator, leveraged his prominence at that time by insisting that the establishment of the AASS take place in December. It was clear to many abolitionists, even then, that Garrison was going to offend a good number of anti-slavery leaders by demanding that the movement follow his uncompromising dictates. The society's organizers acquiesced, met on short notice, and, for the most part, they were only able to attract Easterners to the meeting.[76] The Declaration of Sentiments they drew up was hastily written, but at the society's first annual meeting in May of 1834, their goals were stated more clearly, and there was a better geographical representation of abolitionists from across the North.[77]

During the 1834 annual meeting of the AASS, young men from the Lane Seminary in Cincinnati presented an impressive report on the dramatic consequences of anti-slavery debates held a few months earlier that resulted in the conversion of almost all of the school's students to the abolitionist cause. Following the convention, the national society decided to concentrate its resources on mailing anti-slavery literature and pamphlets throughout the states, and this campaign was accelerated the next year. The society's corresponding secretary announced that the AASS was "making arrangements with all possible expedition to use the press on a larger scale."[78] The national society also hired several agents to give abolitionist lectures and to encourage the establishment of local anti-slavery societies.

When the national organization was started, the AASS leadership was dominated by New York abolitionists who were leery of Garrison's radicalism and the extremism of many of his loyal allies from Boston. Garrison was placed on the national organization's executive committee but assigned to the minor position of secretary for foreign correspondence. He continued to spend the bulk of his time and energy to *The Liberator*, and initially accepted a secondary role with the national society.[79] Garrison and his camp did not have the conformity of religious backgrounds that Tappan's group had in New York. Garrison's followers included Quakers, Orthodox Congregationalists, Unitarians, and some Transcendentalists. His Boston constituency was made up of individuals who were more liberal in their religious points of view, and as a group, they could be a feisty lot.[80] Historian George Frederickson aptly articulated the basic division between the Tappan brothers' New York-based abolitionist operators and Garrison's more radical Massachusetts followers:

> Lewis Tappan, the wealthy New Yorker who financed many abolitionist activities, wrote anxiously to George Thompson, the British abolitionist: "The fact need not be concealed from you that several emancipationists so disapprove of the harsh, and, as they think, the unchristian language of *The Liberator*, that they do not feel justified in upholding it." This, in general, was the feeling of the Executive Committee of the American Anti-Slavery Society in the early years of the movement. Undoubtedly, the Society itself was not diverted from its aim of abolishing slavery because of Garrison's immoderation; they were concerned lest others be alienated.[81]

Garrison and his band of abolitionists attempted to bring about the emancipation of slaves by means of harsh attacks and abrasive accusations. They didn't hesitate to alienate their opponents by stinging their adversaries with intemperate insults. The New York-Ohio Wing of the anti-slavery movement, of which Weld was a part, instead employed methods of conversion. They tried to persuade their adversaries and readers by presenting compelling examples, personal testimonies, historical precedents, statistical analysis, and logical comparisons. Both groups agitated and used appeals to conscience and high principle. There were many individuals in both camps who used both tactics; but for the most part, Garrisonians would goad while Weldites would entreat.[82]

The AASS had a shaky beginning in the mid–1830s. It was difficult to convince the average American that slaves should be emancipated then or at any time in the future. Reactions to the efforts of the AASS were overwhelmingly negative. A proslavery spirit predominated Northern thinking and the vast majority of all Americans reviled the expression of abolitionist ideas. Lewis Tappan's house was burned and the Tappan brothers found it necessary to employ armed men to protect their store from being vandalized and destroyed. Most newspapers condemned the society's leaders as dangerous troublemakers, businessmen predicted that the nation's economy would be severely damaged if slaves were freed, and on numerous occasions, lecturers for the national society were attacked and mobbed. During July of 1834 in

New York City, rioters damaged, looted, and burned black schools, businesses, churches, and homes.[83]

By 1837, the General Association of Connecticut had grown so upset with anti-slavery crusaders they agreed to exclude abolitionists from Congregational Church pulpits.[84] Connecticut's reaction to the work of abolitionists was particularly negative and this was due to a significant degree to the quantity of ivory imported into the state. In the 19th century, the opportunity to bring music into numerous American homes and churches required the construction of pianos made with ivory keys. Piano keys had previously been made of wood, which warped, cracked, and stuck; but ivory keys were smooth and moved fluidly. As more and more people in America were able to improve their standards of living, pianos came to be particularly valued, and they were also something of a status symbol. In North America, by the middle of the nineteenth century, as many as three hundred thousand pianos were constructed in one year.

In order to meet the demand for ivory, exporters of this product slaughtered untold numbers of elephants in Africa. The tusks were torn from the elephants and carried to East African ports by slaves, and clipper ships took the ivory to Europe and New England.[85] Connecticut became the primary importer of ivory in North America. When the ivory arrived in Connecticut, powerful windsaws were used, which cut an entire piano keyboard from a single tusk. The scraps of ivory were used to make canes, pipes, knife handles, billiard balls, fans, cameos, carved animals, and inlays for decorative furniture. By 1840, a ton of ivory was cut up each week in Connecticut. Slavery now also served the nation's aesthetic lifestyle.

When the AASS was founded, Democrat Andrew Jackson was serving his second term in the White House, and the national society's progress was also stymied by the nation's seventh President. Jackson was a slaveholding anti-abolitionist who loathed the men who put the national organization on its feet, so much so he once delivered an unfettered attack against abolitionists in his annual message to Congress. He called for "severe penalties" to put down the "unconstitutional activities" of abolitionists. Although Jackson's name has long been linked to the triumph of democracy for the general populace, that certainly did not include blacks, women, or, for that matter, Native Americans. When the American Anti-Slavery Society's publications were not distributed throughout the South, usually because the materials had been destroyed by local postmasters, Jackson ignored this affront to federal authority and refused to demand an end to these actions.

This is not to suggest that abolitionists were tolerated by most Whigs. The majority of Northern Whigs labeled abolitionists as "crackpots" and "incendiaries."[86] Although some Whigs were willing to abide anti-slavery crusaders, many others "stoned abolitionists, demolished black churches, and razed black districts ... both parties, it could be argued, supported slavery."[87] The nation's two most powerful political parties were, not surprisingly, wedded to white male voters. Abolitionist historian Merton Dillon asserts, "When anti-slavery Whigs and Democrats were elected, as happened on a few occasions, they could accomplish little for the anti-slavery cause. If they made the attempt, they soon were confronted with party discipline and the demand for party regularity."[88] When hard-core abolitionists went to the polls in the 1830s, they usually felt that both parties' candidates were unacceptable choices.

The American Anti-Slavery Society's firm position that slaveholders should not be reimbursed for freeing their slaves left their field agents with no room to compromise. This meant that AASS agents confronted the difficult task of convincing their fellow citizens to relinquish something central to most American's value system — namely people's strong belief in the right of personal ownership, the right to keep whatever they had financially invested in, the right to private property. Even if a person listening to an anti-slavery speaker recognized the inherent wrong of one person holding another person in bondage or agreed that slavery seemed to contradict the core tenants of Christ's teaching, the vast majority of Americans could not bring themselves to believe that slaveholders should be required to give up what they legally owned for nothing.

Even so, between late 1835 and 1838, the American Anti-Slavery Society experienced higher degrees of success. The national organization continued to use an anti-slavery mailing program, but at its annual meeting in May of 1836, it reduced this effort considerably because this approach had only limited success.[89] Nonetheless, the AASS mailing campaign did stir widespread controversy throughout the South. Historian Lacy K. Ford has described the reaction to the campaign as bordering on "apoplexy." These anti-slavery publications caused "an overwhelming majority of southern whites ... to suppress anti-slavery sentiment," and their literature was viewed as "nothing short of a terrorist attack."[90] John C. Calhoun insisted that the real intention of the American Anti-Slavery Society, by sending its literature into the South, was to instigate slave insurrections. In 1835, a Georgia statute approved the death penalty for individuals found guilty of publishing anything that would cause slaves to revolt.[91] Ironically, Southern whites' reaction to abolitionist writings resulted in their restricting their own freedom of speech and in censorship of themselves.[92]

However, the American Anti-Slavery Society's most effective efforts in the North came about after it employed a larger number of agents as abolitionist lecturers and organizers of local anti-slavery societies. This strategy, also decided upon at the 1836 national gathering, contributed significantly to convincing some Americans to oppose slavery, or at least recognize that the institution of slavery must cease to exist at some point in the future.[93] As agents spread the abolitionist message, they managed at the very least, to inspire a debate on slavery on a national scale. These agents unleashed attacks on slavery with a fury and voice that harkened back to speeches reminiscent of Samuel Adams and Patrick Henry in Revolutionary times. Each agent helped create numerous anti-slavery organizations throughout New England and across the nation's mid-northern states.[94] But mob attacks against these orators continuously took place in both urban and rural settings.

By the mid–1830s, free northern African Americans were starting to form vigilance committees to help prevent kidnapping of blacks and to provide aid to fugitive slaves. Historian Benjamin Quarles maintains that these committees represented "the greatest" of all black self-defense organizations.[95] The help given included shelter, food, medical attention, and clothing, to say nothing of psychological support. The creation of these committees also helped galvanize support, to a degree, for the anti-slavery cause in urban areas. David Ruggles[96] was the leading force behind the establishment of the New York Vigilance Committee in 1835. On two occasions, kidnappers tried to abduct Ruggles himself, who openly confronted slave catchers, frequently demanded that city officials grant trials to blacks, and also sought out lawyers to give African Americans legal aid. In addition, Ruggles courageously helped support efforts to track down people who had gone missing.

In 1836, Robert Purvis[97] established a similar committee in Philadelphia, and other Northern cities organized vigilance committees as well. Purvis worked closely with William and Letitia Still in Philadelphia. Later, William Still was secretary of the Vigilance Committee in the city, and he was one of the most important Underground Railroad operators in the North. He housed fugitive slaves, helped them send messages to relatives, and sometimes arranged reunions.[98] Black abolitionist Theodore S. Wright, who served on the Executive Committee of the AASS from 1833 to 1840, did not hesitate to point out that these committees were necessary because the national society did not devote sufficient attention to the plight of fugitive slaves nor to the problem of kidnapping.

One measure of the degree to which abolitionists were starting to affect public policy decisions in the mid–1830s was their influence on the debate surrounding bringing Texas into the Union after the Lone Star State became a republic in 1836. Many Americans feared that admitting Texas as a new state might invite war with Mexico. The Independence of Texas had not been acknowledged by Mexico. Another powerful voice against such action came from Northerners who opposed admitting a new slave state, thereby increasing Southern strength in Congress. Abolitionist Benjamin Lundy published two pamphlets, *The Origins and True Causes of the Texas Insurrection* and *The War in Texas*, that accused Southerners of wishing to carve "five or six states" out of Texas.[99] John Quincy Adams delivered such strong denunciations in the U.S. House of Representatives against making Texas a state it helped to force President Jackson to break away from supporting annexation in order to avoid fracturing the Democratic Party. Abolitionists included anti–Texas themes in their petitions to Congress, and when Democrat Martin van Buren became President, he also decided to stand against the admission of Texas[100] so as to not "jeopardize the strength of the party in the North."[101] It was also the case that the foes of annexation were able to leverage the nation's financial collapse in 1837 as a warning against how a war with Mexico would drain an already shrinking national treasury.

In 1838, Texas withdrew its application for admission into the Union. The Mexican War did not start until the spring of 1846, but from the late 1830s until open hostilities erupted, some members of the very young American Labor Movement viewed the South's proslavery agenda in the Southwest with suspicion. When the New England Workingman's Association met in Boston in 1846, they announced their opposition to the War. Even before the fighting broke out, many rank and file laborers demonstrated in Northern cities against letting Texas become a state "unless provisions were made for the extinction of slavery in her borders."[102] When Texas finally joined the Union, abolitionists asserted that its admission only proved what they had been arguing for years — the United States government was basically corrupted by its subservience to slave holders.

An additional manifestation of the impact of the abolitionist movement in the 1830s was the decision by more Americans to involve themselves with the operation of the Underground Railroad. Although fugitive slaves had received support during their flights to freedom before the '30s, many more northern whites joined free blacks in providing assistance after the AASS was established by attaching themselves to the UGRR. Freedom seekers headed out of the nation's slave states in every direction: across the Caribbean Sea, into Mexico, and as far west as California. But by 1840, a remarkable network of northern "conductors" was giving aid and providing safe havens for fugitive slaves from Maine to Nebraska. Northerners who joined the Underground Railroad movement were moving beyond vocal criticisms of slavery by taking the more dangerous step of actually breaking the law in their opposition to human bondage. Those who gave help to hunted fugitives faced heavy penalties, meted out by both the federal and state statutes. Nothing galled slaveholders more than the protection fugitives were given by Underground Railroad agents. The American Anti-Slavery Society's satellite societies across the North helped establish much of the structure of the UGRR network.

Women's contributions to the success of the Underground Railroad were significant. Historian Jesse Macy maintains, "Women were not a whit behind men in their devotion to the cause of freedom."[103] By the middle of the 19th century, black and white women were central to every operational aspect of the Underground Railroad, from raising funds to feeding and clothing freedom seekers. The city of Philadelphia, where many women were deeply committed to abolitionism, was a particularly important UGRR center. Fugitive slaves moved out of the Philadelphia to New York, and then headed northward, staying close to the course of the Hudson River. Escape routes followed by freedom seekers also snaked along the Connecticut River Valley, extended through the regions of Lake Champlain, and stretched into the whole of northern New England.[104] Highways to freedom crisscrossed Pennsylvania, moved through all parts of Ohio, spanned eastern and central Indiana, and ranged across western Illinois.

Southerners frequently attacked abolitionist leaders for helping to create an atmosphere that encouraged the violation of the country's Fugitive Slave Law. Most Underground Railroad agents were secretive about their nefarious activity, which was usually carried out surreptitiously involving only family members and trusted friends. The majority of Underground Railroad "conductors" did not even discuss the aid they gave to freedom seekers with their children, and they never spoke to strangers about it, fearing retribution and bounty hunters seeking rewards. But a small number of operators actually flaunted the aid they gave to African American freedom seekers, and by so doing they enraged supporters of slavery in both the South and North. One such audacious Underground Railroad conductor was American Anti-Slavery Society agent John Cross. After working for the national society in the East, he moved to the Middle West where he became a professed Underground Railroad activist. His efforts resulted in helping numerous freedom seekers find refuge in Northern states and Canada.[105]

The Abolitionist Movement and the Underground Railroad were not synchronized. There were UGRR station masters who were not affiliated with any Abolitionist Societies, and in turn there were individuals who joined anti-slavery organizations but refused to break the law by aiding fugitive slaves. But nonetheless, the two movements were closely intertwined. UGRR historian Fergus Bordewich has observed:

> The two networks existed, however, in a symbiotic relationship, with the societies serving as a fertile recruiting ground for clandestine activists, and the Underground Railroad in turn supplying abolitionist lecture halls and fund-raisers with a steady stream of flesh-and-blood fugitives, who, like figments come to life from the nation's collective nightmare, were living proof of slavery's inhumanity.[106]

The decline of the American Anti-Slavery Society's influence came about quickly when the national society began to unravel towards the end of the 1830s. By then, as historian Stacey Robertson observes, it was "divided into separate, competing organizations. Little middle ground remained."[107] A number of things had occurred by the end of the decade that made this almost inevitable. First of all, William Lloyd Garrison had by then alienated almost every clergyman who was associated with the national society. In 1836, Garrison's *Liberator* was espousing intolerance of any church or minister that did not uphold his anti-slavery ideals. The Methodist Church was described as a "cage of unclean birds;" the Congregationalists were "foes of god and man;" the Presbyterian Church was called an "anathema."[108]

In addition, Garrison was at the same time denouncing the United States Constitution. The Constitution was, he said, an "atrocious compromise ... a libel of democracy ... stained with blood." It was, Garrison announced, an "agreement with hell."[109] He completely disassociated himself with any point of view that wished to take the abolitionist movement in a political direction, but by then many members of the AASS had concluded that "moral suasion" was not, in fact, the most effective way to fight slavery. They were calling for the anti-slavery movement to become political and work within the bounds of the nation's legal system. Many of these individuals concluded that moral arguments simply would not compel conscience stricken slaveholders to free their bondsmen. By 1839, Lewis Tappan had decided that abolitionists should be thinking in terms of "party, party, party" as the "watchword" because "moral questions are lost sight of too frequently."[110] Garrison and his followers overwhelmingly rejected this notion.[111] Taking the crusade in a political direction, they said, would be a farce dooming it to failure on the slippery slope of compromise.[112]

A third important influence that led to the demise of the American Anti-Slavery Society was the growing desire of state and local anti-slavery societies to fund their own efforts and take care of their own affairs. They increasingly rejected the idea that they needed the direction of a national organization, and this had the effect of decentralizing the national society. Numerous local societies expressed a desire to raise funds for their own organizations and not send money to the national office. This was in large part a result of the economic hardships experienced throughout the United States brought about by the "Panic of '37." The American Anti-Slavery Society's funds were shrinking dramatically.[113] In early November of 1839, only three years after the American Anti-Slavery Society had swelled its number of agents to nearly seventy lecturers, the national society was forced to inform their last twenty agents that they could no longer pay their salaries.[114]

The fourth, and the most important reason for the virtual collapse of the American Anti-Slavery Society was the so-called "Women's Question."

During the early phases of the anti-slavery crusade, many men had spoken for women, but they never allowed women to speak for themselves at meetings. Among the first women to do so were the Grimke sisters. Sarah and Angelina Grimke moved to Philadelphia from the home of their aristocratic, slave-holding parents in South Carolina, and once there, they both became Quakers and were touched by the reforming spirit. While living in Philadelphia, Angelina Grimke was introduced to *The Liberator*, and she started reading pamphlets published by the American Anti-Slavery Society. In 1836, she wrote *An Appeal to the Christian Women of the South*, which called for an end to slavery. That same year Sarah Grimke published *Epistle to the Clergy of the Southern States* that enraged Southerners to the point that Charleston author-ities instructed police to arrest her if she ever attempted to return to her native state. These publications by the sisters were banned by postmasters in the South, but in the North they put both women in the spotlight.[115]

In December of 1836, the Grimke sisters attended a training session for American Anti-Slavery Society agents in New York; and following this con-vention, both women started lecturing publicly against slavery. They were without question remarkably powerful speakers who inspired audiences lis-tening to their abolitionist lectures. Their speeches in 1837 were delivered throughout New England to mixed audiences of men and women. On numer-ous occasions, very large crowds turned out to hear them speak; but they were always dogged by anti–abolitionists during their speaking tour. A third of a century later, Wendell Phillips said:

> No man who remembers 1837 and its lowering clouds will deny that there was hardly any contribution to the anti-slavery movement greater or more impressive than the crusade of the Grimke sisters through New England states.[116]

But during the course of these lectures, the Grimke sisters also received harsh criticism from numerous men for their decision to deliver public lec-tures. Indeed, some women, like Catherine Beecher, joined the chorus of those decrying these appearances. Before the Grimke sisters started their lec-turing tour, many leading American abolitionists did not hesitate to point out that slavery in the United States clearly contradicted the basic message of equality and liberty articulated in the Declaration of Independence. But after the sisters' popularity grew and parallels started to be drawn between women's second-class citizenship in the nation and the status of slaves, numerous abo-litionists stopped making reference to the Declaration. Influential clergymen came down hard on the Grimke sisters for their unorthodox conduct, and they complained that their public presentations challenged Biblical references to a woman's place in society. The sisters appearance in church pulpits, they said, was a violation of church decorum.[117] The Congregational Church condemned female public behavior as "unnatural" in their 1837 Pastoral Letter. Angelina responded to her critics by saying:

> We cannot push Abolitionism forward with all our might until we take up the stumbling block out of the road... If we surrender the right to speak in public this year, we might surrender the right to petition next year, and the right to write the year after, and so on. What then can woman do for the slave, when she herself is under the feet of man and shamed into silence?[118]

Sarah Grimke responded to the ministers thus:

> The Lord Jesus defines the duties of his followers in his Sermon on the Mount... Men and women are Created Equal! They are both moral and accountable beings, and whatever is *right* for men to do, is right for women.[119]

A Pandora's box had been opened by the Grimke sisters' success that divided the abolitionist movement thereafter.[120] William L. Garrison and most of his comrades supported the sisters. Theodore Weld and others represented a third position in this controversy. They supported "abolitionists who favored sex equality." But they "believed that issue ought to be played down so as to enable the movement to recruit the many people who were ready for abolitionism but not yet enlightened enough to accept women's rights."[121] The individuals who took this third view thought that once people took up the slaves' cause, they would be inclined later to embrace a broader attitude towards

Angelina Grimke Weld (courtesy Massachusetts Historical Society).

Sarah M. Grimke (courtesy Massachusetts Historical Society).

human rights. But there is no question that Weld emphatically defended the Grimkes' right to speak before "promiscuous assemblies."[122]

The Grimke sisters letters to Weld in late 1837 clearly show the extent to which the women had been worn down and fallen into poor health due to all of the controversies they had endured that year:

Sarah Grimke to Weld — November 7, 1837
Dear Brother Weld,
    I have only time to say that we have concluded to pass the winter here [Boston]. We hope it is a right conclusion. A. is sick with a slight fever owing to over exertion. I do not know when she will be fit for service again.
                                                              Thy Sister, S.M. Grimke

Sarah Grimke to Jane Smith — November 8, 1837
    ...On last first day evening Angelina lectured at Kingham. We had had a most fatiguing week previously and were much worn, but hoped by keeping entirely quiet all first day that she might get thro.' I wanted her much to let me lecture instead of her, but as I tried it on the preceding 6th day and found my breast weak, she would not consent. She spoke an hour and twenty minutes, and then had to leave her lecture unfinished being too much exhausted to proceed. She had a fever-ish night; the next morning we came 15 miles in the stage to Boston; as soon as we arrived she went to bed but set up all the morning yesterday and part of the morn'g and afternoon today. She has fever every day and considerable head ache, but as I believe it is the result of over exertion, I hope that rest will restore her...
                                                          Thine in tender love, S.M. Grimke

Sarah and Angelina Grimke to Weld — November 30, 1837
    ...It was delightful after 5 months of constant traveling and lecturing to feel all my responsibilities rolled off at once and to stretch myself on my bed of ease and be too sick and yet without any pain to do anything. I was downstairs for the first time today... Farewell in love of the Lord and the bond of the slave.
                                                                              A.E. Ge[123]

By the end of 1837, exhausted and tense, the sisters decided to step away from the lectern.[124] In the spring of 1839, Abby Kelley visited the Grimke sisters and was astonished to discover the extent to which Angelina's health had been broken. Kelly shared the following impression of what she found in a letter to Anne Warren Weston:

I went there with a determination to rebuke them severely for absenting them-selves from the N.Y. meetings, but found to my own mortification that I had passed judgment before examining the witnesses. Angelina is truly very feeble. Their opinion is, that her labors in lecturing were altogether too great for a con-stitution naturally very slender and that she will never recover from it. Shock. Then last winter she applied herself too closely in assisting to get out "Slavery as it is," which has entirely prostrated her physical as well as mental energies. How many changes have come over "the spirit of her dream." *Look at her history.* Sarah did not think it proper for her to leave A under such circumstances, as they expected much company and as A exerted herself far too much in order to keep up *appearances* when in company.[125]

The sisters resumed lecturing again in early 1838 but stopped speaking publicly altogether that spring. In May of 1838, Angelina Grimke married Theodore Weld, and thereafter she and her sister worked closely with him on nearly every kind of project with which he was involved.

The controversy over women's involvement in the anti-slavery movement was not limited to the Grimke sisters alone. Garrison and his supporters were also pushing hard for women to play a more significant role in the affairs of the AASS. In fact, they wanted to put women in leadership roles of the national organization. When the American Anti-Slavery Society held its annual meeting in 1839, the "women's issue" was directly confronted.[126] A resolution was put before the society's convention, proposing that women delegates should have equal voting rights with men. After a lengthy debate, the resolution passed. Garrison was elated when this transpired, for he now saw an opening that might lead to his gaining control of the national organization; but at this 1839 gathering of the national society, he did not quite have enough votes for this to happen. However, at the 1840 meeting of the AASS, Garrison did gain control of the society. This was achieved primarily because of the overwhelming support he received from female delegates. The Garrison wing had chartered a boat that left Lynn, Massachusetts, for the national society's meeting in New York City. A large number of pro-Garrison delegates were onboard, and this group of people was particularly crucial when the vote was taken that signaled Garrison's triumph at the convention. The irony was that by then Garrison had alienated himself from nearly every man who had previously held a leadership role in the national organization. Garrison's uncompromising pronouncements regarding abolitionism had driven them away from wanting anything to do with him. When feminist Abby Kelley[127] was elected to the executive committee by a vote of 557 to 451 the "conservative membership," also called the New York Committee, withdrew from the floor.[128] The majority of these men went on to establish the American and Foreign Anti-Slavery Society.[129] The new organization, for all intents and purposes, was dominated by Lewis Tappan, who framed and directed the affairs of the AFASS. But Tappan's AFASS lieutenants represented the core of the old AASS leadership.

By the time the dissolution of the American Anti-Slavery Society took place, "a radical abolitionist," for the most part, was someone who believed, as Garrison did, that American society in both the North and South was fundamentally flawed morally. They believed that slavery was America's worst sin, but they envisioned the reorganization of the nation's basic moral character and structure. A "conservative abolitionist" was, more often than not, a reformer "rather than a radical in that they considered Northern society fundamentally good and believed that abolition of slavery would eliminate a deviation from its essential goodness and thereby strengthen and preserve its basically moral arrangements."[130] But it was also true, and this distinction should be clearly understood, that there were "conservative abolitionists" who agreed with Garrison that anti-slavery societies should embrace a broad membership.[131]

However, by the summer of 1840, the American Anti-Slavery Society had ruptured and, in effect, collapsed. The national organization had become little more than an empty shell of what it had formerly been. Garrison became its leader, and remained so for twenty-five years. But the society's funds had fallen to almost nothing, and its once robust membership dramatically dipped. It could not even find funds sufficient enough to publish an annual report and its national conventions were only attended by a handful of delegates.[132] However, between 1840 and 1870, the AASS was able to print the *National Anti-Slavery Standard*, which was a weekly publication. The most important thing it did do under Garrison's direction was to hire Frederick Douglass as one of the society's agents in 1841, thereby helping to launch his remarkable career. There were also some places, like locales in parts of New York and Massachusetts, where the AASS continued to carry out effective work.

The nature of the anti-slavery movement was also being changed in the late 1830s and early 1840s as a result of more extreme ideas expressed by some black abolitionists. The American Anti-Slavery Society always had three blacks on its executive committee who supported the organization's basic ideas and nonviolent strategies. But by the late '30s, a growing number of black anti-slavery leaders and Underground Railroad operators raised questions about discrimination, and some were advocating more overt proposals about how the end of slavery should be achieved. In 1837, black minister Theodore S. Wright condemned Northern racial prejudice during a meeting of the New York State Anti-Slavery Society. In 1839, Charles B. Bell, owner and editor of the *Colored American*, was expressing the view that blacks should articulate their own ideas and affirm their demands.[133] Some blacks felt they could no longer afford the luxury of high-minded approaches to emancipation. In 1840, black abolitionist Charles Lenox Remond, while traveling in Great Britain, told the Glasgow Anti-Slavery Society "that he would welcome a war between the United States and England over the Canadian border in as much as such a development would bring about the freedom of slaves."[134]

The famous *Amistad* incident most certainly had an impact on how both blacks and whites looked at the use of violence by slaves in an effort to gain their own freedom. On July 1, 1839, slaves seized the ship *Amistad* and killed the captain and other captors. As they were unfamiliar with navigating a ship, the Africans drifted at sea until the vessel was discovered off Long Island. The blacks on board were then incarcerated in New Haven, Connecticut. Months of litigation followed, but the case was finally heard before the United States Supreme Court in January of 1841. The incarcerated Africans were freed by a majority of the judges after John Quincy Adams successfully defended them before the court. Joshua Levitt, one of the stalwarts of the abolitionist movement, helped Adams prepare the defense. The high court in no way endorsed slave rebellions when they handed down their decision, but the fact remained that the enslaved Africans on the *Amistad* had managed to achieve their freedom by killing some of their captors.

Historian R. J. M. Blackett correctly points out that black abolitionists were "the bona fide representatives of millions of repressed human beings who they successfully portrayed as the pariahs of American society. Unlike white abolitionists, blacks were constrained neither by the niceties of ideology nor by the competition within the movement."[135] By 1843, black abolitionist Henry Highland Garnet, who had graduated from the Oneida Institute with honors, was calling for open revolt and the striking down of slaveholders.[136] Black abolitionist newspaper man Samuel Cornish, who had been the pastor of the first African American Presbyterian Church in New York City and served on the AASS executive committee, was pointing out that "moral weapons" meant very little to free blacks and fugitive slaves who were confronted by kidnappers. In New York City, a clan of white scoundrels called Blackbirds existed "for the purpose of capturing [free blacks] as fugitives and selling them as slaves to Traders."[137] Increasingly, a small but vocal group of Northerners, both black and white, were embracing the idea that slaves had a right to use violence in order to escape slavery. As early as 1838, white New Hampshire abolitionist Nathaniel P. Rogers had asserted that "the enslaved of the country are so much entitled to their liberty as any of us ... [that] they have a right to throw off all violation of it by force ... nay, it is their duty to do so, if they can."[138] In 1843, the class motto of the Anti-Slavery Mission Institute in Quincy, Illinois, was "Universal freedom or death on the battlefield."[139] In 1845, Joshua Levitt maintained that it would certainly be the case that white men would use "cold steel" to rescue their loved ones.[140] By 1849, even Frederick Douglass had come to believe that slave insurrections were justifiable. This repudiation of pacifism represented yet another division among abolitionists and it clearly rejected that group of anti-slavery advocates who had adopted principles of nonresistance in the 1830s.

In truth, in the 1840s, both the American Anti-Slavery Society and the American and Foreign Anti-Slavery Society were fundamentally overshadowed by the fact that the anti-slavery movement was becoming political. By the early 1840s and through the years that followed, most abolitionists accepted the fact that sermons about brotherhood and lectures appealing to conscience would need to give way to political action as the primary tool to effect change. Most anti-slavery activists did not endorse violence as a legitimate means; but believed instead that in order to destroy slavery, they would need to change laws by influencing the agendas of political parties, and do so by winning elections. Historian Dwight L. Dumond believed that by then,

> the vast network of antislavery societies throughout the Northern states was now an integral part of the political pattern. Men seeking public office could no longer ignore the votes of antislavery constituents, the power of antislavery news-papers, the direct challenge of preelection antislavery questionnaires. Abolition-ists constituted a powerful pressure group in a constantly increasing number of Northern communities. They captured control of the local offices, particularly the school boards, the justices of peace, the sheriffs, and the county courts. Their influence was felt in the state governments.[141]

Abolitionists did, of course, keep using moral arguments, and many of them continued to influence the leadership of churches and religious denom-inations. But by the early '40s, the preponderance of anti-slavery crusaders favored a political and legal strategy. Abolitionists were also recognizing by then the need to more fully focus on the North's symbiotic relationship to the Southern slave system. "Although some anti-slavery societies continued to operate after 1840, they had, by that time, been largely superceded by the new political organizations."[142] There were abolitionists in the 1840s and 1850s who did not adopt this political view, but they represented a distinct minority.

By 1840, when the AASS split apart, the Liberty party was created. By 1848, the Free Soil party, a vastly expanded version of the Liberty party, was established; and by the mid–1850s the Republican party was formed. By the time Democrat James Buchanan was elected president in 1856, the anti-slavery movement was dominated by the political and judicial process. Most hard line abolitionists by then were disenchanted with the Republican Party because they felt that the new party had adopted an extremely watered down version of anti-slavery advocacy.[143] Nonetheless, during the fourth and fifth decades of the 19th century, this political phase of the abolitionist movement saw numerous men and women who had been part of the anti-slavery crusade in the 1830s continue to dedicate themselves to the cause. Weld's dream in the '30s of sending abolitionists into Illinois, Wisconsin, and Iowa in fact came to fruition in the 1840s and '50s, although by then, most of these crusaders were no longer agents of the AASS. A good number of these individuals had previously been agents of the AASS, and still others had been influenced by Weld when they had been associated with him years earlier at the Oneida Institute, the Lane Seminary, and Oberlin College.[144]

On April 9, 1870, following the passage of the 13th, 14th, and 15th Amendments, and with Reconstruction well underway, the American Anti-Slavery Society was dissolved. Most of the people who had been associated with the national society, some of whom had been working for the AASS since its founding, decided that there was no longer a need for the society to exist.

What follows, however, is an account of the American Anti-Slavery Society's work during its most fruitful years, in the 1830s, when Theodore Weld and his loyal AASS agents gradually increased the number of Americans who committed themselves wholeheartedly or partially to abolitionism. As historian Edward Magdol explained:

> As part of his "Band of Seventy," they propagandized and proselytized for the American Anti-Slavery Society.... In an era of change that loosened the cement of social order, these modern missionaries grasped modern means of suppressing sin, which they saw personified more by aristocratic slaveowners than by any other element of the social scene. Their rhetoric blended some of the more pessimistic tones of evangelism with the optimistic accents of republicanism.[145]

During this time, the American Anti-Slavery Society also helped establish a framework that dramatically shaped and energized the future of the anti-slavery movement in the United States from the 1830s until the end of the Civil War.

Chapter 2

Laying Emancipation's Groundwork

Throughout the course of American history, no other crusade for change can eclipse in importance the nineteenth century campaign to end slavery. Those who first came together to advocate the abolition of slavery represented a small percentage of Americans. During the 1830s, the individuals who committed themselves to the anti-slavery cause with real dedication were more often than not harassed and vilified at the very least, and, at worst, were attacked, beaten, and at least one of them was killed. Perhaps the most remarkable collection of people ever assembled for the sole purpose of destroying slavery was organized in 1836 when the American Anti-Slavery Society recruited a substantial group of "agents" to carry forth the abolitionist message. They, along with several other agents previously employed by the society, were called the Seventy or "Weld's Seventy," named after Theodore Dwight Weld, one of America's most important anti-slavery crusaders.[1]

It was Weld, along with Henry B. Stanton and John Greenleaf Whittier, who recruited the Seventy, but Weld was given the primary responsibility for their selection and training.[2] In the mid–1830s, in Ohio, Weld started teaching agents to deliver spirited abolitionist speeches. Many were former fellow students with him at the Lane Seminary in Cincinnati.[3] In 1834, Weld helped organize a debate at the school centered on the slavery issue that was conducted over two and a half weeks. He was almost certainly aware of the remarkable impact that debates about slavery had on students at the Oneida Institute near Whitesboro, New York, in June of 1833.[4] Weld was unquestionably the leader of the Lane student body; Lyman Beecher, Lane's president, said that Weld's classmates at the school in Walnut Hills, just outside the city limits of Cincinnati, looked upon him as a god. By the time the Lane debates ended in the winter of 1834, nearly all of the students who had participated were radicalized about slavery.[5] Historian Donald M. Scott has correctly pointed out that the term "debates" is really a misnomer because it was in fact a "revival."[6]

The seminarians formed a student anti-slavery society and took subsequent actions in the community for the benefit of African Americans, like setting up Sunday schools for children, establishing classes, and putting together a modest library. They also organized social gatherings and assisted blacks seeking employment. During this time, Weld made it a point to attend black weddings, funerals, and Bible classes. The black population of Cincinnati, at the time of the student debates at Lane, represented about one-third of all African Americans then living in Ohio.

The students' actions outraged most of the people in the community and alarmed President Beecher, along with the majority of the Seminary's Trustees.[7] Well over half of Lane's trustees were men who had business affairs tied to the South.[8] Faculty members scolded the seminarians for trying to organize widespread political upheaval instead of performing their primary responsibility, which was studying theology. The Seminary's authorities eventually demanded that the students cease their abolitionist efforts and dissolve their anti-slavery organization. The school's administration also moved to have Weld expelled. Before he was officially removed, Weld, and the overwhelming majority of Lane's students, withdrew from the Seminary, and shortly thereafter, many of them made their way to Oberlin College in northern Ohio. This sudden influx of former Lane students sealed the future of Oberlin College, and the school eventually became the most famous abolitionist institution

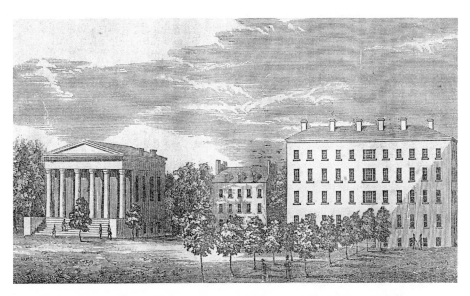

Lane Seminary, Walnut Hills, near Cincinnati (Special Collections and Archives, Knox College Library, Galesburg, Illinois).

of higher learning anywhere in the nation.[9] Thirty-two Lane Rebels enrolled at Oberlin, and more than a third of them became anti-slavery lecturers.[10]

By late 1835, the leaders of the American Anti-Slavery Society were understandably frustrated by the fact that they had not achieved as much progress as they had initially hoped for when the society was founded. Violent attacks on their membership and a sense that the public, instead of favoring their abolitionist agendas, was holding with the status quo, added to their discouragement. In the fall of 1835, famous English abolitionist George Thompson tried to deliver a speech in Boston, but he was confronted by a mob that included many eminent citizens of the community. He barely escaped unharmed. The mob was outraged at the gall of an Englishman expressing condemnation of how Americans conducted their affairs. Thompson, who came to the United States to aid the anti-slavery cause in 1834, met harsh opposition everywhere he went, and finally returned to England in November of 1835.

Abolitionist Charles Stuart was also the recipient of expressions of rage due in large part to his British nationality. In 1835 during a mob disturbance in Connecticut, a retired naval officer challenged Stuart to a duel. He refused to accept the challenge and managed to get away uninjured from other potential manhandlers.[11] During this same period of time, fearing mob attacks, abolitionist Elizur Wright, Jr., felt so unsafe in his residence that he barricaded his door. Lydia Maria Child wrote in 1835, "I have not ventured into the city … 'tis like the times of the French Revolution, when no man dared to trust his neighbors."[12] Historian Leonard L. Richards' meticulous research indicates that the peak of anti abolitionist mob attacks occurred between the summer of 1835 and early 1836.[13] In retrospect, one can see that things were about to change; but in the autumn of 1835, opposition to their reform ideas left the society's executive committee feeling distinctly disappointed.[14]

But in the West, the abolitionist movement, at this very same time, was receiving a much-needed jumpstart. In 1835, after arriving in northern Ohio, Weld began instructing a group of men mostly composed of former Lane students in Cleveland and Oberlin.[15] Weld and the group of reformers that he prepared became very successful at spreading the anti-slavery word in Ohio. Weld's success and that of his young recruits convinced the American Anti-Slavery Society to change their tactics. Previously, the national society had put an emphasis on flooding the nation with anti-slavery pamphlets and literature, but this approach turned out to be largely unsuccessful and their publications barely penetrated the South.[16] The new strategy of the AASS, based primarily on the success of Weld's speaking tours in Ohio, Pennsylvania, and New York, the work of his capable young lecturers in Ohio, and the effective efforts of Henry B. Stanton in Rhode Island, was to vastly increase the society's number of agents.[17] The American Anti-Slavery Society Agency Committee then assigned the recruits to Northern states in order to persuade people, by means of "moral suasion," of the need to emancipate slaves. The AASS had employed agents before this but their numbers were not nearly as large.

By the spring of 1836, the new strategy had improved the morale and optimism of the American Anti-Slavery Society's leadership. The majority of the lecturers and organizers, recruited in the north, were clergymen. When these men made this vocational commitment, they became full-time spokesmen for the abolitionist crusade. A final group of handpicked agents were called together in New York City on November 15, 1836, for training and strategy sessions that lasted until Friday, December 2.[18] Anti-slavery luminaries like Beriah Green, Charles Stuart, the famous Tappan brothers, Arthur and Lewis, and even firebrand William Lloyd Garrison helped with the instruction, but Weld was unquestionably the leading figure during the two and a half week period of inspirational teaching.[19] Training sessions took place each morning and afternoon with two hour classes conducted in the evening.

Those who witnessed the work carried out by Weld were thunderstruck by his intensity and the power of his deliveries even though he came down with a terrible cold during the convention.[20] He shared with the new agents ploys and devices he had learned during the course of his own experience as an anti-slavery lecturer. The recruits were fully aware that Weld had been mobbed on numerous occasions. Weld convinced his recruits that the often-present mob element would eventually quiet down after delivering their insults and tirades, and speakers could usually count on getting their message across by patiently waiting for the right moment to speak.[21] He warned his agents that they would sometimes be required to wait until the following day or evening to be adequately heard and that occasionally eggs, stones, pieces of glass, and even bricks would be hurled at them. In some cases, Weld was known to have folded his arms across his chest and stared at the mob, sometimes for incredible periods of time, before the raucous troublemakers would calm down.[22] Finally the curious onlookers would be able to hear what he had to say.

Weld paid a high price for giving this impassioned abolitionist seminar, however. His health had been failing prior to the agents' convention owing to his exhaustive efforts for the abolitionist cause over the previous years. In December of 1835, Weld had started to struggle with laryngitis while delivering lectures in Pittsburg. His normal schedule on the anti-slavery speaking circuit encompassed eight straight days of meetings. Well before the New York City meeting took place, his voice had grown hoarse and when the New York gathering broke up, Weld collapsed. Although he recovered enough to work and write for the abolitionist cause well into the 1840s, other than some speeches delivered many years later, he was not able to give public lectures again because his voice was ruined.[23] In late June of 1841, Weld wrote a letter to Gerrit Smith expressing his concern about Smith's health. In this letter, we learn from Weld's own hand how badly his voice had deteriorated five years earlier in 1836:

> My dear brother. This letter has been waiting for my postscript these ten days, and even now I should hardly have found time to scribble it but for the information just conveyed to us that you are laboring under a very severe affection of the lungs, and confined to the house. The news give us great concern, much moderated however by the recollection that two years ago you had a similar affection produced by a violent cold, which was quite temporary though very severe, and passed off leaving no permanent trace on your lungs.
>
> I know you will join me in thanksgiving to God that my shattered voice is so far bound up again that I have ventured to engage to speak at an anti slavery meeting at Newark on the 4th of July. It is rather a perilous experiment, but my vocal power has so greatly improved within the last three months that I feel it a duty to *try* it. I shall not venture to speak but a few minutes, perhaps not more than five; (dear brother Weed of Ohio will make the main speech) but if God grant me the power once more to make even a five minute's plea for our perishing brethren, my heart shall commemorate his loving kindness with joy and gratitude. It is now nearly five years since my voice failed me. My last lecture I gave on the 4th of July, 1836. For four months after that I was traversing the States getting lecturers into the field. In November of that year, you recollect, we had our convention of three weeks for the agents, editors, etc. In that convention I felt my voice every day breaking down, till finally it terminated in a whisper. From that time till now I have not spoken in public. Nothing but iron determination to resist all importunity and not to speak even for five minutes in any meeting until restored implicitly did under God save my life. If I find from the experiment next Sunday that I can continue to raise my voice without absolute presumption, I shall make an anti slavery speech, God helping me, as often as I can reassure vocal power enough to last me for ten minutes testimony against the climax of human villainy. Now let me tell you what with God's blessing has so much strengthened my voice. Four months ago I left my study entirely and for nearly twelve hours a day on an average I have been hard at work, ploughing, hoeing, felling trees, splitting rails, digging post holes, making fence, digging and hauling rocks, etc., etc. The effect of this vigorous and unusual muscular exertion upon the vocal muscles has been great.
>
> Your brother ever
> Theodore D. Weld
> June 30th, 1841[24]

Weld's health notwithstanding, following the agents' convention in late 1836, his orators, now referred to as the "Seventy," were sent out by the AASS to carry forth their abolitionist beliefs. Over the course of the next few years they enjoyed a remarkable degree of success spreading the anti-slavery doctrine.

This was accomplished by means of effective public lecturing and by helping to organize state and local anti-slavery organizations.[25] Their style of delivery emulated evangelical revivalist ministers and many of them often linked Christian doctrine to the sin of slavery. Slavery, the abolitionists said, was an extraordinary sin, so foul and corrupting as to foreclose any hope of salvation for its defenders. In the course of their public lectures, the principles of liberty and equality were emphasized, and Weld insisted that his agents' remarks be meticulously factual.

By early 1837, due to the effectiveness of these agents' efforts, there was an average of one anti-slavery society being established each day across the North.[26] By January of 1837, a chain of anti-slavery organizations had been forged across Ohio making much of the state a stronghold for abolitionism. On the third of February that year, the Pennsylvania State Anti-Slavery Society was established and in June the Michigan Anti-Slavery Society held its first annual meeting. When the AASS held its annual convention that year, it reported that its auxiliaries had grown to over one thousand with a membership of more than one hundred thousand individuals.[27] On the Fourth of July, on the nearly unpopulated tall grass prairies of western Illinois, the citizens of George Washington Gale's newly founded Galesburg established an auxiliary society of the AASS and pledged to raise one hundred dollars by December 31 in order to support the anti-slavery crusade. Sixteen weeks later, the Illinois Anti-Slavery Society was organized.[28] In New York, the wealthiest and most powerful state in the North, 65 percent of the counties had anti-slavery societies by the end of 1837. New Yorkers were, by then, contributing about one half of all the funds used to operate the AASS.[29]

The American Anti-Slavery Society was reorganized in 1837 in order to better handle the mass of administrative chores associated with organizing the large number of employed agents and the work that accumulated with the anti-slavery petition campaign. James G. Birney was made the chief administrator, Henry B. Stanton took charge of financial affairs, Joshua Levitt was chosen to edit the society's newspaper, the *Emancipator*, and Weld, after his health improved, helped direct the efforts of the agents, and he was also put in charge of the national society's publications.[30] Weld's assignment as the director of publications was the perfect job for him. According to Stanton, Weld would "pick a dry metaphysical bone for a week" and "dig a month with the patience of a Cornwall miner, into a dusty library for a rare fact."[31] There is no doubt that the year 1837 represents the highwater mark of the American Anti-Slavery Society's success. The May 12th issue of *The Liberator* overflowed with enthusiasm and pride regarding the achievements of the national society. The issue reported that only days earlier, at the society's fourth anniversary meeting, the delegates were filled with "heart cheering and spirit-stirring news from all parts of the land ... this is a glorious week for our holy and righteous cause."

There were, of course, at the same time, numerous anti-slavery lecturers who were not paid agents of the American Anti-Slavery Society. Some speakers belonged to state or local societies. Many ministers gave sermons with anti-slavery themes laced into their deliveries. But many anti-slavery speakers, of all stripes, learned from experience that in hostile circumstances, they should, at the very least, be ready to protect their attire:

> Professor Hudson, of Oberlin College, used to say that the injury he most feared was to his clothes. He carried with him what he called "a storm suit," which he wore at evening meetings. It showed many marks of battle.[32]

The majority of people who were central to the abolitionist movement in the 1830s harbored disdain for urban communities. This may explain, at least partially, anti-slavery leaders' remarkable indifference to the plight of working-class Americans employed in cities and company towns. The environmental conditions in most Northern factories were unhealthy and dangerous, and included outrageous exploitation of women and children. The workday at most textile mills lasted from sunup to sunset in the winter and stretched to thirteen hours or more in the summer. Employers were free to conduct business as they saw fit, and as factories grew larger, the cleavage grew betweens haves and have-nots. When economic times were hard, laborers had to bear the burden, and unskilled and semi-skilled workers were barely able to survive. In the 1830s, women's compensation always fell far below that of men, and poorly paid children under sixteen made up two-fifths of the labor force.[33] Children who were orphans, abandoned by their parents, or the victims of illegitimacy worked in factories in order to survive. In the drab factory towns and overcrowded working-class cities, neighborhoods gave way to disgraceful slums. A good number of women in urban centers were only able to sustain themselves by working as prostitutes.

Southerners did not hold back on criticizing these horrendous conditions that bred disease, hunger, and crime. Southern leaders also pointed out the prevalence of frequent unemployment and the general atmosphere of daily despair. A handful of abolitionists, like Nathaniel P. Rogers and John Greenleaf Whittier, sympathized with the lives working-class people led, but for the most part, anti-slavery leaders ignored these problems. There was real tension that existed between most abolitionists and the urban lower classes. Abolitionists, for the most part, had a "blind spot for the ills that beset the working class" and some of them "denied that there was any real labor problem, at least in this country."[34]

As more foreigners came into America, the number of people living below the poverty line grew. This situation helped to increase fear among immigrants and nonimmigrant laborers that the efforts to emancipate slaves would threaten their opportunities for employment. Most wage earners were bitterly prejudiced towards free blacks, and white skilled workers were resentful of blacks who tried to enter into their trades. Numerous white laborers refused to work alongside African Americans.[35] Members of the lower classes openly expressed racism by participating in mob violence towards abolitionists, which reinforced the negative feelings of anti-slavery crusaders towards these people. Many abolitionist agents were so focused on trying to emancipate slaves that they refused to give attention to Northern working conditions:

> Abolitionists shared with other Americans in the preponderance of positive labor incentives in the free states [and they] also generated enthusiasm for the competitive labor market generally ... they were less capable of perceiving how their own belief in the resilience and moral power of the individual might contribute to conditions of exploitation in a free society.[36]

The majority of abolitionists in the 1830s, whatever the reasons, showed general disinterest towards the hardships brought on by the gradual development of industrialization.[37] Labor reformer, Orestes A. Brownson, argued that the best way to bring down slavery was to develop democratic freedom in non-slave holding states:

> Let us correct the evils at our own doors, elevate the free white laborer, and prove by our own practice, and by the state of our own society, that the doctrine of equal rights is not a visionary dream. O we have much to do here at home.[38]

Brownson maintained that even if slaves were emancipated, they would be "a slave still, although with the title and cares of a freedman."[39]

There was one group of laboring wage earners who were sympathetic to abolitionists, however. They were young working women. Historian Bernard Mandel maintains:

> Probably there was no stronger concentration of anti-slavery sentiment anywhere in the United States than among the "factory girls" of New England, whose humanitarianism and devotion to democracy and the rights of labor gave them an ardent hatred of the slavocracy. They were very active in the abolition movement, in spite of intimidation both for their views and for their impudence in transgressing the bounds of female decency by expressing them.[40]

The abolitionist movement did not succeed to any great extent in reducing Northern prejudice towards blacks. However, anti-slavery advocates did slowly help to convince more and more Northeasterners and Midwesterners that slavery was morally wrong. These reforming agitators helped many non–Southerners accept the fact that slavery could not remain as a permanent institution the United States. In some ways, the agents' most significant impact on people was to stir their conscience about the horrors of slavery. Lecturers simultaneously managed to portray slaveholders as arrogant, mean-spirited, self-indulgent, and cruel.

One of the most effective ways anti-slavery orators moved audiences occurred when they gave accounts of what actually took place at a slave auction.[41] Descriptions of what transpired on the slave block caused widespread discomfort to listeners who learned of the miseries experienced by black families separated from each other. The sale of human beings was premised on criteria that rested upon the economics of market forces, and frequently the lust of potential buyers. These horrifying stories staggered many Northerners who absorbed narratives of heartless slave traders and prospective masters assessing each purchase based upon characteristics like the age of a child, the dispensability of a grandparent, the childbearing health of a woman, the physical disabilities of a man, or the sex appeal of an attractive adolescent.[42]

By the 1830s, as the transfer of slaves accelerated westward, more and more families were broken apart.[43] Between 1790 and 1860, historian Peter Kolchin has estimated that one million slaves were sent into the South's western and Gulf states.[44] The price of female slaves peaked when they reached their early twenties, whereas male slaves brought in their highest price by the time they reached their mid-twenties.[45] Attractive, light-skinned young female slaves were often sent to the "fancy-girl market" in New Orleans. These women brought much higher prices. Some of them ended up in bordellos, and others were sold to very wealthy plantation owners and gamblers.[46]

Two notable members of the Seventy helped resolve something that had divided the anti-slavery community throughout the 1830s. The issue that troubled them was the question of what would happen to slaves if they were immediately and unconditionally freed. Some abolitionists genuinely believed that it would be unwise and irresponsible for slaves to be emancipated instantly, fearing they were not equipped or skilled enough to survive. They called for immediate emancipation to be gradually accomplished. Many other anti-slavery exponents, like William Lloyd Garrison, rejected this concept out of hand. "Duty is ours and events are God's," Garrison said[47]; slaves should be given their complete liberty no matter the consequences. To help settle this issue, the agency committee sent two of the Seventy to the West Indies to observe, analyze, and report on what the real implications of instant emancipation of slaves had been in parts of the Caribbean.

Weld convinced the American Anti-Slavery Society's executive committee to spend money on this venture. These men, Joseph Horace Kimball and James A. Thome, returned to the United States in late May of 1837, and published their research, with Weld's help, in a piece entitled *Emancipation in the West Indies*.[48] The bulk of this work's information was gathered in Antigua,

Barbadoes, and Jamaica. The evidence Kimball and Thome collected pointed to the fact that free labor worked better than slave labor. Their report endorsed the idea that complete freedom should be granted to the enslaved without any conditions attached. The overwhelming majority of the AASS leadership and most, but certainly not all of its membership, accepted their conclusions and thereafter abandoned the notion that emancipation should be only gradually achieved.[49]

Meanwhile, Weld's seekers of converts pushed forward in the North. They drew people by the handful, score and hundreds to schools, community meeting halls, barns, churches, private homes, and, weather permitting, to groves of trees or a farmer's field. They faced threatening crowds and mob attacks, and many of them physically overtaxed themselves during these tours. Their health suffered and several agents had to reduce their daily schedules or in some cases withdraw from the field altogether. The American Anti-Slavery Society tended to have agents work with established state and local auxiliaries with emphasis put on trying to find new supporters in previously untapped rural areas. The fertile agricultural regions worked by cash crop farmers in New York, Pennsylvania, Ohio, and Michigan, turned out to be particularly sympathetic to the concepts put before them by American Anti-Slavery Society agents. Before the Civil War, an overwhelming majority of Americans were farmers, worked on farms as hired hands, or resided in the countryside because services they provided were tied to agricultural production.

Weld believed that people who lived away from cities would eventually influence urban populations to join them in the cause. "Let us take hold of the countryside," he said, "leaving the cities to themselves for the present and we shall soon carry the question."[50] Weld's abolitionist mentor, Charles Stuart, agreed that people living in agricultural regions seemed "only to need information to be with us."[51] The idea of generating the anti-slavery movement from small towns and rural regions did not stem from naïve idealism about uncorrupted people living in the countryside. During the 1830s large cities from Boston to New York to Philadelphia to Cincinnati experienced violent anti abolitionist riots. Individuals of the highest social standing joined in on mob attacks.

> Their membership usually included many prominent and articulate men — doctors and lawyers, merchants and bankers, judges and Congressmen. These "gentlemen of property and standing," as contemporaries called them, had so little fear of indictment or public censure that they often made public pronouncement — and sometimes even permitted records of their meetings and membership to be published! The mobs therefore provide a convenient entry to the sources of Northern hostility to antislavery.[52]

Many metropolitan centers were controlled by businessmen and politicians who reaped financial benefits by supporting slavery in America. Most city newspapers also helped preserve the status quo by playing to racial prejudice. These forces encouraged attacks on abolitionists by warning their fellow urban dwellers that emancipation would result in race mixing and lost jobs for whites.

By the mid 1830s Weld's colleague Elizur Wright, Jr., Corresponding Secretary for the AASS, came over to the rural strategy instructing field agents to "take hold of the country — the yeomanry of country towns, leaving the cities to themselves for present."[53] Wright was a Yale graduate who met Weld in the Western Reserve of Ohio and then moved back East to help organize abolitionist sentiment. Wright was always keen on emphasizing to his anti-slavery colleagues that it was not only slave holders who were to be condemned but also "rich northerners anxious to partake" in the plunder by furnishing their capital "for the extension of slave labor." Following the establishment of the American Anti-Slavery Society, Wright was made the organization's Corresponding Secretary. In this capacity, he convinced the AASS leadership to "broaden the financial base of the society to the grass-roots membership."[54] Wright carefully reviewed each agent's monthly expense report and always reminded them of their obligation to be as frugal as possible.[55] Between 1833 and 1839, when Wright left New York, in order to become the editor of the *Massachusetts Abolitionist*, he was at the center of the American Anti-Slavery Society's leadership.

Historian James Brewer Stewart, in his book *Holy Warriors: The Abolitionists and American Slavery*, made this connection to the abolitionist movement's appeal to men and women living in rural areas:

> By the mid–1820's, vastly improved water and land routes had also tied what were to become the antislavery regions of rural Vermont, New Hampshire, and Massachusetts to urban centers...
>
> Serving the farmers in the hinterland, newspapers proliferated in all these smaller towns and created sophisticated networks of communication. They also gave literate citizens a heightened sense of involvement in national issues, such as the mobbing of abolitionists and the ransacking of mailbags...
>
> Viewed from these bustling towns and prospering countryside, the disruptions of the 1830's seemed particularly unwelcome ... many [of these people] could claim that by their own honest toil they had risen from obscure beginnings to respectability. Material progress, they firmly believed, depended on the efforts of "free laborers" — self-employed farmers, artisans, and workers. So did the other hallmarks of a "civilized" society — evangelical piety, family stability, republican governance, and the diffusion of secular knowledge. To them, economic advance, the spread of learning, and orderly republicanism were indistinguishable from God's benevolent plans for mankind...
>
> Abolitionists understood the general characteristics of this emerging antislav-

ery constituency and took steps at once to encourage its progress. They felt increasingly sensitive to what Elizur Wright, Jr., described as the "small men" of the towns and countryside."[56]

In the first part of the nineteenth century, as the rural north was witnessing the expansion of commercial opportunities and the nurturing of educational development while expressing a desire for the government to pay for projects like canals, the rural south was moving in a different direction. Southerners, in general, did not move as fast to develop their banking system, or spend nearly as much tax money hiring teachers and building schools, nor did they commit themselves to advancing a wide variety of business ventures. The states south of the Mason-Dixon Line and Ohio River, with the passage of each year, were establishing a very different culture from their Northern neighbors. In fact, from the very beginning of the republic's establishment, the North and South had quickly grown quite different from each other. The North valued "common labor as the supreme human activity," while the South continued "to think of labor in traditional terms as mean and despicable and fit only for slaves."[57]

Alex de Tocqueville wrote the following to his father from Memphis on December 20, 1831:

> The right [north] bank of the Ohio is a scene of animations and industry; work is honored, no one owns slaves. But cross the river and you suddenly find yourself in another universe. Gone is the spirit of enterprise. Work is considered not only onerous but shameful: whoever engages in it degrades himself.[58]

Social divisions were much more rigid in the South. The large plantation owner sat on top of the social order; small planters, with five to twenty slaves came next, followed by small farmers. Illiterate poor whites ranked well below the top three, scraping by on poor land, trying to grow one crop.[59]

Unfortunately, with the Panic of 1837, the nation fell on hard economic times.[60] This extremely sharp economic decline devastated the nation, and in its wake, free blacks suffered the most. Shortly after Weld's last agents' seminar, the Panic forced the AASS, with its financial resources declining, to drop approximately twenty agents from its ranks within six months.[61] The impact of the Panic drove the American Anti-Slavery Society to stress fundraising at the expense of establishing auxiliary societies. It also seems that some of the agents must have been ineffective and were let go after their efforts were evaluated.[62] This forced Weld, who was by now back at work, and his fellow executive officers in New York, to drop their plans to send agents beyond Ohio and Indiana into the upper Mississippi Valley. Before the financial resources of the AASS were substantially reduced by the nation's economic collapse in 1837, the compensation paid to the national society's agents usually ranged from between $500 to $600 per year. Most agents had their travel expenses covered by the American Anti-Slavery Society as well. Some agents occasionally requested an advance on their salaries, but the agency committee, always concerned about adequate cash reserves, refused prepayment.[63]

The work conducted by the Seventy is difficult to measure because, as previously discussed, it was mostly carried out in remote regions away from cities. Therefore, much of what they did was anonymous. The labors of the Seventy were rarely recorded or reported publicly, other than accounts printed in anti-slavery periodicals. Even so, the agents had a profound effect on changing the minds of many Americans, to one degree or another, about the evils of human bondage.[64] Abolitionist crusaders managed to convince many Northern farmers that Southern slave owners were working against the interests of small, free farmers. In the years ahead, the support these abolitionist agents mustered against slavery was translated into votes cast at the polls for anti-slavery office seekers or at least for politicians who opposed the extension of slavery into the territories of the American West. But even in the mid-to-late 1830s, some Northerners went so far as to be enlisted as full-fledged abolitionists.

One of the mistakes many American Anti-Slavery agents made was similar to the miscalculation Weld made about overextending himself physically.

The agents desire and will to carry out their abolitionist work continuously on a daily and weekly basis was unrealistic. The relentless schedules they attempted to follow ultimately caught up with them and several agents finally broke down. Many of them oftentimes fell ill, rested for a time, and then returned to the same kind of grueling timetable. Still others realized that their lungs and throats were growing worn to the point that they could barely speak loud enough to be heard by their audiences. In addition, some of Weld's crusaders came to understand that the hostility and badgering they so often faced overtaxed them psychologically. Lewis Tappan later recalled that "few persons" had a "true idea

Lewis Tappan (courtesy Oberlin College Archives).

of the insults" they constantly had heaped upon them. They were, among other things, "continually watched ... opprobriously alluded to in the daily press ... followed not infrequently by droves of boys even from places of public resort to their doors ... objects of real or affected aversion or terror ... treated as disturbers of the public peace, and as outlaws in the community."[65]

Eventually, some of these lecturers came to grips with the fact that their zeal was trumped by the reality that there were limits to what they could endure. In July of 1836, James Thome wrote a letter to Weld asking his mentor for advice on how to deal with his exhaustion:

Dear Bro. Weld

I have been threatening for some time past to write you a letter, but uncertainty as to your whereabouts has prevented. In a note to Prof. Morgan, which came, with the bearer, yesterday, you direct letters to be sent to Utica. With this information I will no longer delay writing.

The first thing that I want to talk with you about is touching my health. I have laboured all this summer under the painful apprehension that I should not be able to lecture next winter. My voice seems to have *given way* for the present. I cannot speak for half an hour without getting hoarse. I have tried several times this summer, and under every variety of circumstances, and it seems that in the most favorable cases, speaking induces hoarseness. The origin of this difficulty I suppose was this. Toward the close of the winter, I laboured unusually hard in Lecturing and debating. While I was at Cadiz I brought on hoarseness by lecturing twice a day for a week and then getting engaged in a very warm debate with a talented young man. I then was solicited to visit several other places in succession to lecture. I yielded and made my hoarseness worse and worse. In the midst of the whole I took cold. Ever since that my voice has been as above described. I have not *spoken once*, on any subject, without being hoarse. My general health is also much more feeble this summer than it has been for many years. I fear that last winter's campaign has injured my *lungs* seriously. In a word, it is very evident that, unless my voice improves very much, I cannot think of lecturing next winter. I couldn't deliver one course of lectures without being layed up — not with my throat merely, but utterly prostrate in body. A few weeks since I attended a protracted meeting, which the Brethren of our class were holding in Ridgeville near Elyria. I found that the excitement of a single day's labor, and that praying merely, would so exhaust me that I couldn't attend the evening meetings.

In view of those things, I want you[r] advice as to the course I had better take. How would it do for me to go, this fall, to the West Indies, and act as correspondent for some of the Anti Slavery Papers? This idea has by some means or other been very strongly impressed on my mind for some time. What do you think of it? Have the Ex. Com. Found persons to fill this station? Do you think of any better course for me to take to restore my health?

I fully believe that the present is a *crisis* with me. If I can by a short period of rest and by enjoying a favorable climate, establish my health, I may live to some purpose. As it is at present I feel that my health is not firm and is growing less so daily. I live constantly under the ghastly apprehension that my life may be soon cut off. You can conceive how such an impression must cut the sinews of effort and discourage all attempts both at mental discipline and mental furnishment.

Dear Bro. Weld — do not suspect me of a secret wish to escape the toil and danger of the Anti Slavery field. I do not think I have any such feeling. It is not for me to boast of my attachment to this cause, or of my courage in promoting it amid various dangers...

It *may be* that my present afflictions are temporary, and that by entire cessation from all speaking *until* the Fall, and by active manual labor, I may regain my voice. If I should, I will not, of course, desire to leave the country. Now I wish, if you think it best and if it is practicable, to have the matter so arranged that I can go, in case my health continues as it now is...

Well I must stop. All here are well.

Look for a folio Post in a few days

You Bro. In the bonds of the opprest

James A. Thome[66]

Although religion was the primary connection shared by Weld's lecturers, the other common bond was education. The overwhelming majority of AASS agents were or had been serious students, and many of them came from well-schooled families. A good number of "Weldites," as several of his followers sometimes were called, became teachers at some point in their lives; some helped establish colleges and seminaries.[67] The intellectual qualities and scholarly achievements of these agents were impressive.

The term "Seventy" was not used as the name for Weld's group until the New York agents' convention was over. It appeared days later in anti-slavery publications like the *Emancipator* (December 15, 1836), *The Liberator* (December 17, 1836), and the *Friend of Man* (December 22, 1836).[68] The reference to the Seventy in the *Friend of Man* appeared in a fundraising appeal inserted in the paper by Lewis Tappan as assistant treasurer of the AASS. It read:

To the Friends of the Cause

Seventy agents have been appointed by the executive committee to labor in different parts of the free states, and as the expenditures of the society will thereby be greatly increased, the friends who pledged certain monies at the last anniversary are earnestly solicited to remit the same as soon as possible; and the friends of the cause generally are entreated to make donations to maintain the increased number of agents and the publications of the society. Antislavery newspapers are requested to give this notice an insertion.

The Biblical references to the seventy can be found in both the Old Testament where Moses is commanded "to gather seventy ... of the elders of Israel" and in the New Testament in Luke chapter 10; verses 1–3:

After these things the Lord appointed other seventy also, and sent them two and two before his face into every city and place, whither he himself would come.

Therefore said he unto them. The harvest truly is great, but the labourers are few: pray ye therefore the Lord of the harvest, that he would send forth labourers into his harvest. Go your ways: behold, I send you forth as lambs among wolves.

Most historians who have studied Weld have doubted whether the total number of agents ever, in fact, reached seventy. Historian Dwight L. Dumond, in the course of his comprehensive anti-slavery scholarship, identifies well over 60 possible members of Weld's band.[69] Gilbert H. Barnes and Louis Filler mention many of the same individuals by name, and Barnes includes Angelina and Sarah Grimke as members of the "Seventy,"[70] as does Grimke sisters scholar Gerda Lerner.[71] Dumond also lists Angelina Grimke, but neither she nor her sister Sarah were officially employed by the AASS.[72] It seems therefore, that one could be counted as a member of Weld's band even if not paid a salary by the national organization's agency committee. Historian Larry Ceplair, in his book *The Public Years of Sarah and Angelina Grimke*, describes the sisters as "under the auspicies of, but not officially employed or paid by, the American Anti-Slavery Society."[73] Historian John L. Myers conducted the most notable scholarship regarding Weld's agents, and he includes Weld himself as one of the "Seventy."[74] Myers believes that agents employed by the national society in December of 1836, just after Weld's New York gathering, are the best candidates "to claim membership in the band."[75] Both Myers and Dumond believed that for reasons of death, health, and other circumstances, fewer than seventy agents actually lectured for the AASS. There were, at the height of Weld's involvement, a total of at least sixty-five agents on the rolls of the AASS. Because there is compelling evidence of their participation, Angelina and Sarah Grimke should also be included, bringing the total to sixty-seven. When the American Anti-Slavery Society met at its annual meeting in May of 1837, its minutes report:

> There have been appointed by the Committee, in the course of the year, but chiefly within the last six months, upwards of seventy agents, sixty-five of whom have been in the service of the Society for longer or shorter periods.[76]

Abraham Lincoln scholar Rodney O. Davis, who is very familiar with nineteenth Century American language usage, believes that the expression "upwards of seventy" means "not quite seventy" or "almost seventy." Therefore, if "upwards" carried such a connotation in the mid–1800s, the minutes of the AASS reveal that a total of seventy agents was, in all likelihood, never quite attained.

Two other women were nearly made members of the "Seventy." Lydia Maria Child[77] was offered an appointment by Weld in 1836, but every influential Boston abolitionist, other than her husband David, opposed this idea.[78]

The agency committee also approved a Miss Wheelright (first name unknown), to deliver lectures to women about slavery, but no record of her efforts has been found.[79] It seems probable, however, that Miss Wheelright was Elizabeth Wheelright, who lived in Massachusetts, and was once embroiled in a controversy in her church with her anti abolitionist minister.[80]

The names of most of Weld's crusaders have been long forgotten. Their obscurity makes it difficult to track down detailed information about many of them. But the impact of their anti-slavery work raises the questions: What were their backgrounds? Where did they conduct their work as agents? How were they received? What became of them after they left the service of the American Anti-Slavery Society? In the following chapter, there is a short sketch of each one, but before these crusaders are identified and described, let us first briefly examine the life of Theodore Weld.

Weld was born in Hampton, Connecticut, in 1803, the fourth son of Ludovicus and Elizabeth Weld. His father, a Congregationalist minister, enrolled Theodore for a short time at Phillips Academy in Massachusetts. In the mid–1820s, the Weld family moved to New York where Theodore briefly studied at Hamilton College, but later he enrolled at George Washington Gale's Oneida Institute near Whitesboro.[81] He studied at the Institute, a ministers' training school close to the Erie Canal, for three years. Later Gale established anti-slavery Knox College in Illinois, which became an anchor of the anti-slavery cause in "the West." While a student at the Oneida school, Weld met abolitionist Charles Stuart in nearby Utica and the two men became very close friends.[82] Stuart, a retired British military officer, saw great potential in Weld, helped finance his education, spurred him to embrace abolitionism, and thereafter closely followed his career.[83]

Oneida Institute, Whitesboro, New York (Special Collections and Archives, Knox College Library, Galesburg, Illinois).

It was also in Utica that Weld fell under the spell of Great Revivalist minister Charles G. Finney, who had been converted by Gale to the religious crusade in 1821.[84] Weld was converted, in turn, to the evangelical religious movement by Finney in 1825, and the new believer soon became a committed public orator and advocate of various reforms himself.

Finney became the most influential individual associated with the fervent revivalism of the Second Great Awakening, and he accumulated around him a like-minded group of fellow revivalists known as "Finney's Holy Band." Riding his horse from community to community across New York, Finney gave sermons that lasted all day, and sometimes extended well into the evening. Finney, who

Charles G. Finney (courtesy Oberlin College Archives).

possessed an excellent singing voice, effectively interspersed hymns into his religious services. During the course of his emotional presentations, sinners moved towards the stage to embrace conversion; some were nervous and anxious, while others seemed lost in a state of ecstasy. Finney and his fellow fire-and-brimstone revivalists encouraged these electrically charged and oftentimes raucous religious gatherings. In New York State, the area west of the Catskill and Adirondack Mountains rigorously blazed with such intensity that the region was called the "Burned-Over District."[85]

Unlike the tenets of traditional Calvinism preached by ministers in the old established churches throughout New England, who maintained that only a select few were eligible to enter the kingdom of heaven after death, Finney offered the hope of salvation to anyone and everyone who converted to Christianity. In addition to conversion, however, Finney believed that new believers would need to move forward in life as benevolent Christians. Finney held that salvation occurred at the "beginning of the religious experience" not at the end, as old-line Calvinists believed.[86] This was intoxicating stuff to audiences made up of men and women, many of whom had never belonged to a church or been part of a traditional religious denomination.

In the 1880s, Henry B. Stanton, a Finney convert and one of Weld's closest colleagues, put down this description of his first impression of Finney's speaking style, powerful delivery, and the force of his persuasion:

> A tall, grave-looking man, dressed in an unclerical suit of gray, ascended the pulpit. Light hair covered his forehead: his eyes were of sparkling blue, and his pose and movement dignified. I listened. It did not sound like preaching, but like a lawyer arguing a case before a court and jury ... the discourse was a chain of logic, brightened by a felicity of illustration and enforced by urgent appeals from a voice of great compass and melody ... taken all in all, I never knew the superior of Charles G. Finney. His sway over an audience was wonderful.... As he would stand with his face towards the side gallery and then involuntarily wheel around, the audience in that part of the house towards which he threw his arm would dodge as if he were hurling something at them.[87]

During these years, while crisscrossing the Burned-Over District of New York, Finney seemed to possess an ability to penetrate the psyche of almost everyone who heard him; even people who did not convert on the spot admitted to experiencing a state of anxiety when Finney's sermons were over.

The Great Revival's new evangelical doctrine, with its message of immediate redemption for each person, required that every individual who embraced the new theology be responsible for applying his or her beliefs to moral action for social good. Consequently, many new wave evangelists came to the conclusion that they must adopt the cause of emancipating slaves, who were as deserving of God's salvation as they were. These completely committed "evangelical abolitionists saw themselves as participants in the cosmic drama of sin and redemption."[88] In addition, their religious commitment also meant that various other reforms should also be addressed.

Theodore Weld, at first, devoted himself primarily to speaking for the temperance movement, and he effectively emulated many of Finney's conversion techniques. He unfailingly condoned the right of women to speak and pray at religious services. Gradually, Finney and Weld effectively joined evangelical religion to social reform, including anti-slavery advocacy.[89] Both men became very well known in the course of their public appearances. Finney eventually moved to New York City, where he became a favorite of famous reforming New York philanthropists Arthur and Lewis Tappan, and he later became president of abolitionist Oberlin College.[90]

By 1830, Weld was devoting himself to both temperance and aiding the anti-slavery cause.[91] In 1831, he traveled throughout the west as a general agent of the Society for Promoting Manual Labor Literary Institutions, an effort supported by Lewis Tappan, Gale, and others.[92] Weld had met Tappan at the Oneida Institute after Tappan's two sons had enrolled at Gale's school. Manual labor schools provided a means by which young men could pay for their room and board and achieve an education, while simultaneously doing regular chores and physical labor at a school.[93] During this trip, Weld also agreed to look for a suitable place to locate a theological seminary in the West. He journeyed over 4,500 miles throughout parts of the Middle West and into the South advocating manual labor education and observing slavery first hand. Weld reported that he moved across the country by means of public conveyances, riding horseback, and sometimes by walking.

As a result of this journey, he decided to move to Cincinnati in 1833 to study theology at the Lane Seminary, and he convinced many students at the Oneida Institute to join him at the school not far from the banks of the Ohio River. The river town by then had a population of over thirty thousand and had gained the name Queen City of the West. Though he might very well have been made a member of the faculty at Lane, Weld decided to enroll as a student instead.[94] Following the upheaval of the student rebellion at Lane, Weld went north with most of his fellow Lane Rebels to the Oberlin community. The majority of these young men continued their studies by enrolling at Oberlin College, but Weld decided to turn down the opportunity to teach at the school.[95] Instead, Weld chose a different course, and from that point forward he became an established figure in the nation's anti-slavery cause. Starting in the fall of 1834, his effectiveness as a fighter for freedom in Ohio was remarkable. Weld's success as an abolitionist lecturer and as a recruiter of average people into local anti-slavery organizations, and his reputation as a fearless and powerful speaker before angry audiences, put him at the center of the leadership of the American Anti-Slavery Society.[96] The hostility and violence Weld faced during his speaking tours seemed to only deepen his commitment to the cause. His store of energy was always present, which helped him counter his confrontations with the mobs he faced down. Weld did not randomly select places to lecture but instead chose locations where

Cincinnati (Slab) Hall where Lane Rebels lived after arriving at Oberlin College (courtesy Oberlin College Archives).

he believed there were at least a few friends of the abolitionist cause. These people guaranteed him a base of support and a degree of protection from hot-headed antagonists.

> Most of his addresses were given in the open air. Often in the winter the lecturer spoke to his audience with great coat and mittens on, and with the temperature but little above zero.
> More than once Mr. Weld eluded the smoking tar-kettle and the bag of feathers. Dead cats and carrion were often thrown at him. Once a brickbat struck him on the side of the head and made him insensible. The language used toward him was profane, vile and obscene...
> He was utterly fearless in his work. He could adapt himself to any audience...
> The women were his best helpers in escaping the fury of these assaults. He used to carry with him a big scrap-book, out of which he read extracts that made his adversaries as mad as March hares. Great efforts were made to wrest this book from his hands and burn it and destroy it. Again and again the women took it in charge and saved it from the mob.
> This was Weld's heroic time.[97]

On March 2, 1835, Weld wrote a letter from Putnam, Ohio, to Elizur Wright, Jr. This correspondence conveys what it was like for Weld during his early days of lecturing against slavery throughout Ohio. His experiences described herein, become vivid in his telling, which shows the vehemence of the opposition he faced and the tenacity and fortitude with which he confronted it. The letter stated in part:

> *My dear broth Wright,*— Since my last letter I have lectured at Concord, Ross Co., five times, at Oldtown [Frankfort], seven times, at Bloomingburg, Fayette Co., nine times, and at Circleville, Pickaway Co. fourteen times.... Went next to Circleville, the capitol of Pickaway Co. I had long heard of Circleville as violent in the extreme against abolition. Found two decided and open abolitionists and a few others in a state of transition. The Presbyterian minister, Mr. Benton, said among his people that I was a rebel, had made all the mischief at Lane Seminary, and surely a man should not be countenanced who was such a disturber of the peace. Further, he said, as I was told, that the distinguished faculty of Lane Seminary had felt themselves impelled from solemn sense of duty to warn the public against me, declaring in their official capacity that I was a remarkable instance of "monomania." Through his influence the Presbyterian church was shut against me. Finally, the vestry room of the Episcopal church was procured. At the second lecture, the mob gathered and threw eggs and stones through the window. One of the stones was so well aimed that it struck me on the head and for a moment stunned me. Paused a few minutes till the dizziness had ceased, and then went on and completed my lecture. Meanwhile some of the gentlemen had hung their cloaks up at the window, so that my head could not be so easily used as a target. The injury was not serious, though for a few days I had frequent turns of dizziness. The next day the mob were so loud in threats that the trustees of the church did not feel at liberty to grant the use of the vestry, but some of

them very cheerfully united with other friends, and procured a large room in the centre of the village, recently fitted up for a store and counting room. This would hold comfortably one hundred persons. The next night I lectured there. Room full. Stone and clubs flew merrily against the shutters. At the close as I came out, curses were showered in profusion. A large crowd had gathered round the door. Lamp black, nails, divers pockets full of stones and eggs had been provided for the occasion, and many had disguised their persons, smeared their faces, etc., to avoid recognition. But the Lord restrained them — and not a hair of my head was injured.... As ever, thine perishing. Theodore D. Weld[98]

In some communities Weld's intuition helped him decide to first win a crowd over by delivering a temperance lecture. If he felt that approach had been successful, he would shift to an anti-slavery theme the following evening. His instincts in regard to reading the mood of people he was about to address combined with his appealing personality often worked wonders.

When people knew he was in their part of the country, Weld received written invitations asking him to deliver lectures. The request below was mailed to him by members of the student body at Ohio University in Athens, Ohio:

Mr. Weld,
    Having been informed that you are laboring in the cause of Abolition at Marietta, and being desirous of hearing a course of lectures on that subject, we have deemed it proper to send you this note, requesting you to give us a call as you pass along. We whose names are hereto subscribed are students of the Ohio University. We should therefore be unwilling to take upon ourselves the responsibility of giving you an invitation in the name of the Citizens of the village. We are however warranted in believing that you would meet with a general good reception! We have made some enquiry among the people on this subject. Some of the principal citizens would be *willing* to hear, others would be *glad*. A spirit of enquiry has lately been awakened especially in the Institution. There is however *much*, and some bitter opposition. A discussion, notwithstanding, we think would be safe and we hope profitable.
    With this we subscribe ourselves
                                                            Y[ou]rs., etc.
                                                            J's Wm. Taylor
                                                            A. McFerson
                                                            C. P. Taylor
                                                            N. B. Pringon [?]
                                                            E. P. Pratt
                                                            July, 1835
    P. S. The Rev. Mr. Fullerton is here at this time: he thinks it would be well for you to come.[99]

In 1835, the Ohio State Anti-Slavery Society was established in Zanesville. Weld was one of the individuals who helped form the society that was modeled after the AASS. Ten men who later would be members of the Seventy were in attendance when the state society was organized.

Weld frequently zeroed in on the evil of the slave masters' control. He was extremely effective at attacking the addictive and character-destroying aspect of a slave owner having absolute power over another human being. This unlimited control over a slave had nothing to do with economics. "Arbitrary power is to the mind," Weld argued, "what alcohol is to the body, it intoxicates. Once power is achieved," Weld said, "the stronger the desire for it" and therefore "the more its exercise is enjoyed."[100]

In the winter of 1836, Weld asked the executive committee of the AASS to develop a plan whereby information would be gathered in order to address the needs of free blacks. Weld believed that if such a committee was established, an agent could then be employed to supervise this effort. A little over a year later, the national society created such a committee and eventually, four agents — John Miter, Augustus Wattles, Hiram Wilson, and William Yates — were assigned to this project.[101] Weld was sure that this effort of developing the potential of free blacks would help destroy the myth of African Americans' inferiority.

Despite his poor health, by the late fall of 1836, Weld had put together, from Maine to Indiana, an impressive group of committed anti-slavery crusaders. His bearing, dedication, and work ethic astonished those who closely observed him. Following his success in Ohio and Pennsylvania, he moved across New York State where hundreds of individuals flocked to his lectures.[102] Here, he often passed through familiar parts of the state where he had lived as a young man. In some towns crowds were so large people were turned away. Numerous converts followed in his wake as he moved from one town to the next, although opposition was always present. After his lectures in Rochester, New York, for example, 800 people joined the anti-slavery ranks. In Utica, he converted 600 locals.[103] In Lockport, a nasty troop of disruptive rowdies were waiting to stop Weld from speaking, but four hours later, over four hundred individuals signed on as new members of the Niagara County Anti-Slavery Society.[104] Weld's only defeat took place in Troy, New York, where the uproar over his speeches nearly resulted in his being seriously injured and culminated in a demand from the Mayor that he leave town. He always believed that his unsuccessful effort in the summer of 1836 in Troy was his greatest failure in the field.

Weld's incredible speaking ability was discussed and commented on by numerous individuals and written about in many newspapers. The *Pittsburgh Times* gave this account:

> One of Nature's great orators — not a declaimer, but a logician of great tact and power. His inexhaustible fund of an anecdote and general information, with the power of being intensely pathetic, enables him to give the greatest imaginable

interest to the subject. His powers of teaching are of the first order — this is, his facility for generalizing broadly and regularly, for passing into profound abstractions and bringing his wealth of ideas into beautiful light by clear, striking, and familiar illustrations.[105]

Catherine Birney said that Weld could "command reason and intelligence ... manly courage ... remarkable expression, and a fervent enthusiasm which made him the best platform orator of his time."[106] Wendell Phillips[107] once lamented that he never had the opportunity to hear Weld as an abolitionist lecturer, but everyone told him that he "has never been equaled."[108] Lewis Tappan recalled that when Edwin Stanton, who was later Lincoln's Secretary of War, heard Weld deliver a lecture in Ohio when Stanton was in his youth, he was "swept away." Tappan wrote:

> Previous to delivering the first, he gave notice to the audience that he had no objection to any one taking notes of what he should say. He observed a young man [Edwin Stanton] taking notes, and at the close made inquiries about him. He was told he was a young lawyer residing in the place. On reaching his lodgings, the stranger came to his room introduced himself, and said: "I went to your lecture with the intention of taking down your argument, and replying to it at a future time, but you have entirely swept away the ground of my opposition."[109]

One time Oberlin College President James Fairchild claimed that "it is doubtful whether any community was more profoundly moved by the eloquence of a single man."[110]

Historian Martin Duberman observes that Weld's psychological profile was balanced. He "formed good relationships ... worked with zest and spontaneity" and was able to "be aware of worlds beyond [his] own private horizons."[111] Weld was not a man whose "behavior patterns" were "notably eccentric." Indeed, he disliked self-serving exhibitionism and was put off by pretentious sophisticates.[112] As a young adult at both the Oneida Institute and the Lane Seminary, Weld's demeanor and countenance led to his classmates overwhelmingly recognizing him as a respected leader.

Despite his growing notoriety, Weld, by now known as "the thunderer of the West,"[113] was a shy and modest man who usually chose to avoid public notice when possible. He loathed large cities, never attended annual meetings of the AASS, accepted no office, and explained to people who found this odd that at heart he was "a backwoodsman."[114] This, in fact, was disingenuous, but there is little doubt that Weld was not comfortable in the spotlight until he was called upon to take the platform before a large audience in order to deliver an anti-slavery lecture. This probably helps explain why he is such a little known figure in American History. But, in the summer of 1836, Weld did agree to meet with the Tappan brothers in New York to chart the mission of their new agents.[115] In order to organize and train the new recruits, he was required to live in New York City. Elizer Wright, Jr., remarked that the collection of men the AASS had working together after Weld arrived in July, that included himself, Stanton and Whittier, was a "pestilence, dangerous clump of fanatics all in our little room plotting freedom for slaves."[116] Weld first sought out a group of highly regarded candidates, including individuals who some believed would refuse to join his band of agents. During the summer and fall he scoured Ohio, New York, and New England searching for worthy individuals. His tour of New England gave many abolitionists there the chance to finally meet this man whose remarkable reputation had preceded him. Elizabeth Whittier, John Greenleaf's sister, said after encountering him that his "vision of benevolence" haunted her; Ann Warren Weston rushed from her sickbed to greet him.[117] Weld returned to New York City from New England in early October but then left almost immediately for Ohio. This trip back to Ohio was the result of a strong difference of opinion that gradually came to a head between Weld and Finney. Weld had by now put the anti-slavery crusade at the top of his agenda but Finney, though still dedicated to the abolitionist cause, believed that the evangelical message should come first. In August, Weld received a letter from four fellow Lane Rebels, William T. Allan, J. W. Alvord, Sereno Streeter, and James Thome, informing him that Finney was telling them to make their primary commitment to his religious priority. Weld convinced Allan and Thome to stand with him but Alvord and Streeter decided to remain loyal to Finney. Weld returned to New York City by late October in order to ready himself to instruct his new lecturers. However, the relationship between Weld and Finney was thereafter strained forever.[118]

Once the last group of agents was finalized, they were brought to New York City for intensified instruction. The training sessions were designed to help prepare the servants of the cause for the difficult task ahead and provide them with answers to the tough questions that would be posed to them during their lectures. These included:

1. What would happen to slaves if they were immediately freed?
2. Would former slaves engage in revenge towards former owners and other whites?
3. Would emancipation ruin the nation's economy and destroy the South?
4. Did not the Bible say that Hebrews held slaves?
5. Would freed slaves overrun the North?
6. How should agents conduct themselves before threatening mobs?

The convention was not a secret but the recruits were told not to "bluster at all in regard to the meeting."[119] The AASS realized that due to the expanded employment of agents, they would be required to vastly increase their fundraising effort and therefore set a goal of fifty thousand dollars to meet costs.[120]

By all accounts, the agents' convention was a remarkable event. During the decade of the 1830s, its impact ranks in significance with the publication of William Lloyd Garrison's *The Liberator*, the Lane Seminary Student Debates, and the martyrdom of Illinois abolitionist newspaperman Elijah P. Lovejoy. Garrison believed that with the exception of the original meetings of the New England Anti-Slavery Society and the American Anti-Slavery Society, the agent's convention was "of higher importance than any meeting which has been held to advance the anti-slavery cause."[121] The agents left the convention very well prepared and genuinely inspired. Those who witnessed Weld's zeal and effectiveness at the agents' gathering described him later as a figure larger than life. When the sessions ended each night, he stayed up until two or three in the morning preparing for his presentations the following day. By the time he had finished his classes, his recruits had been schooled on the history of slavery and drilled on understanding the basis of the profitability of human bondage.

Henry C. Wright, one of the Seventy in attendance at the convention, jotted down notes during Weld's presentation. Wright wrote that Weld believed that first and foremost, agents should understand that slavery was a sin. Weld defined slavery as sinful, Wright noted, because of its "holding and treating persons as things. It takes man out of the sphere in which God placed him and puts him in a sphere designed to be occupied by others,"[122] like animals. There were, most likely, thirty-four recruits who attended this last training session before Weld physically broke down.[123] Garrison felt that the comradery established at the meeting was important because by bringing "the agents together" they were able to "see and hear each other, understand each other's feelings and sentiments" and form "a personal friendship with each other."[124] Garrison's *Liberator* reported on December 5, 1836, that because the Grimke sisters were present, they "frequently were appealed to" regarding "the horrors of slavery." The story in the *Liberator* ended by saying, "We do not feel at liberty to go any further with details at present. It is neither necessary nor desirable to trumpet before the agents, ostentatiously and triumphantly: let their work praise them."

Weld helped decide where agents should carry out their work. For example, if a member of the Seventy was an anti–Mason, he was not assigned to regions where freemasonry had a stronghold. Agents who were particularly articulate arguing against the precepts of the American Colonization Society were sent to those areas of the North where colonization was favored. If an agent proved to be ineffective as a public speaker, he was given an administrative assignment. Frequently, the AASS shifted agents: sometimes within a state and sometimes from one state to another.[125]

Newspapers throughout the nation that opposed the work of anti-slavery activists were alarmed after they learned of such a large meeting of abolitionists in New York City. The *New Hampshire Sentinel,* the *Albany Argus,* and the *Richmond Enquirer* wrote scathing articles about the gathering. The *New York Courier* and *Enquirer* went so far as to suggest that Americans should turn to violence as a means of retarding the efforts of the national society's agents.[126] In the 1830s, Whig James Watson Webb, who was the editor of the *Courier and Enquirer,* often attacked abolitionists because their efforts would lead to amalgamation.[127] Webb was one of the most notorious race-baiting journalists writing at that time.[128]

Almost simultaneously, a controversial event was taking place in Congress. In 1836 the House of Representatives passed a rule that forbad any hearing of or discussion about slavery. This came to be called the "Gag Rule." The following resolution was passed by the House in May of 1836:

> *Resolved,* That all petitions, memorials, resolutions, propositions, or papers relating in any way or to any extent whatever to the subject of slavery or the abolition of slavery, shall, without being either printed or referred, be laid on the table, and that no further action whatever shall be had thereon.[129]

The legislators who passed this rule unwittingly did so when the anti-slavery movement was ascending. When Congress withdrew this constitutional right, it created the opportunity for anti-slavery crusaders to ally themselves with thousands of Americans who were offended by this action. Abolitionists charged that the new rule was a violation of the Constitution and many non-abolitionists regarded the policy as an outrage. The anti-slavery movement leaped at the opportunity to take advantage of the public's negative outcry over the Gag Rule, which was perceived by large numbers of Northerners as a challenge to free speech. There followed an intense effort to repeal the Gag Rule that was not achieved until December of 1844.[130] Its repeal was brought about largely by thousands of abolitionists, many of them women, and including many of the Seventy, circulating petitions that were signed and sent to the nation's capital where they flooded Congress. Petitions were left in banks, churches, and places of business where they were picked up and signed by people from all walks of life. The fight against the Gag Rule was led by John Quincy Adams and the petition drive was substantially orchestrated by Stanton, Whittier, and Weld.[131] In 1837, the AASS passed the following resolution urging every one of its county auxiliaries to help with the petition campaign:

> DEAR SIR,— The following resolution was passed by the American Anti-Slavery Society, at its recent meeting in this city:
> "*Resolved,* That it is earnestly requested of the Secretary of each County Anti-Slavery Society in the Union, to forward by mail, immediately, to Elizur Wright, Jr., in the city of New-York, the name of one or more suitable persons, in each

town of said country, with their post office address, to circulate Anti-Slavery petitions for signatures."

It is the intention of the Society, to present to Congress and our State legislatures, at their next sessions, the names of as many petitioners, as possible...

And now, sir, we wish you, whether the Secretary of a County Anti-Slavery Society, or not, to procure and forward, to this office, as soon as possible, the names of one or two thorough and efficient abolitionists, in each of the towns in your country, to whom we can forward petitions...

In forwarding the names, be pleased to write them in a *plain hand*, and be careful to annex to each, *the Post Office address*. If you cannot forward names from *all* the towns, do so from as many as possible. Let the importance of the subject excuse us for again urging you, *to do this without delay*.[132]

The national society also emphasized that petitions be sent to Congress in regard to ending slavery in the territories, rejecting the annexation of Texas as a slave state, and putting an end to interstate slave trafficking.[133]

Lydia Maria Child was one of the leaders of the women's petition campaign against the Gag Rule. Child and her courageous female colleagues frequently faced disapproval and disrespect while taking petitions to people asking for signatures. There were so many petitions sent to Congress that several clerks were hired to process the sea of paper delivered to the capital by the wagonloads. Ironically, the success of the petition campaign helped reduce the need for AASS agents. Local volunteers went from relative to relative, friend to friend, and neighbor to neighbor asking them to put their names on the petitions. Therefore, as the number of local petitioners increasingly took up this work, it was not necessary to bring in outside organizers.[134]

When the Seventy were first spreading out across the North, Theodore Weld was required to concentrate on the recovery of his health. He gradually grew stronger by engaging in a physical fitness program and following the Graham Diet.[135] But by April of 1837, Weld was convinced that his voice was so thoroughly ruined that he could no longer be an agent; he officially resigned as one on April 14. Later that year, he considered taking a trip to England with Charles Stuart but decided not to do so because of his poor health. In a correspondence from Weld to Louis Tappan in early June of 1837, he wrote:

My general health is pretty good, but I become very hoarse if I attempt to *speak* or even to *discuss* in conversation if at all excited. I don't understand it. I wish much to talk with you about the matter broached by you in your letter by Brother B. God willing, we will confer about it when we meet.[136]

Despite Weld's distaste for cities, he moved from the country to New York City. He regained his health while living in a small attic room at night and working in the office building of the AASS by day, but he refused to accept a salary. Here, he directed the work of the society's agents and prepared his two primary publications — *The Bible Against Slavery* (1837) and *American Slavery As It Is: Testimony of a Thousand Witnesses* (1839). The former work, as the title suggests, laid out Weld's biblical arguments against human bondage; parts of the pamphlet were often quoted in other anti-slavery publications. In this work Weld gave particular attention to slavery's violation of the eighth commandment, "thou shalt not steal," and the tenth commandment that forbids coveting "anything that is thy neighbor's."[137] The later work was a major influence on Harriet Beecher Stowe, who later wrote that she "slept with it under her pillow until it crystallized into *Uncle Tom's Cabin*."[138]

By 1840, *American Slavery As It Is,* which was substantially put together and edited by the Grimke sisters, had become one of the best selling books in the country. Weld and the Grimke sisters were certain the text would greatly aid the petition campaign. In the book's introduction, Weld asked his readers to think of themselves as "witnesses" who had been "empannelld (sic) as a juror to try a plain case and bring in an honest verdict." The readers were implored to answer the question: "Is slavery, as a condition for human beings, good, bad, or indifferent? You have common sense, and a conscience and a human heart," Weld said, "pronounce upon" the question.

The book portrayed the treatment of slaves in the American south as heartless and brutal. Slavery allowed slaveholders to indulge in an extravagant lifestyle and showed them as totally lacking in human decency. The text was organized to answer questions the public frequently asked about slaves and slaveholders by individuals who had personally observed the evils of slavery. This work did not hold back on graphic accounts of what slaves regularly had to endure. It described overworked and exhausted men and women who were flogged, mutilated, and sometimes "branded with red-hot irons."[139] The book gave accounts of young boys forced to brutally fight one another for the amusement of their masters, described female slaves bred like livestock, and related stories of runaway slaves shot to death while trying to escape.

American Slavery As It Is gave significant attention to the loathsome character and vicious behavior of overseers. The overseers were responsible for the regular daily operation of slaves' work and functioned as the drivers of large slaveholding plantations. A Rev. Horton Moulton who had moved to Massachusetts from Georgia, described overseers as "generally loose in morals ... those who whip and torment slaves the most are in many instances called the best." Another contributor to the book pointed out that they were men of "low repute" and not "permitted to come to the table of their employers." When slaves committed offenses like stealing, arson, or attempted escapes, overseers were given the job of handing out particularly gruesome punishments for these transgressions. *American Slavery As It Is,* more than anything else, illustrated that slavery could only exist by means of violence or the threat of violence.

In the late 1830s and early '40s, as noted earlier, Weld also effectively reinforced John Quincy Adam's opposition to the Gag Rule. Weld carried out this effort with numerous individuals who were among his abolitionist comrades over the years. In 1841, he moved to Washington, D.C., where he lobbied Congressmen and served as an advisor to Adams. Weld was urged by Ohio's anti-slavery Whig Congressman Joshua Giddings to move to the nation's capital in order to carry out this work. On occasion, Giddings, Weld, and their abolitionist cohorts would huddle outside the House of Representatives in full view of Southern Congressmen.[140] Weld remained in the capital until 1843, when he returned to private life.[141]

Gradually Weld moved farther and farther away from the anti-slavery crusade. He and his wife, Angelina, had three children, and eventually moved to New Jersey, living on a farm near Belleville where they opened a coeducational school.[142] Later, in 1854, they moved to Perth Amboy, New Jersey, and started teaching at the Eagleswood School.[143] In 1863, the Welds moved to Fairmouth, Massachusetts, which later became Hyde Park in Boston.[144] Weld briefly attempted a speaking tour during the Civil War but was physically unable to continue with these lectures because his voice failed him. But in the midst of the War, Weld and the Grimke sisters alerted their fellow Americans of the need to address the exploitation of society's have-nots that were the "dragon-brood" of slavery; "aristocracy, caste, monopoly, class legislation, exclusive privilege and prerogative all legalized oppression of the weak by the strong."[145]

Following the war, he and his wife continued to stand up for the rights of African Americans and women. In 1868, Theodore, Angelina, and Sarah were made officials of the Massachusetts Women's Suffrage Association.[146] In the 1870s, Weld harshly criticized the federal government for negligence in regard to insufficiently enforcing the rights of freedmen in the South. He also dedicated himself to helping to establish and finance the construction of a new library in Hyde Park and he served on the school board.[147] In addition, he helped organize the community's historical society. Angelina died in 1879, but Weld, who by now had grown a long white beard, lived in Massachusetts until 1895. Ten years before he died, Weld described what he recalled about the hardships abolitionists endured during the time of his service to the anti-slavery cause:

[They] were the victims of an indiscriminate ostracism, everywhere they were doomed because they hated slavery and lived out that hate. In thousands of cases [abolitionists] were subjected to personal assaults, beatings, and buffetings, with nameless indignities. They were stoned, clubbed, knocked down, and pelted with missiles, often with eggs, and, when they could get them, spoiled ones. They were smeared with filth, stripped of clothing, tarred, feathered, ridden upon rails, their houses sacked, bonfires made in the streets of their furniture, garments, and bedding, their vehicles and harnesses cut and broken, and their domestic animals harried, dashed with hot water, cropped, crippled, and killed. Among those outrages, besides assaults and breaches of the peace, there were sometimes burglaries, robberies, maimings, and arsons; abolitionists were driven from their homes into the fields and the woods and their houses burned. They were dragged and thrust from the halls in which they held their meetings. They were often shot at and sometimes wounded.[148]

Weld occasionally gave lectures about educational topics and the works of Shakespeare until he was nearly ninety years old. He died in his sleep in 1895 at age 91 and was buried in Boston's Mount Hope Cemetery.

Many scholars have been puzzled over Weld's withdrawal from public life by the mid–1840s. Why did this giant figure choose to permanently disengage himself as a leading spokesman for the abolitionist crusade? Dumond suggests that by then it was the only thing left for Weld to do. The Gag Rule had finally been repealed, and Weld most certainly wanted nothing to do with the extremism of "Garrisonians." Another reason as to why he stepped away from actively associating himself with the movement was his inclination to believe that it was bad timing for the crusade to involve itself with political parties. In addition, Weld was by then responsible for raising a family, and he undoubtedly worried about his health failing again while caring for his children. His son, Theodore, was frequently unhealthy as a child. There can be no question of the fact that he did not want to associate himself with abolitionists who opposed women's involvement with the cause. In a letter Weld wrote to Lewis Tappan in 1843, he clearly explained why he rejected any affiliation with the American and Foreign Anti-Slavery Society because of the society's refusal to allow women to be part of the organization's operation:

Dear brother Tappan,
   I learn from brother Leavitt that the Ex. Com. Of the Am. And For. Anti S. Soc, have appointed me as one of their representative to the London Convention. I write this to beg that my name may not be published as one of the representatives of the A. and F. A. S. S. And for this reason (One which I have no doubt all the committee fully understand) I totally dissent from the *foundation principle* on which the society is based — a *denial* of the equal membership of women — and if my appointment as their representative were made public, I should feel impelled to make equally public the *reasons* forcing me to decline, and to do it *in such a way* as would inevitably bring up anew the questions of women's rights to speak, vote, sit on committees, etc., in connection with the Slave's right to personal ownership with all its attributes and in all its relations.
   Now, free to utter and to act out my convictions upon the subject of women's rights, and doing it at all times and places in my judgement calling for it, as you and all my friends well know, still the agitation of that question in *connection with* abolition societies and their operations I believe always has been, and *must* be, only evil and that continually in its effect on the *slave's deliverance*. I pray

therefore that you will not by *publishing* my appointment, make it necessary for me to set that ball in motion again. The question never would have become, as it has, inextricably twisted into the abolition question, but for the persevering attempt to deprive women of what are, in my estimation, their inalienable rights. *You* most conscientiously thought otherwise, and *acted out your conscience.*[149]

Tappan bitterly remarked later that Weld had gone into "a ditch opposite his house, doing work any Irishman could do for 75 cents a day."[150]

It also seems to have been the case that by the mid–1840s, Weld decided to withdraw himself from working for the abolitionist cause, because he had come to the conclusion that an open conflict between the North and the South was inevitable.[151] But of even greater significance was the fact that Weld's personality had drifted away from that of an evangelical orator, towards a behavior that followed the dictates of gentle restraints. He was no longer the rebel of his youth: he had simply become a different kind of person. Weld was, by then, more of a humanitarian Christian who was no longer drawn to institutionalized religious orthodoxy.[152]

What follows, in Chapter 3, is a listing of Weld's Seventy with comments and anecdotes about each member of his band of agents.

Chapter 3

Members of the Seventy

Theodore Dwight Weld

On November 4, 1836, Elizur Wright, Jr., corresponding secretary of the American Anti-Slavery Society, wrote a letter to Weld just before the commencement of the New York agents' convention, which brought together the last of Weld's recruits. In the second and third paragraphs of Wright's letter, he acknowledged to his friend and colleague the "great responsibility" Weld was about to face. His letter read in part:

Theodore Dwight Weld (courtesy Massachusetts Historical Society).

I know the agents' meeting is a *great responsibility*. But I am more convinced than ever of the need of it. Indeed, as things now are, it seems to me absolutely indispensable to the cause.... We have strongly and seasonably invited Birney; Scott and several others have expressed to me their warmest and most joyous approbation of the measure. No one within my knowledge has hinted any dissatisfaction. I do hope you will never regret *swallowing* your "repugnancies," *modesty* and all. If in this matter we shall be found to have erred, I certainly will not throw any of the blame on *you*.

I think from the first part of my letter you will have seen that we need this meeting almost as much for the sake of our committee, as of the agents themselves. There are some members of our committee, who with all the prominence that has been given to them, have never more than half conceived the magnitude and urgency of the work. They need to have a lodgement made in them of two ideas. 1. This

68

cause is worthy of *more effort than any other*, at this time. 2. Want of *faith* in it is a crime against the Savior. Our friend A. T[appan] should be disabused of the idea that if he and G[errit] Smith and two or three others should fail to pay their notes at *three o'clock* some day, the cause of God's oppressed would fall through! Our committee once in a while falls into a fit of practical "expediency," and puts *prudence* against *faith*. If there ever was a cause where they went together, it is this. The whole of the big fallow is as mellow as an ash-heap and we, forsooth, are too prudent to buy seed more than enough to sow a few patches, for fear we shall not have enough money to pay the harvesters! I do trust in God that when our band of worthies come to pray together and feel together on this subject, they will make such an expression of their views, and give such a pledge of their energies, as will put our silly fears to a shameful rout...

E. Wright, Jr.

[P.S.] I have cautioned all the agents against making any *bluster at all* in regard to the meeting.[1]

William T. Allan

The son of an Alabama slave owner, William enrolled at Lane Seminary with his brother James. Both of the Allan brothers had met Weld as young men at their father's home in Alabama when Weld was traveling through the South. During the Lane Seminary debates, Allan's descriptions of the horrors of slavery had a profound effect on his classmates. He said of human bondage that "cruelty is the rule and kindness the exception." When the debates ended, William was made president of the Lane Student Anti-Slavery Society, and after withdrawing from the school, he went north to Oberlin. He was commissioned as an agent of the AASS in 1835, and became one of the society's most valuable figures. In 1836, Allan wrote to Weld and said that he had concluded "it is my duty to plead directly the cause of the poor and needy ... my brethren are in bonds."

Allan lectured in Ohio, Michigan, Pennsylvania, and New York, where his relentless speaking schedule left him exhausted. Between January 1 and February 3 of 1837, Allan gave thirty-six speeches in thirty-four days. In the fifty-seven days between February 3 and March 27, he spoke fifty times. Over a period of fifty-five days from late March through the third week of May, he spoke nearly every day or evening. By the end of May, in need of "a haven of rest," Allan retired as an agent, remarking that he was relieved to step away from the "tumults and distractions" that he experienced during his lecturing tour. He has been warned to stay away from his boyhood home or have his throat cut.

Allan eventually settled in Illinois, where he became a dedicated Underground Railroad operator, worked for the Illinois State Anti-Slavery Society lecturing passionately for the organization's cause in various counties and became a significant political ally of anti-slavery congressman Owen Lovejoy.

In the early 1860s, Lovejoy informed Weld that he owed his seat in the House of Representatives to Allan, who had been responsible for turning Lovejoy's congressional district into an abolitionist stronghold. Allan was one of the most powerful influences for freedom in Illinois.[2]

Guy Beckley

A Northfield, Vermont, clergyman, a strong supporter of the temperance movement, and an effective solicitor of funds for the AASS, Beckley lectured against slavery in Vermont and New Hampshire, even when warned not to beforehand. His service commenced on September 30, 1836, and while attending Weld's New York agents' convention, he was refused permission to preach in Methodist churches in the city because of his anti-slavery views. Beckley worked as an agent in 1837 and 1838, but was not salaried during his second year of service. He reported that people sometimes left their jobs and came out of the fields in order to hear him speak. Beckley moved to Michigan in 1838 where he later co-edited the anti-slavery weekly, the *Signal of Liberty* with Theodore Foster. The newspaper was published from 1841 until 1848. Beckley was actively involved with the Michigan Anti-Slavery Society, supported the activities of the Liberty party, and while living in Ann Arbor, he became a committed Underground Railroad operator.[3]

Henry Beldon

Born in Greenfield, Connecticut, in 1813, he studied at the Union Theological Seminary, the Andover Theological Seminary, and Princeton. Beldon was a Presbyterian minister who was appointed as an AASS agent in the summer of 1836, but it seems he did not begin working for the national society until that fall. He was recommended to be an agent by Elizur Wright, Jr. Beldon assisted fellow agent Ray Potter as a lecturer in Rhode Island at a time when that state's anti-slavery efforts had become somewhat neglected. He was later assigned by the agency committee to continue abolitionist work in several Pennsylvania counties after Weld's New York agents' convention. In New York Beldon reported being harassed in every building at which he spoke with the exception of private homes. He later served on the executive committee of the American and Foreign Anti-Slavery Society and he also worked for the American Home Missionary Society.[4]

James G. Birney

One of the most prominent figures in the anti-slavery movement, Birney was born in Danville, Kentucky, graduated from Princeton in 1810, and lived for a time in Alabama. While living in Alabama, Birney met Weld at the home of slave-holding, Presbyterian minister James Allan, the father of William T. and James M. Allan. Birney and the two Allan sons were greatly influenced by Weld's anti-slavery positions during the time they were with him in Huntsville.

Birney returned to Kentucky and decided to address the issue of slavery in earnest. He was initially a "colonizationist" and for a time served the ACS as one of their agents. By 1834, he had become "an immediatist" but his views were so unpopular in Kentucky, he decided to move to Cincinnati. In 1835, Birney wrote a letter to Gerrit Smith stating that either "slavery shall be exterminated or liberty destroyed."

In Ohio, he printed the anti-slavery publication *The Philanthropist*; few abolitionists put pen to paper better than Birney. In 1836, an anti abolitionist mob broke into his office and smashed his printing press. Birney managed to convert very influential individuals to the abolitionist cause from the clergy, colleges, various professions and businesses. He became an executive officer of the American Anti-Slavery Society in 1837. Birney condemned churches that did not enthusiastically back abolitionism, and he believed that religious organizations were obligated to refuse financial support from slaveholders. In 1840, Birney was a vice-president at the World Anti-Slavery Convention in London.

A strong proponent of taking the abolitionist movement in a political direction, Birney became the Liberty Party candidate for President in 1840 and 1844. The Liberty Party was a militant organization that did not address other political topics but instead focused exclusively on the anti-slavery cause. In 1845, Birney became an invalid, retired from public life and later moved close to Perth Amboy, New Jersey, where Weld and his family were living.[5]

James M. Blakesley

Blakesley was an Oberlin graduate who conducted the majority of his anti-slavery lecturing and organizing in New York State, often coordinating his efforts there with fellow agent Henry Bowen. While lecturing in New York, Blakesley had to dodge thrown candlesticks, tobacco boxes, and brickbats. In Chautauqua County twenty supporters marched with him to a lecture site and fought off a fist-fighting mob in order to let him speak. In the community of Colden, Blakesley enlisted 200 people to the anti-slavery cause, which represented about one-fifth the town's population. Blakesley also aided Henry B. Stanton's anti-slavery efforts in Rhode Island and he helped establish the Providence Juvenile Anti-Slavery Society. Like other members of the Seventy, when mobs attempted to break up his meetings in public, he moved the gatherings to private residences. As a lecturer, he reported strong support from clergymen. His service as an AASS agent ended in March of 1837, but in 1838, he was selected as an agent by the New York State Anti-Slavery Society. In 1840, Blakesley carried out missionary work in Jamaica with former American Anti-Slavery Society agents Amos Dresser and Charles Renshaw.[6]

Jonathan Blanchard

Born in Rockingham, New York, in 1813, Blanchard graduated from Middlebury College in 1832. He then served as principal of the Plattsburg Academy in New York during which time he defended anti-slavery sentiment. Blanchard was a very effective agent for the AASS in Pennsylvania, and he is given credit for converting Thaddeus Stevens to the antislavery cause. He carried out effective work in south-central Pennsylvania and as many as twenty-five of his meetings were interrupted by anti abolitionists. He was once stoned on the streets of Harrisburg.

Blanchard studied at Lane after the student slavery debates, became the minister of Cincinnati's Sixth Presbyterian Church and also helped James G. Birney edit *The Philanthropist*. He was made the second president of abolitionist Knox College in 1846, where he was involved with Galesburg's Underground Railroad activities. During his tenure at Knox, he consistently appointed abolitionists to the College's Board of Trustees. Throughout the course of his life, he supported the temperance movement and was vehemently opposed to secret societies. Blanchard later became the president of Wheaton College in Northern Illinois, after a falling-out with Knox's founder, George Washington Gale.[7]

Henry Bowen

Bowen entered the Oneida Institute as a supporter of the American Colonization Society, but after the 1833 student debates about slavery at the school, he embraced "immediatism," and helped establish the institute's anti-slavery society. The AASS assigned Bowen to deliver lectures and organize local societies in Western New York state. During the course of his lecturing, he often collaborated with fellow agents James Blakesley and George Storrs. When inclement weather halted his speaking schedule, Bowen reported passing time reading anti-slavery literature in order to improve his deliveries. He devoted much of his time in the field circulating petitions in an effort to defeat the Gag Rule. His service to the national society ended in 1837. Bowen turned down an offer by the agency committee in September of that year to be an agent in Indiana.[8]

Charles C. Burleigh

Born in Plainsfield, Connecticut, in 1810, Burleigh was a founder of the New England Anti-Slavery Society. He was editor of both the *Connecticut Unionist* and the *Pennsylvania Freeman* and was an eloquent speaker with the ability to aptly extemporize. Burleigh, who lectured for the national society in Rhode Island, Connecticut, and Pennsylvania, was known for his shoulder length hair, massive red beard, and shabby attire. In Pennsylvania, in addition to his lecturing, Burleigh spent a great deal of time supporting the state society's organizational meetings. He was twice jailed in Pennsylvania for selling anti-slavery literature.

Poor health often required him to restrict his work as an agent. In December of 1837, he sailed to the West Indies to improve his health but he returned the following May. Burleigh was later an agent of the Pennsylvania State Anti-Slavery Society in 1839 and 1840; he also worked for the AASS in Ohio in 1842. New England abolitionist Parker Pillsbury wrote that "in argument he [Burleigh] had no superior and few equals." He was said to sometimes hold audiences "breathless and silent for hours." He was a talented debater, opponent of capital punishment and supporter of women's rights. In 1845, Burleigh published *Thoughts on the Death Penalty.* When the Women's Rights Convention in Worceter, Massachusetts, was called in 1850, Burleigh was an active participant, and in 1859, he was made Corresponding Secretary of the AASS.[9]

William H. Burleigh

A Yale graduate, William was the brother of Charles C. Burleigh. As a young man, he was an apprentice clothier and printer. He became a temperance advocate, peace movement activist, and member of the Liberty Party. Burleigh possessed an amiable personality, superior intellect, and was a gifted public speaker. In Connecticut, he was the editor of the anti-slavery publication *Christian Freeman* that later became the *Charter Oak*, which was crafted as an anti-slavery family-based newspaper. He was also the editor of the *Christian Witness*, a publication supported by the Pennsylvania state anti-slavery society. A great deal of Burleigh's work as an agent was conducted in Connecticut, where he was once arrested for violating the state's black laws. He also worked as an American Anti-Slavery Society agent in Pennsylvania. Burleigh's volumes of poems, many of which were reform-based poetry, were published between 1841 and 1849. Later in his life, Burleigh was involved with the Liberty party, served as both harbor master and port warden in New York, and was corresponding secretary of the New York State Temperance Soci-ety.[10]

W. L. Chaplin

Born in Groton, Massachusetts, and educated at Harvard, Chaplin became a lawyer in Farmington, New York. He helped establish an anti-slavery society in Lowell, Massachusetts, and later was made general agent of the New York Anti-Slavery Society. The AASS agency committee had him work in various New England states, but illness limited his service for the national society in late 1836 and early 1837. In Auburn, New York, after he delivered a single lecture, more than one hundred people enlisted in the abolitionist cause. In 1838, when the national organization was starting to show signs of division, Chaplin expressed dissatisfaction with the American Anti-Slavery Society's dictatorial policies and consequently, he came to support the notion that state societies should fund their own programs. He later became a very influential member of the Liberty Party and helped launch the new political organization. Chaplin was a particularly active Underground Railroad operator and he was once jailed for helping fugitive slaves escape.[11]

Ichabod Codding

Educated at Middlebury College, at an early age Codding committed himself to the temperance movement. As a college student, Codding grew distressed with what he learned about slavery, asked for a short leave of absence in order to lecture for abolitionism and when Middlebury's administrators refused, he withdrew from the school.

Codding was one of the American Anti-Slavery Society's most remarkable agents. Abolitionist historian John L. Meyers maintains that he should be included in a list of the most influential anti-slavery advocates in the nation between 1837 and 1840. Codding lectured throughout Vermont, but carried out particularly effective anti-slavery work in Maine. He also lectured for a very brief time in New York and Massachusetts and he later preached in Connecticut for two years. He was a famous orator, whose spellbinding speeches often left his audiences awestruck.

After Codding moved to the Middle West, he continued to be a champion of abolitionism in Illinois and Wisconsin. He was involved with Underground Railroad activities while living in Illinois, worked tirelessly for the Liberty Party, supported women's involvement in the abolitionist cause, and also helped establish Wisconsin's first anti-slavery newspaper. Codding vigorously opposed the Kansas-Nebraska Act and when the Republican Party was founded, he was one of its earliest converts.[12]

Nathaniel Colver

Colver was born in Orwell, Vermont, in 1794. In 1829, being suspicious of secret societies, he joined the anti–Mason movement. He was a tanner, a War of 1812 Veteran, a Vermont and New York clergyman and an agent for the American Anti-Slavery Society in New York, Pennsylvania, Connecticut, and Massachusetts. In 1835, Colver helped establish the New York State Anti-Slavery Society; he was recommended to be an AASS agent by Charles Stuart. In Redding, Connecticut, in 1838, only hours after he delivered an anti-slavery lecture, the building in which he had spoken was bombed.

He was an excellent debater who possessed an eloquent speaking style; John Quincy Adams once said that Colver "was the best off-handed speaker I ever heard." Colver, who was a very popular temperance lecturer, held ministerial posts in Detroit, Cincinnati, and Chicago. He decided to decline an offer by the agency committee to work for the anti-slavery cause in Indiana in 1837. While attending the World Anti-Slavery Convention in England in 1840, he opposed women's inclusion at the gathering. He founded the Tremont Temple in Boston to educate black clergymen, and Colver Institute, which eventually merged with Wayland Seminary to form Virginia Union University.[13]

John Cowles

The son of a temperance advocate, Cowles was educated at Yale and later graduated from Oberlin in 1836. Admired for his keen mind, he was the principal of Oberlin's Preparatory School and a mathematics professor at the college. He opposed the college's move to establish joint education for men and women. Cowles was a charter member of the Oberlin Anti-Slavery Society and was highly respected by his fellow anti-slavery agents, who unanimously recommended him for AASS service. His brother, Henry, was also a respected teacher at Oberlin and a committed abolitionist. John Cowles was aligned with the anti–Garrison faction of the anti-slavery movement. While lecturing in Michigan, he was instrumental in establishing the state's anti-slavery society. He once faced a vicious attack in Pontiac where a local sheriff intervened in order to prevent bloodshed when a member of a mob waved a knife towards him.[14]

John Cross

Born in Ashfield, Massachusetts, in 1797, Cross prepared for the ministry at the Oneida Institute, where he befriended the school's founder, George Washington Gale. He revelled at calling attention to the abolitionist cause.

Cross lectured as an agent for the American Anti-Slavery Society in New York and Pennsylvania. In the course of his lectures, he reported being burned in effigy, learning how to avoid missiles being hurled at him, and dealing with individuals who tried to prevent him from being heard by playing loud music. He significantly aided the Underground Railroad movement in Michigan.

He was sent by the AASS to Illinois in 1839, where he had to personally finance most of his anti-slavery efforts. Cross helped organize and launch the Liberty Party in the Prairie State and his audacious UGRR efforts in Illinois were openly advertised in newspapers and posted notices. In 1844, Cross drew an illustration to advertise his efforts aiding fugitive slaves and printed his sketch, with his name attached, in the anti-slavery newspaper, *The Western Citizen*. The advertisement depicted freedom seekers on a UGRR train that disappeared into a tunnel. In 1846, he affiliated himself with the Wesleyan Methodists and for the next five years was a circuit riding preacher. In the late 1850s, Cross continued his abolitionist efforts in southern Iowa.[15]

Amos Dresser

A Lane Seminary Rebel, Dresser studied at the Oneida Institute and graduated from Oberlin in 1839. Dresser worked for the anti-slavery cause in several states, but he carried out very significant work in Massachusetts and also lectured in Rhode Island. While traveling through Tennessee in 1835 selling Bibles, Dresser was discovered carrying anti-slavery literature. He was seized and flogged by mechanics and workmen before a large crowd. The beating gave him notoriety, and he was a focus of attention at Weld's 1836 New York convention. Dresser was a missionary in Jamaica from 1839 to 1841, but he overworked himself there and returned to the United States. He later lectured for a time in the British Isles. Dresser was involved with the Peace Movement and in 1849 published *The Bible Against War*. He was also a teacher at Olivet Institute in Michigan and was a clergyman in Ohio and Nebraska.[16]

Edward Henry Fairchild

Born in Stockbridge, Massachusetts, in 1815, Fairchild was educated at Oberlin. Fairchild was a minister and brother of James Fairchild, the third president of Oberlin. In 1835, Edward Fairchild became a member of the Oberlin Anti-Slavery Society. He lectured in Erie and Crawford Counties in Ohio and was also an abolitionist crusader in western Pennsylvania, serving the AASS as its only agent in that part of the state in late 1836 and early 1837. An anti abolitionist once drove Fairchild and his listeners from a lecture site by causing the room to fill with sulfur fumes.

He briefly taught at a black school in Cincinnati and was, for several years, a minister in Ohio, Michigan and New York. Fairchild became principal of Oberlin's Preparatory Department in 1853 and wrote the pamphlet *Historical Sketch of Oberlin College*. Fairchild later became President of Berea College in Kentucky. Berea, which flourished under his leadership, was established in the mid–1850s to promote the education of blacks and whites, men and women. He vastly expanded Berea's physical plant and increased the school's enrollment.[17]

Hiram Foote

A Lane Seminary Rebel, Foote studied at the Oneida Institute where he initiated the student Gravel Debate about slavery in 1833. He was the first president of the institute's anti-slavery society and, following the society's establishment, the school's colonization society gradually disappeared. Foote, a Finney convert, took part in the New York temperance convention in 1833. He completed his education at Oberlin and was an abolitionist lecturer in Ohio. Foote later became a minister in Illinois and Wisconsin where he was an Underground Railroad activist. He was a delegate to the first anniversary meeting of the Illinois State Anti-Slavery Society in 1838. Hiram Foote's brother Horatio was also an abolitionist, an admirer of Charles G. Finney and a trustee of Illinois' Knox College. Hiram Foote eventually became secretary of the American Tract Society, worked for the American Sunday School Union, and was a trustee of the Wisconsin Institute for the Blind. Foote also worked as a home missionary in New York and Minnesota from 1865 to 1886.[18]

Samuel Gould

A Lane Seminary Rebel, Gould successfully raised money for the AASS; only Henry B. Stanton raised more funds for the national society. Gould was particularly effective at making sure that pledges made to the American Anti-Slavery Society from state and local societies were in fact collected. In 1835, he was employed by the Rhode Island Anti-Slavery Society and was also assigned to that state by the AASS in October of the same year. He reported very favorable reactions to his anti-slavery work in Rhode Island.

Gould worked in Pennsylvania for the national society for eleven months. During one stretch of time, he traveled over one hundred miles, delivering fourteen lectures in an eight-day period. Gould once stirred a great controversy by delivering a speech to a black audience in Harrisburg. The community's town council announced that his speech had excited "the colored population" and instructed him to "desist from his efforts." He also lectured in Ohio,

Massachusetts and New York and on one occasion in Poughkeepsie, barely escaped serious injury with only a torn coat when a mob threatened to have him tarred and feathered. During Weld's New York's agents' convention in 1836, Gould aided in the training of the society's new recruits. In June of 1838, Gould stepped down as a lecturer when he experienced serious throat problems.[19]

Angelina Grimke

Born in South Carolina, Angelina, as a young woman was a Presbyterian, but her convictions caused her to withdraw her membership because of the church's attitude toward slavery. She converted to the Quaker faith after moving to Philadelphia, where she attached herself to the abolitionist cause. Angelina was particularly influenced to join the anti-slavery crusade after she learned of Garrison being mobbed in Boston. She was a leading women's rights advocate and a gifted, riveting speaker who helped vindicate a woman's right to speak publicly. She was a strong supporter of Free Produce Principles and consistently argued against the idea of compensating slaveholders if their slaves were emancipated. In 1851, Angelina attended the Women's Rights Convention in Rochester, New York, and in 1863, she was a delegate to the National Convention of Women in New York City. Although she abhorred violence, she strongly supported the Union cause during the Civil War. Her notes of attendees at Weld's 1836 New York agents' convention helped verify names of many who were present at the gathering.[20]

Sarah Grimke

Thirteen years older than her sister Angelina, Sarah moved to Philadelphia in 1821, became a Quaker, and like her sister, rejected her aristocratic, slave-holding family in South Carolina. Their mother was the daughter of Governor Smith of North Carolina, and their father was a justice of South Carolina's Supreme Court. As a girl, she revolted against restraints on female education. Unlike her sister, Sarah was not gifted at public speaking but she recognized and often pointed out similarities between the status of women and the enslaved. "Men," she said, "have attempted to drive women from almost every sphere of moral action." In 1838, Sarah was the author of *Letters on the Equality of the Sexes*. That same year, she and her sister Angelina were disowned by the Quakers; Angelina for marrying Theodore Weld outside of the faith, and Sarah for attending the wedding. She strongly supported the petition campaign to repeal the Gag Rule, and later joined Weld and her sister as an educator. Sarah Grimke died at the age of 81 in 1873.[21]

Cyrus P. Grosvenor

Grosvenor was educated at Dartmouth and the Princeton Theological Seminary. He was a Baptist minister in New Haven, Boston, and Salem, who served as an AASS agent in Massachusetts and Rhode Island. In Massachusetts Grosvenor's efforts were sometimes carried out with fellow agents Amos Dresser and Henry B. Stanton. Grosvenor was one of the leading Baptist clergymen in the anti-slavery movement and he served for a time as editor of the Baptist weekly newspaper, *The Christian Reflector*. He often quarreled with the national society's leadership about their policies regarding expense reimbursements which is most likely the reason his service ended in January of 1837. Grosvenor was selected as the president of Central College in Cortland County, New York, in 1837. Throughout his life he supported equal education for men and women. Grosvenor vigorously backed the idea of the anti-slavery movement becoming political and eventually worked for the Liberty Party. He attended the World Anti-Slavery Convention in London in 1840.[22]

Jonathon Hazelton

A native of New Hampshire, Hazelton was a Methodist minister who abandoned support of "colonization" and embraced immediate emancipation in the mid–1830s. He was hired as an agent in August of 1836, attended Weld's New York convention in November and December and was assigned by the agency committee to his home state of New Hampshire, where he conducted a very strenuous speaking tour that fall. Hazelton felt that his effectiveness as a lecturer was enhanced because of his reputation in his home territory. He carried out effective work in the state's three northwestern counties. Hazelton reported opposition to his efforts by individuals who claimed his lectures would cause civil unrest and pit neighbor against neighbor. He was characterized as "zealous in the cause" and during a three-week period in January of 1837, Hazelton delivered fifteen lectures. His period of service as an anti-slavery lecturer was relatively short, as he was one of several agents released by the American Anti-Slavery Society by the middle of 1837.[23]

Oliver Johnson

Born in Peacham, Vermont, in 1809, Johnson was, it seems, William Lloyd Garrison's most devoted follower. Garrison, said Johnson, "was raised up by Divine Providence to deliver the Republic from the sin of slavery." He was an editor and writer for *The Liberator, The National Anti-Slavery Standard, The Anti-Slavery Bugle, The New York Independent*, and for a time assisted Horace Greeley at the *New York Tribune*. When Garrison was in England in

1833 and again when Garrison was ill, Johnson took charge of *The Liberator's* publication.

He helped establish the New England Anti-Slavery Society and drafted the society's constitution. The NEASS made Johnson the first agent they assigned to Vermont. Johnson's goal was to successfully combine his Quaker beliefs with his devotion to the cause of liberty. He held in particular esteem fellow agents, the Burleigh brothers, Charles C. and William. Throughout the 1830s, Johnson openly condemned churches he believed demonstrated hostility to the anti-slavery cause. Johnson was a committed Underground Railroad operator and he lectured for the AASS in Vermont, Pennsylvania, and Rhode Island. He also ventured into Ohio in the early 1840s on behalf of the AASS. An executive of the Philadelphia Anti-Slavery Society, Johnson was also the author of *William Lloyd Garrison and His Times*.[24]

Joseph Horace Kimball

Kimball was born in Pembroke, New Hampshire, in 1813 and became the editor of the *Herald Freedom* in Concord, New Hampshire. He was employed as an AASS agent in September of 1835. The national society sent Kimball and fellow agent James Thome to investigate the impact of the immediate emancipation of slaves in the West Indies. Kimball suffered terribly from consumption before he departed for the Caribbean and hoped that by spending time in a warmer climate, his health would be restored. But he did not recover, and was unable to travel extensively about the islands. Kimball did, however, make substantial contributions to information both men gathered about emancipation in Jamaica. He died of tuberculosis within a year of returning to the United States in 1837.[25]

William McCoy

A Methodist minister from Lyndon, Vermont, McCoy was also a pastor in Rochester, Brookfield, and Northfield. His employment as an agent of the national society began in September of 1836. McCoy joined five other American Anti-Slavery Society agents who lectured throughout Vermont, and he reported speaking to numerous people who told him they knew very little or nothing about the crusade to emancipate slaves. He stepped away from his lecturing tour in November in order to attend Weld's New York agents training convention. McCoy concentrated his work in his native county of Caledonia and in the counties along the Quebec frontier. His service to the AASS ended in September of 1837, due to the national society's insufficient funds.[26]

James McKim

Born in Carlisle, Pennsylvania, in 1810, McKim graduated from Dickinson College in 1828, and became a Presbyterian minister. He helped establish the American Anti-Slavery Society and wrote for the *Anti-slavery Standard,* a publication that influenced the abolitionist cause throughout the nation. McKim was an agent of the Pennsylvania Anti-Slavery Society, served as the publishing agent for the society, and was also actively involved with the Underground Railroad in the Keystone State. In 1849, fugitive slave Henry Brown had himself mailed in a box from Virginia to McKim in Philadelphia. The story of Henry "Box" Brown's escape became one of the most celebrated tales of Underground Railroad lore. McKim succeeded John Greenleaf Whittier as editor of the *Pennsylvania Freeman,* supported John Brown's family after the Harper's Ferry raid, and was a strong advocate of enlisting black soldiers during the Civil War. He was selected as secretary of the Freedman's Relief Association in 1863, holding that post until 1865. McKim was also the First Secretary of the American Freedman's Union Commission.[27]

James Milligan

Milligan was a schoolteacher who became a Reformed Presbyterian minister. He maintained that Christians should not feel loyal to religious denominations or governments that supported slavery. Milligan was born in Scotland and came to the United Stated in 1802. He was one of the first individuals in Vermont to openly advocate unconditional abolition of slavery in the United States. Milligan was one of six American anti-slavery agents dispatched to Vermont. He was a distinguished scholar of the classics and was characterized as a gifted, eloquent speaker. He was made vice-president of the Vermont Anti-Slavery Society in 1835, was a vocal supporter of William Lloyd Garrison's radical abolitionist positions and once delivered an impassioned lecture to the New England Anti-Slavery Society. Milligan later carried out Underground Railroad operations and abolitionist work in Pennsylvania and Illinois.[28]

John J. Miter

A native of New York, Miter worked as a cabin boy on his brother's boat when he was a teenager. He studied at the Oneida Institute, was a Lane Seminary Rebel and, after leaving Lane, enrolled at the Troy Seminary in New York. He was assigned by the agency committee to work with fellow agent William Yates to provide aid to free blacks in hopes of improving their social, intellectual and moral condition. Miter, a temperance advocate, helped established the New York State Anti-slavery Society. He labored for the abolitionist cause in Newark, New Jersey, and was commissioned to work in Illinois for the American Home Missionary Society. Miter briefly served as a minister in Chicago, and then became a clergyman in western Illinois, where he lectured against slavery in several small towns until 1841. He was closely connected to anti-slavery activists at Knox College. Miter eventually left Illinois in order to serve as a minister in Wisconsin, where he continued abolitionist advocacy.[29]

John Monteith

Monteith was a graduate of Jefferson College and the Princeton Theological Seminary. He was a follower of Charles G. Finney, and was selected as the first president of the University of Michigania, later the University of Michigan. He supported practical education and the manual labor academy concept. Monteith worked for the American Home Missionary Society and was also an ancient languages professor at Hamilton College. He lectured for the AASS in Ohio and also supported Underground Railroad activities. Monteith was a founding member of the American Anti-Slavery Society and was one of the older members of the Seventy at the time of his agency service. His efforts on behalf of the AASS were gradually reduced because of weakness in his lungs. He was also a minister at the First Presbyterian Church in Elyria, Ohio.[30]

Leonard S. Parker

A native of New Hampshire, Parker became a Lane Rebel. Parker was a lifelong supporter of Charles G. Finney after first hearing the evangelist preacher when he was a youth at the Boston Latin School. He enrolled at Oberlin in 1835 and graduated from the college in 1838. Parker served the abolitionist cause in Ohio, frequently carrying out work there with fellow agents Hiram Foote and Edward Fairchild. Parker and Foote were once furiously mobbed in Johnston, Ohio. Parker often encouraged local abolitionists to assist him as speakers. His service as an agent of the American Anti-Slavery Society was quite short, for he only served the agency committee until February of 1837, when the national society's finances began to suffer during the collapse of the national economy. Parker later became a clergyman in Ashburnham, Massachusetts.[31]

Samuel Fuller Porter

Born in Whitestown, New York, in 1813, Parker was a graduate of the Oneida Institute and a Lane Seminary Rebel who completed his theological training at Oberlin in 1836. Porter, an anti–Mason and Temperance advocate, briefly worked with John Monteith in December of 1836. His brother-in-law was fellow agent Edward Weed. Porter lectured throughout Ohio, was a minister in Chatham, and then became a blacksmith. He was often reclusive and sometimes fell into deep fits of depression. Porter was a minister in Kingswood, New Jersey, from 1843 to 1857 and in Malta, Illinois, from 1857 to 1863. He was a Civil War chaplain, serving near Memphis and Vicksburg, where he frequently preached in hospitals. He died at the age of 97 in 1911, the last of the Lane Rebels.[32]

Ray Potter

A bookkeeper, a schoolteacher, and a Baptist minister, Potter was initially a "colonizationist." He helped organize the Pawtucket, Rhode Island, Anti-Slavery Society, and was also vice-president of the Providence Anti-Slavery Society. He was a founding member of both the Rhode Island Anti-Slavery Society and the American Anti-Slavery Society. Potter was the only agent of the national society to be given a permanent assignment in Rhode Island. Potter was the publisher of the monthly pamphlet *The Pure Testimony*, a theological publication that was scornful of Methodists. He was a supporter of the Anti-Masonic Movement. He was, for a time, the minister of the Sixth Principle Baptist School in Pawtucket. Potter's effectiveness as an abolitionist crusader ended about the time of Weld's New York agents' convention because of a scandal involving him and an unmarried woman.[33]

E. C. Prichett

Recruited as an AASS agent while attending school at Amherst in July of 1836, Prichett carried out important abolitionist activities in upstate New York, and sometimes coordinated his work with agent Thomas B. Watson in the Northeast part of the state. Both men met strong hostility from more than 100 locals when they were organizing an anti-slavery society in Clinton County. In 1837, Prichett was praised for his effective work in New York. He also worked for the national society in Pennsylvania and helped establish the Pennsylvania Anti-slavery Society. Prichett's AASS agency service was completed in September of 1837, but he was later made corresponding secretary of the New York State Anti-Slavery Society in 1840. The *Friend of Man* reported that he also served as an agent for the state society.[34]

Asa Rand

Born in Rindge, New Hampshire, in 1793, Rand was a Dartmouth graduate and Congregational minister in Gotham, Maine. He edited the *Christian*

Mirror in Portland, Maine, from 1822 to 1825. Although many of the men who became members of the Seventy were greatly influenced by or loyal followers of Charles G. Finney, Rand, in the early 1830s, was openly critical of Finney's popular evangelical theology. In 1832 he published *Teacher's Manual for Teaching English Grammar*, and the following year, he established a bookstore and printer's shop in Lowell, Massachusetts. Rand helped establish the American Anti-Slavery Society, and he conducted anti-slavery work in Massachusetts, New Hampshire and New York. In December of 1836, while caring for his ill daughter in New Haven, he agreed to deliver an abolitionist speech, but was jeered and harassed by Yale students.

His work as an agent ended in the spring of 1837, and he then resumed his career as a minister in the state of New York. In 1838, he was the author of *Law and Testimony Concerning Slavery*. In 1852, he wrote a widely circulated and well-received pamphlet entitled *The Slave Catcher Caught in the Meshes of Eternal Law*. Rand was later a clergyman in two Massachusetts communities.[35]

A. T. Rankin

Brother of Ohio's most famous Underground Railroad conductor, John Rankin, A. T. was a Presbyterian minister posted by the American Anti-Slavery Society in both Ohio and Indiana. He was recommended for service by agent Edward Weed and began working for the national society in November 1836. He sometimes worked in conjunction with his Rankin relatives and James G. Birney in Ohio. Rankin was also an active Underground Railroad operator in both Ohio and Indiana, and he promoted the idea that local anti-slavery societies should call their gatherings "library meetings," in order to protect their members from harassment and intimidation. He carried out especially effective anti-slavery activity in Fort Wayne, Indiana. Rankin left Indiana in 1844 and moved to Buffalo, New York.[36]

John Rankin

Not to be confused with New York abolitionist John Rankin, the Ohio John Rankin was a Presbyterian minister and one of the nation's most famous Underground Railroad operators. He was one of the country's leading opponents of slavery before 1830. "Slavery," he said, "is opposed to all the original properties of human nature." Henry Ward Beecher said that Rankin was "the man most responsible for the abolition of slaves in America." In 1828, he was selected as the president of Ripley College. His safe haven house for freedom seekers in Ripley, Ohio, stood overlooking the Ohio River. He stirred controversy by advocating violence to bring about an end to slavery.

He was conscientious about collecting funds for the national society after becoming an agent. At first, Rankin felt insecure about his public speaking ability, but over time he developed a powerful and effective style of delivery. He endured threats from drunken thugs, fought off ambush attacks while riding horseback along country trails, and lived with the knowledge that posted notices in Kentucky offered rewards for his assassination. Rankin was a driving force behind the establishment of the Ohio Anti-Slavery Society. His wife, Jean, joined his UGRR efforts, coordinating their work with black Underground Railroad conductor John Parker, who lived close to the Ohio River in Ripley. In the late 1830s, when members of the AASS argued over the issue of women's involvement in the activities of the society, Rankin sided with the women. Weld started his Ohio anti-slavery lecturing campaign in Ripley.[37]

Charles S. Renshaw

Renshaw came from a family of Southerners who supported slavery. He was educated at the Oneida Institute, was a Lane Seminary Rebel, and continued his education at Oberlin. He was converted to the evangelical religious movement by Charles G. Finney. A close friend of fellow agent William T. Allan, he lectured in upstate New York, often working closely with Allan in the northwest part of the state. In June of 1837, he returned to Oberlin so unhealthy and overextended that Weld expressed concern that he might die. In the fall, Renshaw turned down a second offer from the agency committee to work as an agent. He and Allan dreamed of traveling to Tibet in 1838, but they turned back after reaching the Platte River. Renshaw later carried out missionary work in Jamaica. He briefly served as a minister in Quincy, Illinois, which was by then a community greatly influenced by the abolitionist efforts of Weld's ally, Dr. David Nelson. Renshaw was later a clergyman in Pennsylvania and Massachusetts.[38]

David I. Robinson

A Methodist clergyman, Robinson was made secretary of the Methodist Conference Anti-Slavery Society in 1835. He was hired as an AASS agent in June of 1836 and labored for the national organization in New Hampshire but also carried out work in Maine. He was recommended to serve as an agent by George Storrs, with whom he occasionally lectured in New Hampshire. Following Weld's 1836 convention, illness forced Robinson to stop lecturing for six weeks, but he eventually resumed his work for the national society in January of 1837. One of his closest anti-slavery comrades was fellow agent

Jonathon Hazelton. He was also made a financial agent of the AASS and was later appointed as a financial officer of the New Hampshire Anti-Slavery Society.[39]

Marius Robinson

Born in Dalton, Massachusetts, in 1806, Robinson was converted to evangelical religion after attending a revival in 1825. He longed to be a minister but lack of funds forced him to learn the trade of printing instead. Robinson eventually graduated from the University of Nashville. As a young man, Robinson taught at a Cherokee mission school. He decided to study at the Lane Seminary, worked at the school's printing shop, and was vice-president of the Student Anti-Slavery Society. He was highly regarded by his abolitionist comrades. He lectured in Ohio, but in 1837 was attacked, and severely beaten in the town of Berlin. Robinson never fully recovered from the injuries that he suffered during his beating. He later became the editor of the *Anti-Slavery Bugle* in Salem, Ohio, a community prominently involved with the Underground Railroad. The *Anti-Slavery Bugle* replaced *The Philanthropist* as the primary organ of the Ohio State Anti-Slavery Society. Robinson became the president of the Ohio Mutual Fire Insurance Company following the Civil War.[40]

David Root

Root was a Middlebury College graduate and an avid proponent of manual labor schools. In an 1835 sermon Root said, "Slavery, like an incubus, presses upon the heart of this Republic.... It stirs the wrath of heaven ... blacks are here and must remain here." In July of 1836, Root was one of fifteen agents appointed by the AASS and he was given the title, Agent for Special Missions. Root helped establish the New Hampshire Anti-Slavery Society, and in 1838, he conducted work in Ohio for the national society. He was a respected clergyman in Ohio and New England and is remembered for delivering a moving memorial address following the death of E. P. Lovejoy. Root was also an agent of the Massachusetts Abolitionist Society from the fall of 1839 until the spring of 1840. He later endowed professorships at Beloit College and the Yale Theological Seminary.[41]

William P. Russell

A native of New York, Russell attended Vermont's Bennington Academy, and was a graduate of the Oberlin Theological School. He was ordained in

1842. Russell was recruited by Weld and was then assigned by the AASS to lecture in New York State. He once barely avoided being tarred and feathered by a violent mob in Hamburg but those who threatened him decided to back down. Russell's short service as an agent for the national society ended in January 1837, only weeks after Weld's New York agents' convention was concluded. He turned down a second AASS commission offered to him in 1839. Russell was an agent of the American Missionary Society after the Civil War and was a minister in Ohio, New Jersey, Massachusetts, and Michigan from 1841 to 1880.[42]

Alvah Sabin

Born in Georgia, Vermont, in 1793, Sabin was dramatically affected as a child by reading the book *Horrors of Slavery*. Sabin graduated from Columbian College, which later became George Washington University. He was a delegate to the first American Anti-Slavery Society Convention in Philadelphia. As an influential Vermont Baptist minister, he lectured in his home state for the AASS. He rejected an offer to be an agent in the summer of 1836 but Weld convinced him to accept the commission that fall. Although records are unclear, he seems to have started lecturing for the AASS shortly after Weld's 1836 agent's convention. Sabin was actively involved with the Underground Railroad in Vermont. He entered politics in 1836 and was elected to a seat in the Vermont State Legislature, where he served for ten terms. In the 1850s, he served two terms in the U.S. House of Representatives and he was also Vermont's Secretary of state for two years.[43]

Orange Scott

Having spent part of his early childhood in Canada, Scott was one of eight children and received very little formal education. Scott was an ordained Methodist minister and frequently clashed with bishops of his church when they tried to silence his anti-slavery advocacy. His sermons were frequently laced with fiery anti-slavery language. Scott embraced the anti-slavery cause in 1834 after hearing a speech delivered by Henry B. Stanton. In the midst of dealing with controversies, his manner was often intemperate and rude, but he was also characterized as sincere and courageous. He organized, with LaRoy Sunderland, the Methodist Anti-Slavery Society in 1833. After joining the "Seventy," he carried out anti-slavery work in Maine, New Hampshire, and New York with the title, Special Missions. Scott also labored for the abolitionist cause in Rhode Island, Connecticut, and Pennsylvania. He was publisher of the *True Wesleyan* and *The American Wesleyan Observer,* and was very much opposed to Garrisonism. Scott decided to withdraw from the Methodist Church in 1843, to become one of the driving forces behind the establishment of the Wesleyan Methodist Church. He said he wanted to establish "a new anti-slavery, anti-intemperance, anti-everything-wrong church organization."[44]

Avelyn Sedgewick

Sedgewick was a Presbyterian minister from Rome, New York, who attended the organizational meeting of the New York Anti-Slavery Society. His service as an agent for the American Anti-Slavery Society started on October 1, 1836. While he was lecturing for the AASS in Verona, New York, a canal boat captain offered $10 to anyone who would silence him, but there were no takers. Sedgewick's work was often carried out in localities that had not been exposed to anti-slavery advocacy. In September of 1837, he informed the agency committee that he wanted to conclude his service as an agent, and he completed his work for the American Anti-Slavery Society in November. Sedgewick then moved to Byson, New York, but continued his commitment to the anti-slavery cause.[45]

Nathaniel Southard

A native of New Hampshire, Southard moved to Massachusetts and helped establish the Boston Young Men's Anti-Slavery Society. He was a delegate to the first meeting of the American Anti-Slavery Society. Southard was very much influenced by and associated with the more radical and controversial abolitionist views of William Lloyd Garrison. He carried out abolitionist work for the AASS in both Massachusetts and Rhode Island. In addition he spent time working closely with Weld in New York City. The national society later made Southard the editor of the *American Anti-Slavery Society Almanac*, a publication initiated to graphically illustrate, among other things, the horrors of slavery. Southard continued to aid the national society in a variety of ways until late 1839.[46]

Henry B. Stanton

The son of a country merchant, Stanton was born to parents who belonged to the Congregational Church in Pachang, Connecticut. He became a very close friend of Weld's. Stanton was a Lane Seminary Rebel who helped recruit many young men from New York to enroll at Lane. He lectured in Northern states from Maine to Indiana and was probably mobbed as frequently as any abolitionist speaker. He maintained that approximately 150 of his anti-slavery gatherings were broken up. Stanton conducted remarkably effective work in Rhode Island and was particularly articulate arguing before the Massachusetts Legislature the case for abolishing slavery and the slave trade in Washington, D.C. He cogently argued that slavery's existence in the nation's capital brought shame upon the United States. In 1837, Stanton expressed his hope that AASS agents would not only successfully wage war against slavery but also wage warfare against prejudice, as well.

Stanton was brilliant at extemporaneous speech and his lectures were passionately delivered with sarcasm and wit. Stanton attended the World Anti-Slavery Convention in London in 1840 where many nations were represented. He married famous women's rights activist Elizabeth Cady and after his marriage, he studied the law and became a patent attorney in Boston. He was actively involved with the Free Soil Party and served in the New York Senate in 1850 and 1851. In 1855 he helped organize the New York State Republican Party in Syracuse.

Between 1848 and 1857, Stanton's articles were published in Albany newspapers and he later wrote for Horace Greeley's *New York Tribune*. When the Civil War ended, he became an editor of the *New York Sun*. He was the author of *Sketches of Reforms and Reformers in Great Britain and Ireland*. Henry Ward Beecher characterized Stanton as someone with personality traits similar to John Adams —"able, staunch, patriotic, full of principle, and always unpopular." He was one of the most able administrators involved with the anti-slavery movement and possessed a particular facility for managing the national society's financial affairs.[47]

George Storrs

Storrs was born in New Hampshire, and, after serving as a Congregational minister, he became a Methodist clergyman. He studied at Princeton, graduated from Andover Theological Seminary, and was a professor of theology at Western Reserve College in Ohio. In 1828, he lived in South Carolina where he observed the grim reality of a slave's life. Historian John L. Meyer maintains that from the early spring of 1835 until the late spring of 1836, the anti-slavery movement in New Hampshire "revolved around the efforts of George Storrs."

The sometimes impetuous Storrs was censored by the Methodist General Conference for his controversial anti-slavery activities and in the midst of an anti-slavery lecture in Northfield, Vermont, in December of 1835, he was once dragged from a speaking platform and jailed for being a "common railer." He was also jailed on another occasion in Pittsfield, New Hampshire in 1836. Storrs also lectured in New York and in Livingston County, a blacksmith's anvil was fired at a building where he was speaking and on the same occasion, an attempt to blow up the structure was prevented. His most significant work as an agent was accomplished in his native state of New Hampshire. He concluded his work as an agent in October of 1839 and by that time had become one of the American Anti-Slavery Society's most competent agents. Storrs published *The Bible Examiner* from 1845 until his death in 1879.[48]

Charles Stuart

Born in Jamaica, Stuart became a British Army captain, retired from the military, and settled in Canada. He was a dashing figure remembered for his kilt and stylish hat. In 1822, he moved to New York to become principal of the Utica Academy. Stuart greatly influenced Weld's adoption of anti-slavery beliefs and helped advance Weld's career, but the friendship between the two men faded over time due to differences about religious beliefs. In 1829, Stuart returned to England to support the British Agency Committee's efforts to eliminate slavery in the Empire. While lecturing against slavery in England, he often carried a replica of a slave ship with him.

He returned to the United States in 1834 where he was an outspoken critic of the American Colonization Society. Stuart developed strong friendships with abolitionists Gerrit Smith, James G. Birney, and Beriah Green. He was a prominent member of Charles G. Finney's "Holy Band" of preachers and became an agent of the American Anti-Slavery Society. Stuart regularly mailed parcels of information about the progress of the abolitionist movement in America to Great Britain. As an agent, Stuart was a weak public speaker, but nonetheless, he conducted anti-slavery lectures for the AASS in Ohio and New York and served the abolitionist crusade throughout New England. He was once hit by a hurled brick bat while lecturing in Western New York; though badly shaken, he recovered and resumed his speech. In 1841, he was the author of *Oneida and Oberlin: Expiration of Slavery in the United States.* Stuart later helped establish the Anti-Slavery Society of Canada in Toronto.[49]

James A. Thome

Thome was one of the most effective student speakers during the Lane Seminary slavery debates. In 1834 he traveled with Henry B. Stanton to the AASS annual meeting and delivered a powerful speech entitled *The Southern Slave Kitchen, the Sodom of the Nation.* The son of a slave-holding owner of a Kentucky flour mill, who came to reject slavery, he co-edited, with J. Horace Kimball, *Emancipation in the West Indies.* Thome conducted most of the investigative work in the Caribbean due to Kimball's severe illness. He lectured in several Ohio communities, and once had to flee from Oberlin in order to avoid extradition to Kentucky for aiding a fugitive slave. He encouraged the activities of women in the abolitionist crusade. A member of the Oberlin College faculty from 1838 until 1848, he was elected to the school's board of trustees in 1851. Thome was a clergyman in Cleveland from 1849 to 1871.[51]

David Thurston

A leading spokesman for the abolitionist cause in Maine and active in the state's underground railroad affairs, Thurston was the first chairman of the Maine Anti-Slavery Society. He was a founding member of the AASS, and in the summer of 1836, his work as an agent in his home state commenced. Thurston was described as a man "without guile." He effectively employed Weld's strategy of remaining in a community for several days until a core groups of anti-slavery supporters were organized.

When Thurston stepped down as an agent, he wrote, "Never was my mind more deeply convinced of the truth, the righteousness, or the magnitude of the abolition enterprise." When the national society split apart in 1840, Thurston helped establish the American and Foreign Anti-Slavery Society. A vocal member of the AFASS, he argued that the Mexican War was primarily fought to gain more slave territory. He actively supported the peace movement, the Liberty Party, and in 1850, Thurston was a delegate to the Frankfurt Peace Conference. Thurston became a minister in several communities in Maine and was president of the American Missionary Society in 1859.[50]

Wilson Tillinghast

A Rhode Islander, Tillinghast worked for the AASS for a relatively brief time. He attended several of Weld's lectures in order to learn a more powerful abolitionist rhetoric and style of delivery. Tillinghast was hired as an AASS agent in the summer of 1836 and was assigned to lecture in New York State. He initially worked for the national society on Long Island from late July until September. Tillinghast's period of service for the national society lasted for no more than six months and the only record of reimbursement for his travel and postage expenses was ten dollars. The American Anti-Slavery Society's agency committee reassigned Tillinghast to Pennsylvania in November of 1836, but it seems he never worked in the Keystone State as an agent after Weld's 1836 New York agents' convention was concluded.[52]

Joseph Towne

An AASS agent in Massachusetts, Towne was the first regular minister of the Congregational Church in Amesbury where he served from 1834 to 1836. He worked closely in that community with Henry B. Stanton. Towne believed that one could be an abolitionist without adhering to the outspoken radicalism of William Lloyd Garrison, and he vehemently repudiated Garrison in the publication *Clerical Appeal* that he coauthored with the Rev. Charles Fitch. Towne resigned his post as an agent for the national society in December of 1836 and became the minister of the Salem Street Church in Boston. Although advocating a woman's right to share her opinions equally with men, Towne continued to be a bitter opponent of Garrison's well into the 1840s.[53]

Edward Tyler

Born in Guliford, Vermont, in 1800, Tyler was the son of the state's Chief Justice. An 1825 Yale graduate, he was commissioned in April of 1836 to work as an agent in Connecticut, where he met strong opposition and hostility in a state that did not organize a state anti-slavery society until 1838. He was once cheered by people who supported him during a speech in Vermont as protestors simultaneously tried to noisily disrupt his lecture. As a Congregational minister, Tyler conscientiously emphasized the idea that the existence of slavery in the United States ultimately represented a threat to the core principles of a free democratic society. In 1837 he predicted that it was only a matter of time before Americans would be forced "to take one side or the other for this is not a simple question of negro slavery, it is a cause of human rights." Tyler was the author, in 1835, of *Slaveholding: A Malum in Se or Invariably Sinful.* He was the editor of New England religious newspapers after he concluded his service as an agent and joined the American and Foreign Anti-Slavery Society.[54]

Abner B. Warner

Born in North Hampton, Massachusetts, in 1814, Warner attended Williams College, and later, while studying at the Andover Theological Seminary, he was interviewed and hired as an agent by Weld. His classmates at Andover included future members of the Seventy Henry Beldon and Jonathan Blanchard. Warner was an ordained Congregational minister and was assigned by the agency committee to work in Massachusetts. He stepped down as an agent for the national organization in September of 1837 and subsequently graduated from New Hampshire's Gilmanton Seminary in 1838. In 1839, due to his influence, Warner's church in Milford, New Hampshire, became an abolitionist stronghold despite opposition from some members of his congregation.[55]

Thomas B. Watson

A lawyer from Keeseville, New York, Watson convinced the agency committee to let him conduct his lecturing and organizing close to his home in northeastern New York State. His employment as an agent was unusually arranged in that he was selected by the agency committee after submitting a written application to the AASS in the summer of 1836. He started his work as an agent in September of that year. Watson sometimes carried out work in the northeastern part of the state with fellow AASS agent E. C. Prichett. In Essex County Watson reported frustration with "the apathy of people" but he was also encouraged in some locations by farmers holding meetings at "their respective school houses." In the spring and summer of 1839, he was employed as an agent of the New York State Anti-Slavery Society.[56]

Augustus Wattles

Born in Lebanon, Connecticut, in 1807, Wattles was a Lane Seminary Rebel and Oneida Institute graduate. Wattles and Marius Robinson withdrew from Lane in order to set up a school for blacks in Cincinnati. He was an Underground Railroad operator in Ohio, and the AASS put him in charge of industrial training for blacks; most of his work was conducted in Ohio but he also served briefly in Indiana. Wattles invested his own inheritance helping blacks learn about farming, and married "Cincinnati Sister" Susan Lowe. Cincinnati Sisters were a group of women who moved from the East to educate blacks in southern Ohio. Wattles' health broke in the summer of 1837, putting an end to his agency service. He moved to Kansas in 1855 to serve the Emigrant Aid Society and started printing the anti-slavery publication *The Herald of Freedom*. He frequently corresponded with Weld about his abolitionist efforts in the West. While living in Kansas, Wattles offered assistance to John Brown even after Brown was accused of murdering Missouri slaveholders. In 1861, Wattles traveled among Native American settlements in Kansas on behalf of the War Department and reported their predicament as pitiful. He died in 1876.[57]

Edward Weed

Born in North Stamfield, Connecticut, in 1817, Weed attended the Oneida Institute. He was a Lane Seminary Rebel who married Phoebe Mathews, another Cincinnati Sister. An AASS agent and minister in Ohio, he occasion-ally worked with fellow agent John Rankin. During his Ohio lectures in July and August of 1836, he faced incredibly fierce hostility from anti abolitionists. In 1836, newspapers in the east reported that Weed had been killed after having been mobbed and lynched, but the *Chillicothe Gazette* corrected this rumor by reporting that, in fact, after Weed had been mobbed in southern Ohio, one of his attackers had died while resisting arrest. He characterized his opponents as "cowards who curse, throw eggs and snowballs, and get drunk." Weed also helped establish the Michigan Anti-Slavery Society. In 1838, he ended his service to the AASS, and became the minister of the Free Church of Patterson, New Jersey.[58]

J. B. Wilcox

J.B. Wilcox was a forceful supporter of the temperance movement, and while living in Genesee County, New York, he was commissioned as an AASS agent in 1836. He joined fourteen other agents that the national society hired in New York that year. His service for the national society in New York was very brief because he only served in the summer and fall. Despite his relatively short period of employment, Wilcox was a successful fundraiser for the AASS, raising between $300 and $400 for the society in less than four weeks in the fall of 1836. Unlike most American Anti-Slavery agents, Wilcox reported that he rarely met opposition in his efforts and failed to organize an auxiliary society in only one county where he worked. He was employed as a financial agent by the national society from October of 1837 to August of 1838.[59]

Lumund Wilcox

Lumund Wilcox was one of the founders of the New York State Anti-Slavery Society. He was involved with various reform efforts and for a time associated himself with Hiram Foote in the temperance movement. Wilcox was employed as an agent by the national society for a very limited time in the state of New York. Despite the brevity of his service, he reported out-standing success, convincing a good number of people in the communities where he lectured to establish local anti-slavery societies. He convinced at least three hundred people in Delaware County communities to sign up as abolitionists even though most of them had never heard of the concept of immediate emancipation. Wilcox was also hired by the AASS as one of their financial agents in the fall of 1837 when the national society's operating budget had substantially declined.[60]

Hiram Wilson

Born in Acworth, New Hampshire, in 1803, Wilson was a Lane Seminary Rebel, attended the Oneida Institute, and was ordained in 1836 after graduating from Oberlin. Wilson was an AASS agent in both Ohio and Michigan. He moved to Canada, where he traveled and accumulated information about the circumstances faced by blacks who had settled there. Wilson established the British-American Manual Labor Institute that provided relief and educational opportunities for fugitive slaves. His efforts in southern Canada were supported by former Lane and Oberlin students. Always plagued by lack of money, Wilson canvassed northern Ohio, soliciting funds for his projects and also traveled to Illinois in order to gather contributions and supplies for his relief efforts. In a letter to James G. Birney, Wilson described the arrival of so many fugitive slaves north of the border as a situation that would keep "our hands ... full for years to come." He seemed to embrace adversity and thought his mission in life was to combine Christian values with reform by vocation. Wilson and former slave Josiah Henson, who met Wilson in 1836, worked closely with each other helping freedom seekers in Canada. Wilson and his wife eventually resettled in St. Catherines, Canada, where they continued to aid fugitive slaves.[61]

J. G. Wilson

A Presbyterian minister and Underground Railroad conductor, Wilson lived in Southern Indiana. He maintained very strong ties to abolitionists and UGRR operators in Ohio. Wilson supported various anti-slavery efforts in Ohio in 1834 and 1835, and then studied at Hanover College in Indiana in 1836 where he continued his anti-slavery activism. Because Wilson lived so close to the Kentucky border, he was able to make firsthand observations of slavery's cruelty and brutality that Weld and the Grimkes included in *American Slavery As It Is.* The agency committee gave him the title Agent in the West. Wilson was the only member of the Seventy so designated. He and A. T. Rankin were the main AASS agents to work in Indiana in the 1830s.[62]

Samuel M. Wilson

Wilson was a minister of the Reform Presbyterian Church in East Crafsbury, Vermont. There is relatively little known about Wilson's anti-slavery activity as an American Anti-Slavery Society agent. In 1834, Wilson joined a like-minded group of Vermont citizens who were calling for the establishment of a state anti-slavery organization. He then helped establish Vermont's Anti-slavery Society and also served as the organization's vice-president in

1835 and 1836. The agency committee assigned Wilson to conduct his work in his home state. There is but one record of his anti-slavery work for the national society, and that occurred during the formation of the Orleans County Anti-Slavery Society in July of 1837.[63]

John Winebrenner

Born in Fredick County, Maryland, in 1797, Winebrenner was a German Reform minister who established the Church of God in 1830. Winebrenner often voiced scorn towards those who perpetrated violence against abolitionist activists. The agency committee gave him a "special assignment." Because Winebrenner spoke fluent German, he was assigned to work with non–English speaking residents in central Pennsylvania. This action was taken because American Anti-Slavery Society was eager to enlist the support of German speaking immigrants. However, even though he accepted an agency committee appointment on March 15, 1837, there are no known recorded reports of his activities. He was a delegate to the Pennsylvania State Anti-Slavery Conventions in 1837 and 1838. The Harrisburg Anti-Slavery Society made Winebrenner their corresponding secretary in 1838.[64]

James T. Woodbury

Woodbury grew up in New Hampshire, graduated from Harvard, practiced law, and then became a Congregationalist minister. He was assigned to lecture in both New Hampshire and Massachusetts. His conversion to abolitionism occurred while speaking with an elderly slave at Mount Vernon, Virginia, who said he knew nothing about the whereabouts of his family. Woodbury also worked for the AASS in Rhode Island and delivered an abolitionist lecture at the first annual meeting of that state's anti-slavery society. He was an opponent of the Garrison anti-slavery wing and when the AASS made him a local agent in Massachusetts in 1837, abolitionists loyal to Garrison protested his appointment. Woodbury once accused Garrison of wanting to "over throw the Christian ministry." Lucretia Mott once recalled that he was one of the AASS members most opposed to women speaking publicly against slavery. Woodbury remained a clergyman until his death.[65]

Henry C. Wright

Born in Charon, Connecticut, in 1797, Wright attended Andover Seminary, was a trained printer, and eventually became a Congregational clergyman. He was a hardcore Garrisonian and actively involved with the affairs of the Massachusetts Anti-Slavery Society. In the 1830s, he was fervently opposed to the use of coercion or violence and was a leading figure of the nonresistance philosophy. Wright briefly worked for the AASS in Rhode Island. The agency committee appointed him as "Children's Agent," but he abandoned most of his efforts with that program when he accompanied the Grimke sisters on their lecture tour. The AASS eventually assigned him to Pennsylvania; and when that occurred, the Grimke sisters registered their strong disapproval to Weld about Wright's new assignment. Wright was later dropped as an agent after numerous complaints about his arrogance and vanity. He contended that his dismissal was due to his support and loyalty to William Lloyd Garrison. In the 1840s, he traveled throughout Europe lecturing about abolitionism. By the late 1850s, he had repudiated his nonresistance position and was arguing that slaves had a right to use violence against slaveholders and that northerners should not hesitate to incite them to do so.[66]

William Yates

Yates aided free blacks while working with fellow AASS agent John Miter, creating aid societies, supporting the temperance movement, and helping to establish Sunday schools. He vigorously fought discrimination against blacks in the North. Yates wrote reports to the American Anti-Slavery Society about the injustices blacks endured in numerous ways in New York State that reduced them to second-class citizens. Yates served for two years as the secretary of the Troy New York Anti-Slavery Society. He carried out abolitionist work for a time in New York City following Weld's 1836 agent's convention. When the national society's funds were shrinking during the Panic of '37, he continued his work without a salary. Yates, who helped establish the New York Anti-Slavery Society, was a fierce opponent of the Fugitive Slave Law of 1793 and devoted much time to attacking its legal basis. In 1838 he published *Rights of Colored Men to Suffrage, Citizenship, and Trial by Jury.* His work for the national organization came to an end in May of 1838.[67]

Others

There were at least fifteen other people who might be included in the "Seventy." Well before Weld started recruiting lecturers, the AASS had been hiring agents; some of these men may have been assumed to be members of Weld's group. In addition, we know that the agency committee was forced to reduce its number of agents by mid–1837. However, it might have been the case that when other anti-slavery lecturers and agents were hired later they also came to be so strongly associated with Weld's band that their names were lumped together with his recruits. There were also abolitionists associated with Weld who acted as agents for state anti-slavery societies, and some of them might have been thought to be part of Weld's group. The national society also appointed men who were called "local agents," who restricted their work to a very small region. By the middle of June 1837, with its coffers nearly empty, the AASS decided to draw up a list of candidates that would be commissioned as local agents. By October *The Emancipator* reported:

> Some of the first clergymen, lawyers, physicians, and businessmen in the coun-
> try, have accepted of local agencies. If our friends will take advantage of their
> labors, and collect money where they shall lecture, ten times the amount
> expended may be raised.

The newspaper went on to state that these agents could speak in their own regions. By May of 1838, 74 men were appointed as local agents by the national society.[68] If this was the case, then, over time, more than seventy people might have been assumed to be members of Weld's legion. Finally, the 67 individuals identified above are by no means an absolute, proof positive list of the "Seventy." Instead, they are the people who are most likely to have been members of Weld's group. Some historians who have studied this anti-slavery era might very well subtract names from this list or add others. Perhaps undiscovered pieces of evidence will be found in the future that will confirm and verify the exact number of Weld's recruits. In the meantime, we cannot be absolutely sure.

The following men are individuals who seem less likely, but nonetheless were possible members of Weld's "Seventy."

George Allen was a professor at Oberlin and an opponent of Garrison, who later became a chaplain at a Massachusetts insane asylum. He also studied at the Oneida Institute and was a Lane Rebel.[69]

Courtland Avery was a minister in Rochester, New York, and Chilli-cothe, Ohio. He was a Lane Seminary Rebel whose brother, George Avery, helped establish an anti-slavery society in Rochester.[70]

George Beecher was a Presbyterian clergyman, the son of Lyman Beecher and brother of Henry Ward Beecher and Harriet Beecher Stowe. He died tragically at his home in 1843.[71]

Joseph Gould studied at the Lane Seminary and was the brother of AASS agent, Samuel Gould. He carried out abolitionist work in New York and Massachusetts.[72]

A. A. Guthrie was an abolitionist who lectured and organized local anti-slavery societies throughout Ohio in 1837. He was a fearless conductor on the Underground Railroad and was active in the affairs of the Liberty Party in Ohio.[73]

Luther Lee was a self-educated Methodist minister and close associate of AASS agent Orange Scott. He strongly supported Susan B. Anthony and the Women's Rights Movement.[74]

Huntington Lyman was a native of Connecticut and a Lane Seminary Rebel who lectured in Indiana and Ohio. He was a clergyman in six different New York communities and later lived in Wisconsin.[75]

David Nelson was a Presbyterian minister who befriended Weld in the early 1830s and later opened, in Quincy, Illinois, the anti-slavery Mission Institute which was destroyed by arsonists in 1843. He was familiar with several Underground Railroad operators in western Illinois and influenced Elijah P. Lovejoy to join the anti-slavery cause.[76]

Amos Phelps was a graduate of Yale and the Yale Divinity School who worked for the New England Anti-Slavery society and lectured in five states for the AASS. He was the national society's first full time agent. Phelps is the most likely man to have been a member of the Seventy listed with this group of less likely candidates. In 1834, he was the author of *Lectures on Slavery and its Remedy* and was a minister at the Free Church in Boston.[77]

John T. Pierce was a Lane Seminary Rebel who was educated at Harvard and the Oneida Institute, and was the nephew of New York reformers, Lewis and Arthur Tappan. He was a schoolteacher in Illinois, Missouri, and Kentucky.[78]

Asariah Smith worked briefly for the AASS, and then completed his education at Yale. He then became a missionary in Asia Minor teaching religion and serving the needy in Eastern Turkey until his death.[79]

James M. Vickers studied at Lane and lectured for a short time in Pennsylvania before poor health forced him to retire from the field. While lecturing in Pennsylvania, he was an anti-slavery colleague of Jonathan Blanchard.[80]

Samuel T. Wells was a Lane Seminary Rebel who also studied at the Oneida Institute, and equally emphasized temperance and abolitionism as a lecturer. He was a very close friend of both Theodore Weld and Angelina Grimke.[81]

Calvin Waterbury was a Lane Seminary Rebel, Oneida Institute student, close confidant of Weld's, and worked for the AASS in New York and Ohio. He took a very active part in the student anti-slavery debates at the Lane Seminary.[82]

George Whipple was a Lane Seminary Rebel and Oneida Institute student who developed the plan whereby people could buy cheap western land, resell lots, establish schools, and return some profits to benevolent societies. He taught at Oberlin and later worked for the Freedman's Bureau.[83]

Chapter 4

The Seventy in Their Own Words

We will never know what it would have been like to have listened to a lecture given by one of the Seventy. Their dramatic pauses, facial expressions, and the inflection of their tone are forever lost. We can, however, read articles they wrote, and therefore hear their voices in print. The first seven entries of this chapter are taken from written accounts that appeared in *American Slavery As It Is: Testimony of a Thousand Witnesses*. Members of the Seventy who had, earlier in their lives, lived in the South and observed the horrors of slavery firsthand, wrote each of these pieces. It seems possible, indeed likely, that in the course of their speeches, some of these narratives would also have been included in their lectures.

We know that Weld encouraged abolitionists who had lived in the South to relate their experiences about slavery to groups of Northerners. He was convinced that accounts of slavery coming from these people would have real credibility. In 1837, during the Grimke sisters' lectures in New England, Weld wrote to them and said that their attacks on slaveholders would be particularly powerful because "you are Southerners." During the Lane Seminary student debates about slavery in Cincinnati, Weld deliberately selected young men from the South to lead the discussion because of their personal knowledge of slavery. In a letter he wrote to Lewis Tappan in March of 1834, only weeks after the debates, Weld explained that one powerful speaker was "born, bred, and educated in Alabama in the midst of slavery; his father an owner of slaves and himself heir to a slave inheritance." The young man of whom he spoke was William T. Allan, one of Weld's most dedicated American Anti-Slavery Society agents.

Accounts of Slavery by William T. Allan in *Testimony of a Thousand Witnesses*

I was born and have lived most of my life in the slave states, mainly in the village of Huntsville, Alabama, where my parents still reside. I seldom went to a *plantation*, and as my visits were confined almost exclusively to the families of professing Christians, my *personal* knowledge of slavery, was consequently a knowledge of its *fairest* side, (if fairest may be predicated of foul.)

There was one plantation just opposite my father's house in the suburbs of Huntsville, belonging to Judge Smith, formerly a Senator in Congress from South Carolina, now of Huntsville. The name of his overseer was Tune. I have often seen him flogging the slaves in the field, and have often heard their cries. Sometimes, too, I have met them with the tears streaming down their faces, and the marks of the whip, ('whelks,') on their are necks and shoulders. Tune was so severe in his treatment, that his employer dismissed him after two or three years, lest, it was said, he should kill off all the slaves. But he was immediately employed by another planter in the neighborhood. The following fact was stated to me by my brother, James M. Allan, now residing at Richmond, Henry county, Illinois, and clerk of the circuit and county courts. Tune became displeased with one of the women who was pregnant, he made her lay down over a log, with her face towards the ground, and beat her so unmercifully, that she was soon after delivered of a *dead child*.

My brother also stated to me the following, which occurred near my father's house, and within sight and hearing of the academy and public garden. Charles, a fine active negro, who belonged to a bricklayer in Huntsville, exchanged the burning sun of the brickyard to enjoy for a season the pleasant shade of an adjacent mountain. When his master got him back, he tied him by his hands so his feet could just touch the ground-stripped off his clothes, took a paddle, bored full of holes, and paddled him leisurely all day long. It was two weeks before they could tell whether he would live or die. Neither of these cases attracted any particular notice in Huntsville.

While I lived in Huntsville a slave was killed in the mountain near by. The circumstances were these. A white man (James Helton) hunting in the woods, suddenly came upon a black man, and commanded him to stop, the slave kept on running, Helton fired his rifle and the negro was killed.

Mrs. BARR, the wife of the Rev. H. Barr of Carrolton, Illinois, formerly from Courtland, Alabama, told me last spring, that she has very often stopped her ears that she might not hear the screams of slaves who were under the lash, and that sometimes she has left her house, and retired to a place more distant, in order to get away from their agonizing cries.

I have often seen groups of slaves on the public squares in Huntsville, who were to be sold at auction, and I have often seen their tears gush forth and their countenances distorted with anguish. A considerable number were generally sold publicly every month...

The following facts I have just taken down from the lips of Mr. L. Turner, a regular and respectable member of the Second Presbyterian Church in Springfield, our county town. He was born and brought up in Caroline county, Virginia. He says that the slaves are neither considered nor treated as human beings...

He stated that one of his uncles had killed a woman — broke her skull with an ax helve: she had insulted her mistress! No notice was taken of the affair. Mr. T. said, further, that slaves were *frequently murdered*...

One of Mr. Turner's cousins, was employed as overseer on a large plantation in Mississippi. On a certain morning he called the slaves together, to give some orders. While doing it, a slave came running out of his cabin, having a knife in his hand and eating his breakfast. The overseer seeing him coming with the knife, was somewhat alarmed, and instantly raised his gun and shot him dead. He said afterwards, that he believed the slave was perfectly innocent of any evil intentions, he came out hastily to hear the orders whilst eating. *No* notice was taken of the killing...

Mr. Peter Vanarsdale, an elder of the Presbyterian church in Carrollton, formerly from Kentucky, told me, the other day, that a Mrs. Burford, in the neighborhood of Harrodsbury, Kentucky, had *separated a woman and her children* from their husband and father, taking them into another state. Mrs. B. was a member of the *Presbyterian Church.* The bereaved husband and father was also a professor of religion.

Mr. V. told me of a slave woman who had lost her son, separated from her by public sale. In the anguish of her soul, she gave vent to her indignation freely, and perhaps harshly. Sometime after, she wished to become a member of the church. Before they received her, she had to make humble confession for speaking as she had done. *Some of the elders that received her, and required the confession, were engaged in selling the son from his mother...*

At our house [Allan's house] it is so common to hear their ('the slaves') screams, that we think nothing of it: and lest any one should think that in *general* the slaves are well treated, let me be distinctly understood: — *cruelty* is the *rule,* and *kindness* the *exception...*

The great wrong is *enslaving a man*; all other wrongs are pigmies, compared with that. Facts might be gathered abundantly, to show that it is *slavery itself,* and not cruelties merely, that make slaves unhappy. Even those that are most kindly treated, are generally far from being happy. The slaves in my father's family are almost as kindly treated as *slaves* can be, yet they pant for liberty.

Accounts of Slavery by James G. Birney

The preceding testimony of Mr. Clay (overworking of slaves), is strongly corroborated by advertisements of slaves, by Courts of Probate, and by executors administering upon the estates of deceased persons. Some of those advertisements for the sale of slaves, contain the names, ages, accustomed employment, &c., of all the slaves upon the plantation of the deceased. These catalogues show large numbers of young men and women.... We have laid aside many lists of this kind, in looking over the newspapers of the slaveholding states; but the two following are all we can lay our hands on at present. One is in the "Planter's Intelligenteer," Alexandria, La., March 22, 1837, containing one hundred and thirty slaves, and the other in the New Orleans Bee, a few days later, April 8, 1837, containing fifty-one slaves. The former is a "Probate sale" of the slaves belonging to the estate of Mr. Charles S. Lee, deceased, and is advertised by G. W. Keeton, Judge of the Parish of Concordia, La. The sex, name, and age of each slave are contained in the advertisement, which fills two columns. The following are some of the particulars. The whole number of slaves is *one hundred and thirty.* Of these, *only three are over forty years old.* There are *thirty-five females* between the ages of *sixteen and thirty-three,* and yet there are only THIRTEEN children under the age of *thirteen years!*

It is impossible satisfactorily to account for such a fact, on any other supposition, than that these thirty-five females were so overworked, or underfed, or both, as to prevent child-bearing...

Another proof that the slaves in the southwestern states are over-worked, is the fact, that so few of them live to old age. A large majority of them are *old* at middle age, and few live beyond fifty-five. In one of the preceding advertisements, out of one hundred and thirty slaves, only *three* are over forty years old! In the other, out of fifty-one slaves, only *two* are over *thirty-five*; the oldest is but thirty-nine, and the way in which he is designated in the advertisement, is an additional proof, that what to others is "middle age," is to the slaves in the south-west "old age:" he is advertised as "*old* Jeffrey."

Accounts of Slavery by John Rankin

Many poor slaves are stripped naked, stretched and tied across barrels, or large bags, and *tortured with the lash during hours, and even whole days, until their flesh is mangled to the very bones.* Others are stripped and hung up by the arms, their feet are tied together, and the end of a heavy piece of timber is put between their legs in order to stretch their bodies, and so prepare them for the torturing lash — and in this situation they are often whipped until their bodies are covered *with blood and mangled flesh*— and in order to add the greatest keenness to their sufferings, their wounds are washed with *liquid salt!* And some of the miserable creatures are permitted to hang in that position until they actually *expire*; some die under the lash, others linger about for a time, and at length die of their wounds, and many survive, and endure again similar torture. These bloody scenes are *constantly exhibiting in every slaveholding country — thousands of whips are every day stained in African blood!* Even the poor *females* are not permitted to escape these shocking cruelties...

Some time since, a member of the Presbyterian Church of Ebenezer, Brown County, Ohio, landed his boat at a point on the Mississippi. He saw some disturbance among the colored people on the bank. He stepped up, to see what was the matter. A black man was stretched naked on the ground; his hands were tied to a stake, and one held each foot. He was doomed to receive fifty lashes; but by the time the overseer had given him twenty-five with his great whip, the blood was standing round the wretched victim in little puddles. It appeared just as if it had rained blood.—Another observer stepped up, and advised to defer the other twenty-five to another time, lest the slave might die; and he was released, to receive the balance when he should have so recruited as to be able to bear it and live. The offence was, coming one hour too late to work...

A respectable gentleman, who is now a citizen of Flemingsburg, Fleming County, Kentucky, when in the state of South Carolina, was invited by a slaveholder, to walk with him and take a view of his farm. He complied with the invitation thus given, and in their walk they came to the place where the slaves were at work, and found the overseer whipping one of them very severely for not keeping pace with his fellows — in vain the poor fellow alleged that he was sick, and could not work. The master seemed to think all was well enough, hence he and the gentleman passed on. In the space of an hour they returned by the same way, and found that the poor slave, who had been whipped as they first passed by the field of labor, was actually dead! This I have from unquestionable authority...

A Presbyterian preacher, now resident in a slave state, and therefore it is not expedient to give his name, stated, that he saw on board of a steamboat in Louisville, Kentucky, a woman who had been forced on board, to be carried off from all she counted dear on earth. She ran across the boat and threw herself in the river, in order to end a life of intolerable sorrows. She was drawn back to the boat and taken up. The brutal driver beat her severely, and she immediately threw herself again into the river. She was hooked up again, chained, and carried off.

Accounts of Slavery by Charles S. Renshaw

Judge Menzies of Boone county, Kentucky, and elder in the Presbyterian Church, and a slaveholder, told me that *he knew* some overseers in the tobacco growing region of Virginia, who, to make their slaves careful in picking the tobacco, that is taking the worms off, (you know what a loathsome thing the tobacco worm is) would make them *eat* some of the worms, and others who make them eat every worm they missed in picking...

I was told the following fact by a young lady, daughter of a slaveholder in Boone county, Kentucky, who lived within half a mile of Mr. Hughes' farm. Hughes and Neil traded in slaves down the river: they had brought up a part of their stock in the upper counties of Kentucky, and brought them down to Louisville, where the remainder of their drove was in jail, waiting their arrival. Just before the steamboat put off for the lower county, two negro women were offered for sale, each of them having a young child at the breast. The traders bought them, took their babes from their arms, and offered them to the highest bidder; and they were sold for one dollar apiece, whilst the stricken parents were driven on board the boat, and in an hour were on their way to the New Orleans market. You are aware that a young babe *decreases* the value of a field hand in the lower country, whilst it increases her value in the "breeding states"...

One Sabbath morning, whilst riding to meeting near Burlington, Boone Co. Kentucky, in company with Mr. Willis, a teacher of sacred music and a member of the Presbyterian Church, I was startled at mingled shouts and screams, proceeding from an old log house, some distance from the road side. As we passed it, some five or six boys from 12 to 15 years of age, came out, some of them cracking whips, followed by two colored boys crying. I asked Mr. W. what the scene meant. "Oh," he replied, "those boys have been whipping the niggers; that is the way we bring slaves into subjection in Kentucky — we let the children beat them." The boys returned again into the house, and again their shouting and stamping was heard, but even and anon a scream of agony that would not be drowned, rose above the uproar; thus they continued till the sounds were lost in the distance...

The "protection" thrown around a mother's yearnings, and the helplessness of childhood by the "public opinion" of slaveholders, is shown by *thousands* of advertisements (for sales that separated families)...

In a conversation with Mr. Robert Willis, he told me that his negro girl had run away from him some time previous. He was convinced that she was lurking round, and he watched for her. He soon found the place of her concealment, drew her from it, got a rope, and tied her hands across each other, then threw the rope over a beam in the kitchen, and hoisted her up by the wrists; "and," said he, "I whipped her there till I made the lint fly, I tell you." I asked him the meaning of making "the lint fly," and he replied, "*till the blood flew.*" I spoke of the iniquity and cruelty, and of its immediate abandonment. He confessed it an evil, but said, "I am a *colonizationist*— I believe in that scheme." Mr. Willis is a teacher of sacred music, and a member of the Presbyterian Church in Lexington, Kentucky...

In the kitchen of the minister of the church, a slave man was living in open adultery with a slave woman, who was a member of the church, with an "assured hope" of heaven — whilst the man's wife was on the minister's farm in Fayette county. The minister had to bring a cook down from his farm to the place in which he was preaching. The choice was between the wife of the man and this church member. He *left the wife*, and brought the church member to the adulterer's bed...

A non-professor of religion, in Campbell county, Ky. Sold a female and two children to a Methodist professor, with the proviso that they should not leave that region of the country. The slave-drivers came, and offered $50 more for the woman than he had given, and he sold her. She is now in the lower county, and *her orphan babes are in Kentucky.*

When Renshaw was living in Quincy, Illinois, he became acquainted with Dr. Richard Eells, who was a dedicated abolitionist. Eells was once indicted for aiding the attempted escape of a fugitive slave and after he was found guilty at his trial, he was fined four hundred dollars by then judge Stephen A. Douglas. Below, is part of a letter Renshaw wrote that Weld and the Grimke sisters included in *American Slavery As It Is.*

I am sorry to be obliged to give more testimony without the *name*. An individual in whom I have great confidence, gave me the following facts. That I am not alone in placing confidence in him, I subjoin a testimonial from Dr. Richard Eells, Deacon of the Congregational Church, of Quincy, and the Rev. Mr. Fisher, Baptist Minster of Quincy.

We have been acquainted with the brother who has communicated to you some facts that fell under his observation, whilst in his native state; he is a professed follower of our Lord, and we have great confidence in him as a man on integrity, discretion, and strict Christian principle.

Richard Eells.
Ezra Fisher

Quincy, Jan. 9th, 1839.

Testimony.—"I lived for thirty years in Virginia, and have traveled extensively through Fauquier, Culpepper, Jefferson, Stafford, Albemarle and Charlotte Counties; my remarks apply to these Counties.

"The negro houses are miserably poor, generally they are a shelter from neither the wind, the rain, nor the snow, and the earth is the floor. There are exceptions to this rule, but they are only exceptions; you may sometimes see puncheon floor, but never, or almost never a plank floor. The slaves are generally without *beds or bedsteads*; some few have cribs that they fasten up for themselves in the corner of the hut. Their bed-clothes are a nest of rags thrown upon a crib, or in the corner; sometimes there are three or four families in one small cabin. Where the slaveholders have more than one family, the put them in the same quarter till it is filled, then build another. I have seen exceptions to this, when only one family would occupy a hut, and where were tolerably comfortable bedclothes.

"Most of the slaves in these counties are *miserably clad*. I have known slaves who went without shoes all winter, perfectly barefoot. The feet of many of them are frozen. As a general fact the planters do not serve out to their slaves, drawers, or any under clothing, or vests, or over-coats. Slaves sometimes, by working at night and on Sundays, get better things than their masters serve to them.

"Whilst these things are true of *field-hands*, it is also true that many slaveholders clothe their *waiters* and coachmen like gentlemen. I do not think there is any difference between the slaves of professing Christians and others; at all events, it is so small as to be scarcely noticeable.

" I have seen men and women at work in the field more than half naked: and more than once in passing, when the overseer was not near, they would stop and draw round them tattered coat or some ribbons of a skirt to hide their nakedness and shame from the stranger's eye."

Mr. George W. Westgate, a member of the Congregational Church in Quincy, Illinois, who has spent the larger part of twelve years navigating the rivers of the south-western slave states with keel boats, as a trader, gives the following testimony as to the clothing and lodging of the slaves.

"In Lower Tennessee, Mississippi and Louisiana, the clothing of the slaves is wretchedly poor and grows worse as you go south, in the order of the states I have named. The only material is cotton bagging, i.e. bagging in which cotton is *baled*, not bagging made of cotton. In Louisiana, especially in the lower country, I have frequently seen them with nothing but a tattered coat, not sufficient to hide their nakedness. In winter their clothing seldom serves the purpose of comfort, and frequently not even of decent covering. In Louisiana *the planters never think of serving out shoes to slaves*. In Mississippi they give one pair a year generally. I never saw or heard of an instance of masters allowing them *stockings*. A *small poor blanket is generally the only bed-clothing*, and this they frequently wear in the field when they have not sufficient clothing to hide their nakedness or to keep them warm. Their manner of sleeping varies with the season. In hot weather they stretch themselves anywhere and sleep. As it becomes cool they roll themselves in their blankets, and lay scattered about the cabin. In cold weather they nestle together with their feet towards the fire, promiscuously. As a general fact the earth is their only floor and bed — not one in ten have anything like a bedstead, and then it is a mere bunk put up by themselves."

Accounts of Slavery by Angelina Grimke-Weld

I think it important to premise, that I have seen almost nothing of slavery on *plantations*. My testimony will have respect exclusively to the treatment of "*house-servants*," and chiefly those belonging to the first families in the city of Charleston, both in the religious and in the fashionable world. And here let me say, that the treatment of *plantation* slaves cannot be fully known, except by the poor sufferers themselves, and their drivers and overseers. In a multitude of instances, even the master can know very little of the actual condition of his own field-slaves, and his wife and daughters far less. A few facts concerning my own family will show this. Our permanent residence was in Charleston; our country-seat (Bellemont) was 200 miles distant, in the north-western part of the state; where, for some years, our family spent a few months annually. Our *plantation* was three miles from this family mansion. There, all the field-slaves lived and worked. Occasionally, once a month, perhaps, some of the family would ride over to the plantation, but I never visited the *fields where the slaves were at work*, and knew almost nothing of their condition; but this I do know, that the overseers who had charge of them, were generally unprincipled and intemperate men. But I rejoice to know, that the general treatment of slaves in that region of country, was far milder than on the plantations in the lower country...

Why I did not become totally hardened, under the daily operation of this system, God only knows; in deep solemnity and gratitude, I say, it was the *Lord's* doing, and marvelous in mine eyes. Even before my heart was touched with the love of Christ, I used to say, "Oh that I had the wings of a dove, that I might flee away and be at rest;" for I felt that there could be no rest for me in the midst of such outrages and pollutions. And yet I saw *nothing* of slavery in its most vulgar and repulsive forms. I saw it in the *city*, among the fashionable and the honorable, where it was garnished by refinement, and decked out for show...

The following circumstance occurred in Charleston, in 1828:

A slaveholder, after flogging a little girl about thirteen years old, set her on a table with her feet fastened in a pair of stocks. He then locked the door and took out the key. When the door was opened she was found dead, having fallen from the table. When I asked a prominent lawyer, who belonged to one of the first families in the State, whether the murderer of this helpless girl could be indicted, he coolly replied, that the slave was Mr. _____'s property, and if he chose to suffer the *loss*, no one else had any thing to do with it. The loss of *human life*, the distress of the parents and other relatives of the little girl, seemed utterly out of his thoughts: it was the loss of *property* only that presented itself to his mind...

Persons who own plantations and yet live in cities, often take children from their parents as soon as they are weaned, and send them into the country; because they do not want the time of the mother taken up by attendance upon her own children, it being too valuable to the mistress. As a *favor*, she is, in some cases, permitted to go see them once a year. So, on the other hand, if field slaves happen to have children of an age suitable to the convenience of the master, they are taken from their parents and brought to the city. Parents are almost never consulted as to the disposition to be made of their children; they have as little control over them, as have domestic animals over the disposal of their young. Every natural and social feeling and affection are violated with indifference; slaves are treated as though they did not possess them...

In the course of my testimony I have entered somewhat into the *minutiae* of slavery, because this is a part of the subject often overlooked, and cannot be appreciated by any but those who have been witnesses, and entered into sympathy with the slaves as human beings. Slaveholders think nothing of them, because they regard their slaves as *property*, the mere instruments of their convenience and pleasure. *One who is a slaveholder at heart never recognizes a human being in a slave.*

As thou has asked me to testify respecting the *physical condition* of the slaves merely, I say nothing about the awful neglect of their *minds* and *souls* and the systematic effort to imbrute them. A wrong and an impiety, in comparison with which all the other unutterable wrongs of slavery are but as the dust of the balance.

Accounts of Slavery by Rev. James A. Thome

Slavery is the parent of more suffering than has flowed from any one source since the date of its existence. Such sufferings, too! *Sufferings inconceivable and innumerable—unmingled wretchedness* from the ties of nature rudely broken and destroyed, the *acutest bodily tortures, groans, tears, and blood*—lying for ever in weariness and painfulness, in watchings, in hunger and in thirst, in cold and nakedness.

Brethren of the North, be not deceived. *These sufferings still exist*, and despite the efforts of their cruel authors to hush them down, and confine them within the precincts of their own plantations, they will ever and anon, struggle up and reach the ear of humanity...

In December of 1833, I landed at New Orleans, in the steamer W_____. It was after night, dark and rainy. The passengers were called out of the cabin, from the enjoyment of a fire, which the cold, damp atmosphere rendered very comfortable, by a sudden shout of, "catch him — catch him — catch the negro." The cry was answered by a hundred voices — "Catch him — *kill* him." and a rush from every direction toward our boat, indicated that the object of pursuit was near. The next moment we heard a man plunge into the river, a few paces above us. A crowd gathered upon the shore, with lamps and stones, and clubs, still crying, "catch him — kill him — catch him — shoot him."

I soon discovered the poor man. He had taken refuge under the prow of another boat, and was standing in the water up to his waist. The angry vociferation of his pursuers, did not intimidate him. He defied them all. "Don't you *dare* to come near me, or I will sink you into the river." He was armed with despair. For a moment the mob was palsied by the energy of his threatenings. They were afraid to go to him with a skiff, but a number of them went on to the boat and tried to seize him...

The mob, seeing their efforts fruitless, became more enraged and threatened to stone him, if he did not surrender himself into their hands... "I'll die first"; was his only reply. Even the furious mob was awed, and for a while stood dumb.

After standing in the cold water for an hour, the miserable being began to fail. We observed him gradually sinking — his voice grew weak and tremulous — yet he continued to *curse*! In the midst of his oaths he uttered broken sentences — "I didn't steal the meat — I didn't steal — my master lives — master — master lives up the river — (his voice began to gurgle in his throat, and he was so chilled that his teeth chattered audibly) — I didn't — steal — I didn't steal — my — my master — my — I want to see my master — I didn't — no — my mas — you want — you want to kill me — I didn't steal the" — His last words could just be heard as he sank under the water.

Accounts of Slavery by Sarah Grimke

As I left my native state on account of slavery, and deserted the home of my fathers to escape the sound of the lash and the shrieks of tortured victims, I would gladly bury in oblivion the recollection of those scenes with which I have been familiar; but this may not, cannot be; they come over my memory like gory specters, and implore me with resistless power, in the name of a God of mercy, in the name of a crucified Savior, in the name of humanity; for the sake of the slaveholder, as well as the slave, to bear witness to the horrors of the southern prison house. I feel impelled by a sacred sense of duty, by my obligations to my country, by sympathy for the bleeding victims of tyranny and lust, to give my testimony respecting the system of American slavery, — to detail a few facts, most of which came under my *personal observation*. And here I may premise, that the actors in these tragedies were all men and women of the highest respectability, and of the first families in South Carolina, and, with one exception, citizens of Charleston; and that their cruelties did not in the slightest degree affect their standing in society.

A handsome mulatto woman, about 18 or 20 years of age, whose independent spirit could not brook the degradation of slavery, was in the habit of running away; for this offense she had been repeatedly sent by her master and mistress to be whipped by the keeper of the Charleston workhouse. This had been done with such inhuman severity, as to lacerate her back in a most shocking manner; a finger could not be laid between the cuts. But the love of liberty was too strong to be annihilated by torture; and, as a last resort, she was whipped at several different times, and kept a close prisoner. A heavy iron collar, with three long prongs projecting from it, was placed round her neck, and a strong and sound front tooth was extracted, to served as a mark to describe her, in case of escape. Her sufferings at this time were agonizing; she could lie in no position but on her back, which was sore from scourgings, as I can testify, from personal inspection, and her only place of rest was the floor, on a blanket. These outrages were committed in a family where the mistress daily read the scriptures, and assembled her children for family worship. She was accounted, and was really, so far as alms-giving was concerned, a charitable woman, and tender hearted to the poor; and yet this suffering slave, who was the seamstress of the family, was continually in her presence, sitting in her chamber to sew, or engaged in her other household work, with her lacerated and bleeding black, her mutilated mouth, and heavy iron collar, without, so far as appeared, exciting any feelings of compassion...

A punishment dreaded more by the slaves than a whipping, unless it is unusually severe, is one which was invented by a female acquaintance of mine in Charleston — I heard her say so with much satisfaction. It is standing on one foot and holding the other in the hand. Afterwards it was improved upon, and a strap was contrived to fasten around the ankle and pass around the neck, so that the least weight of the foot resting on the strap would choke the person. The pain occasioned by this unnatural position was great; and when continued, as it sometimes was, for an hour or more, produced intense agony. I heard this same woman say, that she had the ears of her waiting maid *slit* for some petty theft. This she told me in the presence of the girl, who was standing in the room. She often had the helpless victims of her cruelty severely whipped, not scrupling herself to wield the instrument of torture, and with her own hands inflict severe chastisement. Her husband was less inhuman than his wife, but he was often goaded on by her acts of great severity...

A friend of mine, in whose veracity I have entire confidence, told me that about two years ago, a woman in Charleston with whom I was well acquainted, had starved a female slave to death. She was confined in a solitary apartment, kept constantly tied, and condemned to the slow and horrible death of starvation. This woman was notoriously cruel. To those who have read the narrative of James Williams I need only say, that the character of young Larrimore's wife is an exact description of this female tyrant, whose countenance was ever dressed in smiles when in the presence of strangers, but whose heart was as the nether millstone toward her slaves.

As I was traveling in the lower country in South Carolina, a number of years since, my attention was suddenly arrested by an exclamation of horror from the coachman, who called out, "Look there, Miss Sarah, don't you see?" — I looked in the direction he pointed, and saw a human head stuck up on a high pole. On inquiry, I found that a runaway slave, who was outlawed, had been shot there, his head severed from his body, and put upon the public highway, as a terror to deter slaves from running away.

On a plantation in North Carolina, where I was visiting, I happened one day, in my rambles, to step into a negro cabin; my compassion was instantly called forth by the object which presented itself. A slave, whose head was white with age was lying in one corner of the hovel; he had under his head a few filthy rags, but the boards were his only bed, it was the depth of winter, and the wind whistled through every part of the dilapidated building — he opened his languid eyes when I spoke, and in reply to my question, "What is the matter?" he said, "I am dying of a cancer in my side." — As he removed the rags which covered the sore, I found that it extended half found the body, and was shockingly neglected. I inquired if he had any nurse. "No, missey," was his answer, "but de people (the slaves) very kind to me, dey often steal time to run and see me and fetch me some ting to eat; if dey did not, I might starve..."

Another fact occurs to me. A young woman about eighteen, stated some circumstances relative to her young master, which were thought derogatory to his character; whether true or false, I am unable to say; she was threatened with punishment, but persisted in affirming that she had only spoken the truth. Finding her incorrigible, it was concluded to send her to the Charleston workhouse and have her whipt; she pleaded in vain for a commutation of her sentence, not so much because she dreaded the actual suffering, as because her delicate mind shrunk from the shocking exposure of her person to the eyes of brutal and licentious men; she declared to me that death would be preferable; but her entreaties were vain, and as there was no means of escaping but by running away, she resorted to it as a desperate remedy, for her timid nature never could have braved the perils necessarily encountered by fugitive slaves, had not her mind been thrown into a state of despair.— She was apprehended after a few weeks, by two slave-catchers, in a deserted house, and as it was late in the evening they concluded to spend the night there. What inhuman treatment she received from them has never been revealed. They tied her with cords to their bodies, and supposing they had secured their victim, soon fell into a deep sleep, probably rendered more profound by intoxication and fatigue; but the miserable captive slumbered not; by some means she disengaged herself from her bonds, and again fled through the lone wilderness. After a few days she was discovered in a wretched hut, which seemed to have been long uninhabited; she was speechless; a raging fever consumed her vitals, and when a physician saw her, he said she was dying of a disease brought on by over fatigue; her mother was permitted to visit her, but ere she reached her, the damps of death stood upon her brow, and she had only the sad consolation of looking on the death-struck form and convulsive agonies of her child."[1]

One of the most important things that antislavery speakers and writers did was attack the notion that slaves living in the South were happy, docile, and treated well. This myth, propagated by Southerners, was a commonly held misconception in the North. But, members of the Seventy managed to undermine this idea to a significant extent, and one very effective way they did so was by giving accounts of slavery like the ones described above. Slowly but surely, more and more Northerners began to reject the Southern arguments that the enslaved were better off in bondage because their masters generously bore all the responsibility for their care. Abolitionist lecturers were especially effective at chipping away at the Southern contention that slaves were basically satisfied with their lot in life by pointing out that slaves were willing to risk brutal punishment and even their lives by trying to escape. Every runaway slave story Northerners heard or read about in a newspaper helped weaken the claim of slaveholders that their slaves were happy. When Northern whites occasionally came into contact with a fugitive slave or, under different circumstances, met or befriended a former slave, then they learned with their own ears the truth about the nightmare of living in chains. Another powerful challenge to the idea that slaves were content with their lives was the fact of slaves committing suicide. In 1838 the *American Anti-Slavery Almanac* published a drawing showing a runaway slave who had hung himself from a tree because, according to a fellow slave, he did not want to "again fall into the hands of his tormentors."[2]

The last four testimonies in this chapter, unlike the previous seven, were written by members of the Seventy who had not lived in the South. The following accounts were penned by Weld and other members of his band of agents who had grown up in the North.

Excerpts from Weld's contribution to *American Slavery As It Is*

It is no marvel that slaveholders are always talking of the *kind treatment* of their slaves. The only marvel is, that men of sense can be gulled by such professions. Despots always insist that they are merciful. The greatest tyrants that ever dripped with blood have assumed the titles of "most gracious," "most clement," "most merciful," &c., and have ordered their crouching vassals to accost them thus. When did not vice lay claim to those virtues which are the opposites of its habitual crimes? The guilty, according to their own showing, are always innocent, and cowards brave, and drunkards sober, and harlots chaste, and pickpockets honest to a fault. Every body understands this. When man's tongue grows thick, and he begins to hiccough and walk cross-legged, we expect him, as a matter of course, to protest that he is not drunk; so when a man is always singing the praises of his own honesty, we instinctively watch his movements and look out for our pocket-books. Whoever is simple enough to be hoaxed by such professions, should never be trusted in the streets without somebody to take care of him. Human nature works out in slave-holders just as it does in other men, and in American slaveholders just as in English, French, Turkish, Algerine, Roman and Grecian. The Spartans boasted of their kindness to their slaves, while they whipped them to death by thousands at the altars of their gods. The Romans lauded their own mild treatment of their bondmen, while they branded their names on their flesh with hot irons, and when old, threw them into their fish ponds, or like Cato "the Just," starved them to death. It is the boast of the Turks that they treat their slaves as though they were their children, yet the common name for them is "dogs," and for the merest trifles, their feet are bastinadoed to a jelly, or their heads clipped off with the scimetar. The Portuguese pride themselves on their gentle bearing toward their slaves, yet the streets of Rio Janeiro are filled with naked men and women yoked in pairs to carts and wagons, and whipped by drivers like beasts of burden.

Slaveholders, the world over, have sung the praises of their tender mercies towards their slaves. Even the wretches that plied the African slave trade, tried to rebut Clarkson's proofs of their cruelties, by speeches, affidavits, and published pamphlets, setting forth the accommodations of the "middle passage," and their kind attentions to the comfort of those whom they had stolen from their homes, and kept stowed away under hatches, during a voyage of four thousand miles. So, according to the testimony of the autocrat of the Russias, he exercises great clemency towards the Poles, though he exiles them by thousands to the snows of Siberia, and tramples them down by millions, at home. Who discredits the atrocities perpetrated by Ovando in Hispaniola, Pizarro in Peru, and Cortez in Mexico, — because they filled the ears of the Spanish Court with protestations of the benignant rule? While they were yoking the enslaved natives like beasts to the draught, working them to death by thousands in the mines, hunting them with bloodhounds, torturing them on racks, and broiling them on beds of coals, their representations to the mother country teemed with eulogies of the parental sway! The bloody atrocities of Philip II., in the expulsion of the Moorish subjects, are matters of imperishable history. Who disbelieves or doubts them? And yet his courtiers magnified his virtues and chanted his clemency and his mercy, while the wail of a millions victims, smitten down by a tempest of fire and slaughter let loose at his bidding, rose above the *Te Deums* that thundered from all Spain's cathedrals. When Louis XIV revoked the edict of Nantz, and proclaimed two millions of this subject free plunder for persecution, — when from the English channel to the Pyrennees the mangled bodies of the Protestants were dragged on reeking hurdles by a shouting populace, he claimed to be the "the father of his people," and wrote himself "His most *Christian* Majesty."

But we will not anticipate topics, the full discussion of which more naturally follows than precedes the inquiry into the actual condition and treatment of slaves in the United States.

As slaveholders and the apologists are volunteer witnesses in their own cause, and are flooding the world with testimony that their slaves are kindly treated; that they are well fed, well clothed, well housed, well lodged, moderately worked, and bountifully provided with all things needful for their comfort, we propose — first, to disprove their assertions by the testimony of a multitude of impartial witnesses, and then to put slaveholders themselves through a course of cross-questioning which shall draw their condemnation out of their own mouths. We will prove that the slaves in the United States are treated with barbarous inhumanity; that they are overworked, underfed, wretchedly clad and lodged, and have insufficient sleep; that they are often made to wear round their necks iron collars armed with prongs, to drag heavy chains and weights at their feet while working in the field, and to wear yokes, and bells, and iron horns; that they are often kept confined in the stocks day and night for weeks together, made to wear gags in the mouths for hours of days, have some of their front teeth torn out or broken off, that they may be easily detected when they run away; that they are frequently flogged with terrible severity, have red pepper rubbed into the lacerated flesh, and hot brine, spirits of turpentine, &c., poured over the gashes to increase the torture; that they are often stripped naked, their backs and limbs cut with knives, bruised and mangled by scores and hundreds of blows with the paddle, and terribly torn by the claws of cats, drawn over them by the tormentors; that they are often hunted with blood hounds and shot down like beasts, or torn in pieces by dogs; that they are often suspended by the arms and whipped and beaten till they faint, and when revived by restoratives, beaten again till they faint, and sometimes till they die; that their ears are often cut off, their eyes knocked out, their bones broken, their flesh branded with red hot irons; that they are maimed, mutilated and burned to death over slow fires. All these things, and more, and worse, we shall *prove*. Reader, we know whereof we affirm, we have weighed it well; *more and worse* WE WILL PROVE. Mark these words, and read on; we will establish all these facts by the testimony of scores and hundreds of eye witnesses, by the testimony of *slaveholders* in all parts of the slave states, by slaveholding members of Congress and of state legislatures, by ambassadors to foreign courts, by judges, by doctors of divinity, and clergymen of all denominations, by merchants, mechanics, lawyers and physicians, by presidents and professors in colleges and *professional* seminaries, by planters, overseers and drivers. We shall show, not merely that such deeds are committed, but that they are frequent; not done in corners, but before the sun; not in one of the slave states, but in all of them ; not perpetrated by brutal overseers and drivers merely, but by magistrates, by legislators, by professors of religion, by preachers of the gospel, by governors of states, by "gentlemen of property and standing," and by delicate females moving in the "highest circles of society." We know, full well, the outcry that will be made by multitudes, at these declarations; the multiform cavils, the flat denials, the charges of "exaggeration" and "falsehood" so often bandied, the sneers of affected contempt at the credulity that can believe such things, and the rage and imprecations against those who give them currency. We know, too, the threadbare sophistries by which slaveholders and the apologists seek to evade such testimony. If they admit that such deeds are committed, they tell us that they are exceedingly rare, and therefore furnish no ground for judging of the general treatment of slaves; that occasionally a brutal wretch in the *free* states barbarously butches his wife but that no one thinks of inferring from that, the general treatment of wives at the North and West.

They tell us, also, that the slaveholders of the South are proverbially hospitable, kind, and generous, and it is incredible that they can perpetrate such enormities upon human beings; further, that it is absurd to suppose that they would thus injure their own property, that self interest would prompt them to treat their slaves with kindness, as none but fools and madmen wantonly destroy their own property; further, that Northern visitors at the South come back testifying to the kind treatment of the slaves, and that the slaves themselves corroborate such representations. All these pleas, and scores of others, are bruited in every corner of the free States; and who that hath eyes to see, has not sickened at the blindness that saw not, at the palsy of heart that felt not, or at the cowardice and sycophancy that dared not expose such shallow fallacies. We are not to be turned from our purpose by such vapid babblings. In their appropriate places, we propose to consider these objections and various others, and to show their emptiness and folly.

The foregoing declarations touching the inflictions upon slaves, are not haphazard assertions, nor the exaggerations of fiction conjured up to carry a point; nor are they the rhapsodies of enthusiasm, nor crude conclusions, jumped at by hasty and imperfect investigation, nor the aimless outpourings either of sympathy or poetry; but they are proclamations of deliberate, well-weighed convictions, produced by accumulations of proof, by affirmations and affidavits, by written testimonies and statements of a cloud of witnesses who speak what they know and testify what they have seen, and all these impregnably fortified by proofs innumerable, in the relation of the slaveholder to his slave, the nature of arbitrary power, and the nature and history of man.[3]

Jonathan Blanchard

In October of 1845 Jonathan Blanchard, pastor of the sixth Presbyterian Church in Cincinnati, debated N. L. Rice, pastor of the Central Presbyterian Church in Cincinnati on the questions: Is slave holding in itself sinful, and is the relation between master and slave a sinful relation? The debate took place over the course of four days. Blanchard supported the affirmative and Rice the negative. It seems likely that many of the points Blanchard made during this debate would have been concepts he used in the late 1830s when he was an agent for the AASS. The following are excerpts from Blanchard's remarks.

The question which we are to-day met to discuss, to my own mind, borrows a melancholy interest from the slave-coffles which, in increasing numbers, are passing from the upper to the lower slave-country at this time. Three days since, sixty-four men chained together and separated from their wives and daughters, passed by our city on their way to the South.

While we are debating and you are listening, anxious to know the truth on this important practical question, the slave-pens of a sister city, Louisville, are increasing their number and enlarging their dimensions, to receive slaves brought in from the upper country to send to the lower states for sale. This infernal traffic has been stimulated by the late movements in Lexington against the property and person of Cassius M. Clay; and by the kidnapping of white men on the borders of the State of Ohio, and a practical refusal of bail; by which they now lie in prison in a sister State.

That human beings should be now suffering such inhuman usage in our midst, gives, in my mind, a painful interest to this debate; and must, I think, produce a tender and melancholy sentiment in the breast of all who hear it, independent of the points in dispute.

The question, however, must be considered and decided upon general principles, independent of, though it cannot be separated from, contemporaneous events. It ought therefore to be set forth with great distinctness, to enable us to apprehend clearly and fully the bearings of the argument. It is this. "*Is slaveholding in itself sinful, and the relation between master and slave a sinful relation?*"

To explain and set this question distinctly before you, I observe that, so far as I know, all well informed persons, believers in Christianity, hold, that there are two classes of human practices, as it respects church-discipline — one class, right, the other wrong: practices which ought, and practices which ought not to be received by the church into fellowship. We hold communion with persons engaged in the various vocations of life. If a man is a farmer and tills the soil, we commune with him. If he is a blacksmith, we commune with him. If he is engaged in trade, and conducts his business honestly and uprightly, we commune with him — because those vocations are good and right. But there are on the other hand, practices, such as smuggling, swindling, gambling, selling lottery tickets, &c., with which we hold no fellowship, but which ought to be met and questioned at the threshold of the church. Now the naked question before us to-day, and for the three following days, is, to which class of human practices does the holding of human beings as property belong? Ought the church to object to it?—is it wrong, or is it right?

...Let me tell you, fellow citizens, when they have canonized slave-holding as sinless, and set it up in the church of God; when they have persuaded us that they have God's warrant for the property-holding of *man*, be he colored or white; for keeping him in slavery, because his ancestors were enslaved by others; seizing his infants for slaves as soon as born;—Oh! Sirs, they well know that all the rest of slavery follows. They know that the property power, by fatal necessity, draws every other slave law after it! Does not the gentleman know that if the State of Indiana, or any other State, should enact and enforce a law making its laborers property, that all the other laws of slavery would follow of course? Aye; my friend knows, and God knows, that such is the quality of human nature, that when you have put a bridle in the mouth, and a saddle upon the back, of one man, and vaulted another into the saddle, with whip in hand, and spur on heel, and placed the reins fully within the grip of the rider, it is but insulting misery to cry—"Pray, sir, don't use him as a horse." He is property.—You have made him property; and he will be used as property.

...A money-loving, hardened man, in southern Pennsylvania, told me that when he put his hand to paper to sign a bill of sale for the transfer of a human being, his arm trembled and shook to his shoulder-blade. There is not a power, principle, or faculty included in the awful circle of humanity but shudders at the emotions of this horrid property-power, as the trees of Eden trembled at the movements of Satan in the fall of man. You may go, Kentuckians, to your homes, but the truths to which you here listen, apart from any power of argument, by their own vital force, will abide with you as omnipresent blaze, showing you everything about your negro-quarters in a light in which you never beheld them before, and making you one in understanding and heart with the promoters of liberty, and friends of the slave.—For the truth is God's, and God's unseen power is in it.

...I now come to the last argument, which, if I had placed them in the order of the importance, would have been first. With God's help, I mean not to leave one stone upon another of his argument from scripture which shall not be thrown down. I have once read the texts upon which he founds his doctrine, and it is not necessary to re-read them. I attempted to show, first, that, even though the Hebrew bond-servants had been slaves, that would not answer the purpose of justifying Kentucky slavery, any more than would the fact that the Israelites were permitted to borrow jewels from the Egyptians without returning them, justify modern swindling or stealing.... Slaves are men held in hereditary and perpetual bondage: they are "*property to all intents and purposes forever. That* is slavery. Slaves are *property,* as cattle are property...

And now—*Gentlemen and fellow-citizens*—with many and sincere thanks for your long and patient attention, during this debate, (having no time to recapitulate,) I bid you an affectionate farewell.... For me, I know that when a few days are come, a thousand miles shall stretch between your dwellings and mine—and when, hereafter, this toil-worn frame shall be sinking to its last earthly rest, it shall please my failing memory to remember, that my last effort among you was in vindication of the oppressed.[4]

William Yates

A few members of the Seventy concentrated on the issue of discrimination against free blacks in the North. No American Anti-Slavery Society agent was more concerned about this injustice than William Yates. The following excerpts are taken from Yates' 1838 work *Rights of Colored Men to Suffrage, Citizenship, and Trial by Jury: Being—A Book of Facts, Arguments, and Authorities, Historical Notices and Sketches of Debates—With Notes*:

Introduction

Object Stated

The object of this book is to call to mind, from the records of the past, some of the many testimonies to be found of the rights and services of colored men. The exclusion of this class from social intercourse, throws them into the shade. Comparatively, they are withdrawn from general observation; and this circumstance, of itself, tends to a forgetfulness of their claims. It is a fact, that in proportion as the services they have rendered the country have faded from the memory, so it seems a callousness of feeling towards them has increased.

It is not with the present generation of men, as with the generation who preceded it. Then, when the country had just emerged from the revolutionary struggle—when the services and sufferings of men of color were fresh in the memory—then, as says one who participated in the conflict—"The war over and peace restored, these men returned to their respective States and home; and who could have said to them, on their returning to civil life, after having shed their blood in common with the whites, for the liberties of the country—'You are not to participate in the rights of liberty for which you have been fighting?' Certainly no *white* man." But it is not so now; as is painfully evinced by the successive disfranchisements with which they have been visited, in the constitutions of New Jersey, Connecticut, New York, and by the recent vote of the Reform Convention of Pennsylvania.

History of Service—Materials

It is to be regretted that effectual efforts were not made at an early day to furnish a history of the services of men of color. Even if it had been a collection of facts and testimonies merely, similar to the present attempt, it would have been a work of interest. Then the materials were more abundant—a greater number than at present were living, who were witnesses of their services; then the task would have been comparatively easy; but even as it is, the subject is a rich one. The present work does not exhaust it; it scarcely more than opens the way; other sources of information exist, which the compiler has not had access to; these should be explored and their hidden treasure brought to light. The records of the pension department at Washington, if examined with this view, would doubtless disclose important facts; and it may be, that, from private letters and correspondence of gentlemen who at an early period took an interest in the abolition of slavery, which may yet be preserved, much valuable information and testimony might be gleaned; and so, doubtless, there are other sources.

Facts should be collected and published.

There are a multitude of acts, as well relating to the present as the past history of this subject, which the friends of human rights should industriously and systematically seek out; and these as fast as elicited should be sent forth in a constant stream upon the public mind, through all the channels by which that mind is reached. It is by having heard from day to day, and (with the present generation it has been) from youth to manhood, the vulgar contumely and indignities cast upon men of color, that the public mind has become perverted, and their name connected with injurious associations. And it is only by a *counter* effort, by an exhibition of the opposite side of the picture — by a diligent presentation of truth — by frequent references to services past, and to evidences of merit existing at present; and, generally, to be found wherever men of color are found, that this perversion of the public sentiment can be corrected. It is thus the name of color may be rescued from associations which now attach to it, and connect itself with what is noble in character, and generous in virtue.

People of color are too often pre-judged by those unhappy specimens of humanity which are sometimes seen, and from which no people, whatever their color, are exempt. This is unjust, and the more so as their peculiar circumstances render them liable to this treatment. Excluded as they are from the common intercourse of society, their progress in refinement, social improvements, domestic comforts, the moral worth and influence of many in the circle in which they move, pass unobserved — and their true merits become but little known. Their worth, therefore, moral and social, should be drawn from its obscurity — the curtain should occasionally be lifted, that the world may see how false and unjust are the common imputations thrown upon them; and if in every community some individual would interest himself to gather up the facts of this kind which his neighborhood furnishes, and send them forth to the world, there would soon be found afloat in the public mind, an array of proofs, under whose influence prejudice would gradually subside.

Prejudice Against Color

It is an object of this book to exert an influence, tending to the repeal of laws recognizing distinctions of color. Such laws are the results of prejudice — hatred of men for the complexion it has pleased their Maker to give them. And to remove these out of the way, it is necessary to undermine the basis upon which they rest. Every successful attempt to destroy the objections of prejudice, is a step towards the accomplishment of the object. And prejudice against color, let it be understood, is the battleground between the friends and foes of human rights in a contest for equal laws; especially in the free States, where a question of property does not embarrass the subject. Every legal disability — the exclusion of colored men from militia service, from naturalization, or the basis or representation; denying them the rights of citizenship or suffrage, or the benefit of the public schools; and rendering them incompetent to hold real estate, or to give testimony in court; wherever these exist, they are monuments of the force of prejudice. They all point to the existence of this hateful feeling, from which they originated, which lies back of, and supports them all. They are out-posts on the frontier ground of this disputed territory, and will remain impregnable while the people bow to this dark power; but as soon as *they* are won from the delusion, these defences will surrender at discretion.

The subjects, with reference to which the selections in the following pages have been made, are three, viz.: The Right of Suffrage, of Citizenship, and Trial by Jury.

1. The right of suffrage, by citizens of color.

The notice of this subject is comprised in "Sketches of Proceedings and Speeches in the Convention of New York, held for amending the Constitution of that State, in the year 1821." The order in which the topics involved in the notice of this subject are presented, is the one chosen by the different speakers. This reserves the harmony and continuity of the arguments of each. And this mode of arrangement is according to the design of the work. The leading points which properly belong to a discussion of the subject, are noticed. And it is believed that, with more readers it will have more influence than it would have in any other form, because it expresses the views of some of the most eminent men of the country on the subject, such as Platt, Jay, Van Vetchen, and others, whose arguments are given. By dividing the remarks of gentlemen into suitable paragraphs, and affixing to each a brief designation of the firmation or comparison of ideas, is rendered easy. In regard to the original writing and matter introduced, (and this remark applies to the whole work,) it is proper to say, that, with a few exceptions, but little more has been attempted than was necessary to link the facts and arguments together, so as to enable the reader to follow the chain.

2. Citizenship of persons of color.

In regard to citizenship, this is a subject of great importance — an exclusion from suffrage is a withholding of political rights only, but the question of citizenship strikes deeper; deny a man this, and his personal rights are not safe. He may be hindered from going into a State- or, if he enters it, he may be expelled, or treated as an alien. On this principle Missouri attempted to prohibit free colored men from coming into, or settling in the State, on any pretext whatever. And Connecticut undertook to deprive those of the benefits of a school, who came for the laudable purpose of education.

The selections made have reference (1) to the general principles of citizenship; and (2) to the two memorable instances in the history of the country in which the question has been raised and discussed, viz. the Missouri question, and the case of Prudence Crandall. This subject was also noticed in the debates in the recent Reform Convention of Philadelphia, on the insertion of the word white in the clause relating to suffrage.

3. Trial by jury.

The last subject of this book is trial by jury. It is introduced with a view to consider its application to the case of fugitive slaves, or, as they are styled, "fugitives from labor." The general agitation of the question in the aspect throughout the country, at this time, in legislative bodies, courts of justice, popular meetings, labor, is a valid law or not, under which *any free citizen of a State may be seized as a slave,* or apprentice who has escaped from servitude, *and transported to a distant part of the Union without any trial, except a summary examination before*

*a magistrate, who is not even clothed with power to compel the attendance of wit-
nesses.*[5]

David Root

It is difficult to truly gauge the extent to which the murder of abolitionist
Elijah P. Lovejoy galvanized the antislavery cause in the United States. But
his murder in November 1837, in Alton, Illinois, caused a very real shift in
the attitudes in many Americans regarding abolitionism. Owen Lovejoy said
of his brother, Elijah, that he had "done more by his death than living and
unopposed he could have done in a century." Following Elijah Lovejoy's murder, the antislavery movement received increasing attention. John Quincy
Adams said Lovejoy's death "gave a shock as of an earthquake throughout the
continent."[6] One of the most important eulogies delivered following Lovejoy's
death was given by David Root, a member of the Seventy. Below are excerpts
from Root's remarks:

> My Christian brethren and fellow-citizens, an occasion of rare and affecting
> interest has summoned us in solemn convocation this evening. Not merely that a
> fellow man has expired, not merely that a Christian has departed, not merely
> that a beloved brother minister of the Gospel has gone to his rest; but that an
> American citizen, in the exercise of his rights, rights guaranteed to him by God
> and the constitution of his country, has fallen by the hand of violence, "fallen by
> the fury of a free people murdering in defence of slavery," fallen a martyr in sup-
> port of principles dear to every Christian, every American bosom.
>
> Yes, Lovejoy is no more. That beloved brother, that champion of liberty, that
> Christian hero, that uncompromising friend of the defenceless, down-trodden
> slave, whose movements in the cause of the oppressed for the last six months we
> have contemplated with admiration, has been sacrificed, by wicked hands, upon
> the altar of his country's liberty, in bearing testimony to the truth, and his name
> is henceforth to be enrolled upon the calendar of Christian martyrs.
>
> Brethren and friends, while with grief of heart, we drop the tear of sorrow
> upon the grave of our departed brother, thus early fallen by the wrath of his ene-
> mies, a martyr to this Christian firmness in the cause of God and man, let us
> remember, for our consolation, that the Lord reigns, and that "the wrath of man
> shall praise him and the remainder of the wrath will he restrain."
>
> Brother Lovejoy, whose lov'd memory we would henceforth embalm in our
> hearts, was a New-England man, and as we have been informed; a native of
> Albion, Kennebec County, Maine. His Rev. Brother is, at this time, the settled
> minister of Orono, Maine. And there too, or in that region, reside his afflicted
> mother and sisters.
>
> Elijah P. Lovejoy, the subject of our present contemplation, was graduated at
> Waterville College in 1828. He afterwards practiced law at St. Louis, and was
> Editor of a political paper there. At that time, it seems, his sentiments were
> highly skeptical. But being converted to the Christian faith and hope, by the

instrumentality of Dr. Nelson, during a revival of religion in that place, he conferred not with flesh and blood, but devoted himself to the work of the ministry, after having spent some time at Princeton in preparatory studies. He was subsequently employed as "an Agent for the Sunday School Union, which station he occupied with eminent success, and the entire approbation of the Society."

"By common consent, he was selected as the proper person to conduct a religious paper at St. Louis. The duties of an Editor he discharged with much talent and faithfulness." His benevolent spirit, his firmness and decision of character, his self-devotion to truth and righteousness, early and greatly endeared him to the friends of morality and religion.

When Dr. Nelson was persecuted with abuse, outrage, and violence for his abolition sentiments, and he himself was censured and threatened for the freedom with which he exposed error and condemned vice, and bore testimony against American oppression, Mr. Lovejoy came out in a very able, patriotic, and Christian defence of the right of free discussion. He took his stand upon the Constitution and upon the Bible, that ancient charter of human liberty, and pledged himself to sustain the freedom of speech and of the press at every hazard. It was a noble prediction breathing the spirit of '76, and worth the days of martyrdom.

When a slave was burned to death near St. Louis, by Lynch law, and Judge Lawless published his infamous and *lawless* charge to the grand jury, Mr. Lovejoy raised the note of remonstrance, and rebuked the savage outrage. For this he was banished from the State. He then located his press in Alton, Illinois, a free State. The persecuting, diabolical spirit of slavery, however, did not leave him unmolested when he had left the domain of bonds and blood. It still pursued him with unrelenting virulence and malignity, and soon became rampant in Alton.

About this time, July, 1837, Mr. Lovejoy became thoroughly convinced of the truth and importance of the abolition doctrines, and, at the request of several respectable and influential individuals, made a public declaration of his view, an extract from which we beg leave to introduce in this place.

Anti-Slavery Principles of the Rev. Elijah P. Lovejoy, published in the Alton Observer of July 20th, 1837, for maintaining which he was murdered!...

First Principles.

1. Abolitionists hold that "all men are born free and equal, endowed by their Creator with certain inalienable rights, among which are life, LIBERTY, and the pursuit of happiness." They do not believe that these rights are abrogated, or at all modified by the colour of the skin, but that they extend alike to every individual of the human family.

2. As the above mentioned rights are in their nature inalienable, it is not possible that one man can convert another into a piece of property, thus at once annihilating all his personal rights, without the most flagrant injustice and usurpation. But American slavery does this—it declares a slave to be a "thing," a "chattel," an article of personal "property," a piece of "merchandise," and now actually holds TWO AND A HALF MILLIONS of our fellow-men in this precise condition.

3. Abolitionists, therefore, hold American Slavery to be a *wrong*, a legalized

system of inconceivable injustice, and a sin. That it is a sin against God, whose prerogative as the rightful owner of all human beings is usurped, and against the slave himself, who is deprived of the power to dispose of his service as conscience may dictate, or his Maker requires. And whatever is morally wrong can never be politically right, and as the Bible teaches, and as abolitionists believe, that "righteousness exalteth a nation, while sin is a reproach to any people," they also hold that slavery is a political evil of unspeakable magnitude, and one which, if not removed, will speedily work the downfall of our free institutions, both civil and religious.

4. As the Bible inculcates upon man but one duty in respect to sin, and that is, immediate repentance, abolitionists believe that all who hold slaves, or who approve the practice in others, should *immediately* cease to do so.

5. Lastly. Abolitionists believe, that as all men are born free, so all who are now held as slaves in this country were born free, and that they are slaves now is the sin, not of those who introduced the race into this country, but of those, and those alone, who now hold them, and have held them in slavery from their birth...

Emancipation — what is meant by it?

Simply, that the slaves shall cease to be held as *property*, and shall henceforth be held and treated as human beings. Simply that we should take our feet from off their necks. Perhaps we cannot express ourselves better than to quote the language of another southerner. In reply to the question what is meant by emancipation, the answer it —

"1. It is to reject with indignation the wild and guilty phantasy, that man can hold *property* in man.

2. To pay the laborer his hire, for he is worthy of it.

3. No longer to deny him the right of marriage, but to 'let every man have his own wife,' as saith the apostle.

4. To let parents have their own children, for they are the gift of the Lord to them, and no one else has a right to them.

5. No longer to withhold the advantages of education and the privilege of reading the Bible.

6. To put the slave under the protection of law, instead of throwing him beyond its salutary influence."

Now, who is there that is opposed to slavery at all, and believes it to be wrong and a sin, but will agree to all this?

How and by whom is emancipation to be effected?

To this question the answer is, by the *masters themselves*, and by no others. No others can effect it, nor is it desirable that they should, even if they could. Emancipation, to be of any value to the slave, must be the free, voluntary act of the master, performed from a conviction of its propriety. This avowal may sound very strange to those who have been in the habit of taking the principles of the abolitionists from the misrepresentations of their opponents. Yet this is, and always has been, the cardinal principle of abolitionists. If it be asked, then, why they intermeddle in a matter where they can confessedly do nothing themselves, in achieving the desired result, their reply is, that this is the very reason why they do and ought to intermeddle. It is because they cannot emancipate the slaves that they call upon those who can do it. Could they themselves do it, there would be no need of discussion — instead of discussing they would act, and with their present views the work would soon be accomplished....

I ask you, my hearers, to contemplate this tragical event, as the future and impartial historian shall contemplate it. Let it be recollected, that he contended for the right of free discussion, and in consequence, his press and life were exposed. He cast himself upon the civil authorities, but they refused him protection. His press was destroyed, but there was no disposition "in the powers that be" to repair his loss. He called, however, upon the friends of liberty, and they rallied to his help and replaced his press. But again and again was the glorious engine of freedom destroyed. "He rose in the high purpose of a man, a patriot, and a Christian, and resolved on liberty or death."

Amidst all these dangers and dissuasives, Lovejoy quailed not, neither turned back from his noble purpose. His heart was fixed, trusting in God. At length the crisis came. The press arrived. It was known that there would be violence. The city authorities knew it, but refused to act. A few of the friends of liberty and law, however, with himself, collected in the building belonging to one of them, where the press was, and acting under the authority, and by the instructions of the Mayor of the city, determined to defend it. They had a right to defend it. It was their home, their castle. And they were noble, generous hearts.

Then came on that dreadful night-scene, the rallying of the mob from the coffee-houses, and tipling-shops, and all the hell-holes of Alton, with horrid curses, and howlings, and yells. You may imagine the infernal world disgorging her frightful progeny, and the master spirits of hell, with bloody intent, hurrying to the scene of action.

They plant themselves before the devoted edifice. Forthwith volleys of stones and other missiles are hurled through the windows and doors. But not satisfied with this mode of attack, their assailants soon leveled upon them with fire-arms. The balls whistled through the building, but no one was hurt. The firing without was returned from within. Presently the hoarse, rough cry is heard, "set the building a fire, set the building a fire! Burn them out, burn them out, and shoot the d —-d abolitionists as they go," with curses and yells that rend the air. To prevent the firing of the building, Lovejoy ventured out, and soon fell pierced with three buck shot. It was announced to those without that Lovejoy was dead. And another hideous shout was raised, as if it were an echo from hell.

But the guilt of this bloody deed is not confined exclusively to the immediate actors in Alton. It covers the land. And inasmuch as this horrid crime was perpetrated by the ferocious spirit of slavery, not only those who have connived at the prostration of law and order, but all who have attempted to justify that execrable system of oppression, must be regarded as having been accessary. What shall we say of that portion of the American church, the American press, those statement and divines, and the great mass of the people, all who for the last five years have either countenanced riots or justified that odious system of injustice, crime, and cruelty whence they most frequently proceed? What shall we say of those ministers of the Gospel who have proved recreant to their high vocation and refused to lift up the warning voice against the crying *sin* of this land ; those statesmen who, for the sake of office and emolument, have been deaf to the claims of eternal justice; those editors, guardians of the public press and the public weal, who, for patronage, have cowered to the despotic spirit of slavery, and to curry southern favor, by showing their hostility to the deliverance of the captives, have consented to misrule and violence; those merchants, who for fear of interrupting a lucrative trade with the south, have tried to stifle the voice of humanity; and all those professing Christians, who for fear, or favor, or prejudice, have refused appropriately to remember their brethren in bonds; what shall we say of them? Are they not guilty?

But in the next place. Have we nothing to do with slavery? If we have nothing to do with slavery, you may now see that slavery has something to do with us. Its dark, despotic and diabolical spirit is invading our constitutional rights, stabbing the peace and comfort of our fire sides, and disgracing our country in the eyes of the world.

"Is it nothing to us that it renders us "The Christian's scorn, the Heathen's mirth!"

Are we to rest calmly with the brand of infamy hissing up on our foreheads in consequence of our connexion with its bonds of blood? Ought we not at least to wash our hands of all acquiesce in its wrongs and guilt?

Its blighting, withering effects upon our free institutions are every where visible. It is the prolific source of vice, strife, and havoc, sending forth its malignant influence into the very midst of us, waging war upon all we hold dear. And if ever our country is dismembered and thrown into a state of anarchy and ruin, it is more than probably that slavery will do it.

7. Brethren, how noble, how sublime is the abolition enterprise, possessing a moral grandeur equalled only by the redemption of the world by the mission of the Son of God! Contemplate its principles and measures. You have just heard them as from the dead. What objection have you, can you have to them? Do they not commend themselves irresistibly to your consciences?

And the, how benevolent, how philanthropic, how patriotic its object. It proposes the deliverance of two millions of long neglected captives, and in their deliverance, the salvation of our country. And though thus worthy of all commendation and all cooperation, you behold it unaided and unprotected, struggling against legislative sanction and popular violence, against "principalities and powers and spiritual wickedness in high places."

The Missionary enterprise is justly regarded as one of great moral sublimity. But it fails altogether in the comparison, whether we consider their respective objects, or the moral courage required in their prosecution. For it requires vastly more moral heroism, in these times of apostacy and persecution, to be an abolitionist than it does to be a Missionary...

Brethren, I have one last request. It is that you identify yourselves with the antislavery enterprise, now consecrated and baptized with blood, that, in the fear of God, you commit yourselves to its claims. You have heard our principles tonight from one who sealed them with his blood. You know that they are the principles of eternal truth; and you cannot but feel the conviction, that we are right; that our cause is the cause of God and must prevail.

Yes, brethren, our confidence is in One who is mighty to save, Who redeemed Israel with a strong hand and an outstretched arm, and sunk Pharoah and his hosts in the depths of the sea ; "for his mercy endureth forever," and who is pledged "to deliver the oppressed out of the hand of the spoiler."

We beseech you then, rally round this benevolent, holy enterprise. There is no neutral ground upon which you can stand. He that is not for us is against us. As you then value your country's freedom, the rights of conscience and protection from the violence of midnight ruffians ; as you regard the claims of suffering humanity in the persons of your oppressed countrymen, or respect the blood of your martyred brother, who suffered not for himself, but for us, in defence of principles dear as life to us all; as you would save *yourselves* from bondage and your land from the judgments of heaven; above all, as you would obey God and secure his favor, we entreat you, identify yourselves with this persecuted people who are laboring to establish justice and redeem the captives.

Brethren, our brother has fallen, nobly fallen. His career was short, but splendid, glorious, triumphant. He accomplished much in a little time, and was soon summoned to his reward. His joyous spirit now mingles with all the martyred throng before the throne of God, "who have come out of great tribulation and washed their robes and made them white in the book of the Lamb."

God grant that we may imitate his unbending integrity, his unreserved devotion to truth and righteousness, his fellow feeling for the suffering and the dumb, his unblinking confidence in God, his Christian heroism in witnessing a good confession. And that his bereaved widow and fatherless children may share richly in the blessings of the God of the widow and fatherless, is the earnest prayer of him who is permitted to address you on this mournful and most affecting occasion — Amen.[7]

Chapter 5

Acting on What They Preached

Just as the abolitionist movement became better organized in the 1830s, so too, did the Underground Railroad. The Underground Railroad headed away from Southern states in every direction but in the 1830s and into the '40s and '50s, a remarkable maze of UGRR stations was put into place from New England to the Great Plains. The network of Underground Railroad operators included both individuals who only occasionally supported the movement of fugitive slaves and men and women who provided sustained aid to freedom seekers. Some UGRR conductors tended to work with other station masters who lived close by or in neighboring counties. Other agents communicated with comrades over very long distances.

However, all Underground Railroad activists shared some things in common no matter where or how they carried out their efforts. First and foremost, they were scrupulously careful about the necessity for trust in and the reliability of other conductors similarly involved. It was against the law to aid runaway slaves so failure to be cautious and secretive about this kind of work could jeopardize both fellow operators and the fugitives they were helping. Secondly, it was normally the case that adults did not discuss their illegal activities with their younger children or other people who might unwittingly reveal what was going on to the wrong person. Finally, Underground Railroad carriers were always heedful not to mention what they were up to with strangers who might report them to the authorities or try to cash in on rewards posted by slave owners who wanted their human property apprehended. In addition to staying clear of slave trackers, bounty hunters, and law enforcement officers, Underground Railroad activists had to endure harassment from fellow citizens who thought they were troublemakers or law-breakers. But, for Underground Railroad operators who were or had formerly been antislavery agents, this harassment was usually trifling compared to the violent mobs they had faced as abolitionist lecturers.

It was frequently the case that local or regional UGRR operators passed messages to fellow agents by word of mouth or sent a family member to the next station to outline a plan on how to transport fugitives they were hiding. But in some instances, a note or letter was mailed to an underground comrade residing in another state. Fugitive slaves were transported on horseback, hidden in wagons, escorted on foot close to rivers, put on boats and even secreted in railroad cars. Some runaways were simply given directions and told to travel on their own. Untold numbers of fugitives traveled as stowaways on boats or ships. Innumerable freedom seekers escaped without receiving any help at all, but occasionally they were lucky enough to come upon an Underground Railroad operator by pure chance. Many runaway slaves who were understandably leery of seeking aid from anyone who was white, readily accepted help from free blacks. However, a good number of freedom seekers did not seek aid from anyone black or white. Although real safety was not achieved until escapees entered Canada, large numbers of fugitive slaves took the risk of taking up residence in northern states. If fugitives remained in the United States, it meant living with the constant risk of being apprehended.

A significant number of American antislavery agents were involved with UGRR operations at some point in their lives. Credible verification is difficult to find regarding the Underground Railroad efforts of many American Anti-Slavery Agents even though their involvement with the movement seems very likely. Nonetheless, there is solid evidence that many members of Weld's band involved themselves in Underground Railroad activity. Some of these individuals were helping fugitive slaves escape when they were working for the national society and others became UGRR operatives in later years. What follows are accounts of Underground Railroad agents who belonged to the Seventy.

William T. Allan

In 1838, William T. Allan settled in Illinois a year after marrying Oberlin student Irene Ball. Although Allan's days as president of the Lane Student Anti-Slavery Society, as a pupil at Oberlin, and as an antislavery lecturer in the East were behind him, his efforts as an abolitionist agitator were far from over. He first stayed with relatives in Carrollton but in the fall of that year, he moved to Macoupin County. Allan reconnected with former fellow AASS agents John Miter, Charles Renshaw, and Hiram Foote at a meeting of the Illinois State Anti-Slavery Society in Farmington that October.[1] In 1839, he was reappointed as an agent of the American Anti-Slavery Society and he also agreed to work at that time for the Illinois Anti-Slavery Society. His efforts on behalf of the state society continued until the organization faded away in the mid–1840s.[2] During this time, he lived in Chatham, Springfield, and Peoria while lecturing throughout Illinois. In 1840, Allan reported that the majority of people he encountered were loyal to slaveholders. "The great mass of people in this section are inaccessible to this subject. They will not come to the light but notwithstanding all this, there are many warm friends to the slave, and the cause is slowly but steadily advancing." But, for the most part, he found that "the tenacity and strength of the people's ignorance are indeed astonishing."[3] In 1843, a mob in Peoria successfully stopped Allan from establishing an Anti-Slavery Society in the rivertown.[4]

In 1844, Allan moved to Geneseo where he lived for the rest of his life. His brother, James, had settled in the community in the late 1830s where he had established himself as a prominent figure. By the time William started living in Geneseo, many of its residents had already developed close ties to the abolitionist stronghold in Galesburg, forty-five miles to the south. By the mid 1850s, the *Missouri Republican* identified Galesburg as "the chief city of abolition in Illinois." Allan had many good friends in Galesburg and he once delivered an antislavery speech in the college town. The Western Illinois com-

William T. Allan (courtesy Massachusetts Historical Society).

munities of Geneseo in Henry County, Galesburg in Knox County, and Princeton in Bureau County, represented key Underground Railroad centers in the upper Mississippi Valley. Famous abolitionist Benjamin Lundy spent the last few years of his life living in nearby Putnam County where he revived the *Genius of Universal Emancipation* until his death in 1839.[5]

In the July 18, 1913, issue of the *Geneseo Reporter*, a story entitled "Tales of Operation of the Underground Railroad" discussed the antislavery activities of William and James Allan. The newspaper account extensively quoted Harriet Cohen Miller, who "was a member of the band of colonists that founded Geneseo." Her recollections included the following:

I came to Geneseo with my parents when but a little girl, in 1836. Our family was part of a religious colony which emigrated from New York, settled the place and named it. One of the articles of their creed was antagonism to human slavery, so practically the entire population of the town was composed of abolitionists. Our ideas of right caused us to be violently opposed to everything connected with slavery and among us were some so zealous in the cause of freedom as to give little heed to laws that were designed to assist in perpetuating the institution.

These radical and practical abolitionists organized in about the year 1838 or 1839 and established the "Underground railway" with a station at Geneseo, and my father was selected as its keeper. There was an "L" attached to our house in which was located the well and the wood house. Over this was an attic without windows and entered only by a trap-door from the wood house, the opening being concealed in the construction of the building so that it could not be detected from below. Access to this loft was had by means of a ladder which was concealed elsewhere. When fugitives arrived at our house they were announced by a peculiar signal given in rapping on the door. The fugitives were conducted to the loft by means of the ladder and there concealed until opportunity came to send them on to the next station.

As I was the oldest child in the family I was admitted to the secret and it was my duty to carry food and water to the concealed fugitives by means of the ladder and the trapdoor...

Another thing that aroused the interest of the locality in the slavery question was the coming of the Allan brothers to Geneseo — William and James. They were born and reared in Alabama. Their father was a minister and a slave holder but their mother was opposed to slavery. The boys took the mother's side of the case and came north...

On the death of the elder Allan, William and James fell heir to quite a number of slaves all of which were liberated. One of them who had been long with the Allan family and had cared for the children when they were young, refused to leave them and came to Geneseo and lived with the Allans the remainder of his life. Even under these conditions efforts were made to return this negro to slavery although his pursuers never owned him.[6]

On June 11, 1896, Emma Chapin, William T. Allan's adopted daughter from his second marriage, wrote the following letter to Underground Railroad historian Wilbur Siebert, author of *The Underground Railroad from Slavery to Freedom*. This correspondence described in vivid detail the Underground Railroad activities of her father:

Mr. Siebert,

I have tried my best to give you the information you desire. Have written to my sister in Utah & to friends of my father before I knew him. But I fear I can not tell you very definitely of the road in general. If you will write to Prof. Churchill of Knox College, Galesburg, Ill., he can tell you of the work there, and what was, I am told a strong centre. Nearly all who were active in the work here have passed to the beyond and I was young at the time & my memories are somewhat vague. I will record what I can & you can perhaps cull out something of the much my step-father did for the slave.

If you will write to Mrs. Maltie Whalon (wife of Capt. Whalon & daughter of Dea[con] Millikin) of Lyndon, Ill,) she will tell you of the connections from there.

In 1843 Father Allan went to Peoria to serve as pastor of the Main St. Pres. church. Born in the South of pro-slavery & slaveholding parents, he saw enough of the evils of the institution, to hate it from the depths of his heart. He held that slavery should be abolished, and then instead of colonizing the negroes, they should be made citizens of their own native land of America. Cut off in his father's will for his, to him, extreme & offensive opinions, he entered the ministery poor, but resolved to enjoy the liberty of free speech, & determined to "remember those in bonds as bound with them" & do all in his power to befriend them. His father liberated his slaves by will, & some of them followed Father to Peoria & settled there. One came to Geneseo, with a brother of my father & lived here the rest of his life.

The Peoria Pres. church was called an anti-slavery church & during the time Father Allan had charge of it he was in the employ of the Ill. Anti-Slavery Society & lectured a good deal through the state. At an anti-slavery meeting in his own church one evening, a mob assembled, headed by a saloonkeeper. They carried off one wheel from the carriage of Mr. Pettengill, a friend of my father & a prominent anti-slavery [man] spoke in the wheel of the church [?] The meeting was broken up and threats were made to take my father down to the river, cut a hole in the ice & "chuck him in." His friends besought him to leave the city, but he stood his ground and was not hurt. When I think of the many times his life & property were threatened, it seems strange he escaped from mob violence & unjust law. But God stood within the shadows keeping watch over the right & giving his helpers courage & strength.

At Hennepin, Putnam Co., he had help & sympathy from the Quakers & met Esther Lundy, daughter of Benj. Lundy.

At a lecture, given, I think, in Southern Ill., three Quaker ladies came to Father before meeting & asked to be allowed to sit with him in the pulpit — "to bear testimony." He tried to dissuade them but they made it a matter of conscience. The house was full of roughs and rotten eggs began to fly. Father spoke with one eye on his audience & the other on the immaculate drab bonnets & shawls beside him. The serene sisters [sat] in quiet patience, while eggs broke above them & trickled down over their silk garments.

By & by Father saw an egg coming, aimed straight for his mouth. He used to say in relating the incident, he thought a good deal in short-time. Should he show the white feather by dodging, with such an example of meekness at his side? How would it taste? would it stop the flow of his eloquence? Perhaps he dodged rather by instinct than intention, & the egg, an uncommonly foul one, popped on the wall behind him. He went on but was only able to escape by climbing through a back window.

The Underground Railroad did not run through Peoria, but through the Harkness settlement near Farmington, Fulton Co. It was frequently used at that time. Eli Wilson was an active agent there & though some fugitives were captured, many were sent [from there] on to liberty.

In 1844, Father moved to Geneseo, where his wife died & he married my mother. Here he did efficient work in assisting in the escape of fugitive slaves. I think those who came here, came from near Knoxville, where Father had friends, [the fugitives] stopping on the way at Dea[con] Buck's station at Andover.

Here the work found staunch supporters, Dea[con] Ward, Mr. McFarlance & the Wilcox & Bernard brothers, especially. I well remember the pity and sympathy excited in our young minds by these bondsmen pursued by the terrible fugitive slave law. They usually came after dark & were secreted in the cellar till late at night, or if [the] unfavorable weather, till the next night; when Father or Mr. Wilcox would carry them to the next station north; located at Lyndon, & kept by Dea[con] Millikin & Dea[con] Hamilton. I think. Some were brought here from stations below; some groped their way alone, with only the north star to guide them, that went before them and led them to the goal of their hopes, as the star in the east led the wise men of old. Sometimes two or three were in company, and the terror & loneliness were lessened by being shared, as they hid in the forest by day, or burrowed in some farmer's [hay]stack on the treeless prairie, & patiently picked their way by night, thro storm, cold & heat.

I remember the low uncertain rap they gave at our back door, their hearts in their mouth in fear lest they had mistaken the place, & would meet those who would give them up to the officers of the law & claim the reward. Some of our neighbors spoke openly against those who boldly defied the statutes & tried to steal from their masters their rightful property. But little did my father heed them, for owed allegiance to the higher law of justice & humanity. So my mother gave them a hot supper & led them to the cellar & when it was late, my father hitched his span to the double carriage, buttoned down the side curtains and, placing the trembling fugitives on the back seat, often with Mother on the front seat to better conceal them, he would drive to the next station, fifteen miles north, where friends would assist them on to Canada. One man I can never forget, for my soul cried out in indignation as he slipped off the ragged jacket that was his only upper garment & showed us the long red welts down his back that the whip had made in his cruel beatings. Such a strong frame & manly face he had too. The man with him looked cowed & discouraged, but he looked like one who "could not be a slave." Another I remember, said he had had none but kind masters, & when questioned as to why he ran away, if he was kindly treated, he said, "O massa, I wanted to be free; How would you like to have some one own you?" One told of being long hidden in the swamp & being tracked by bloodhounds & suffering from hunger.

But he was to be sold farther south & that meant giving up all hope & he resolved on liberty or death. He had a knife in his belt & said he would never be taken alive. They were mostly young men & those in middle life, but many had families they must leave, sometimes with the hope of their following to share the home in the promised land. One man brought his wife & two children with him having succeeded in evading pursuit so far. The poor woman's eyes looked like those of a hunted deer. Dea[con] Ward, a neighbor of ours, hired a fugitive, whom we always called Black Henry, who worked for him. But his owners tracked him & it was said they were coming in hot pursuit; swearing to have him, dead or alive. Henry was concealed in the barn & friends armed themselves with axe, pitch fork, &c in his defence & he was saved & got away as soon as it was safe to start. One time when father was away three blacks came to our house. They were placed in a back chamber to wait till they dared go on, for they had an idea they were pursued. Next day men came to search the house, claiming to have a warrant, Mother refused them admittance, told them they had no warrant & could not get one. They went away but the house was watched all day & when Father came home, Mother would not let him arouse suspicion by doing anything for a day or two more. [Then] when they were taken to a farmhouse & from there helped on their perilous journey. Once when Father was driving three colored men at night, he heard pursuers gaining on him. He turned around & drove toward them. They asked Father if he had met Mr. Allan. He said No. & they hurried on & [it being] too dark to recognize him, he was able soon to follow at a slower pace to a safe shelter. The last runaway who came I remember, came after the railroad was built in 1855, & he was smuggled on the train when it stopped at the water tank, a little way below the station. Could all the incidents have been gathered up 30 years ago, while the friends of the cause were on earth, & these days fresh in their memories, what an interesting book might have been made. I can give you no more — and doubtless have used more words than needful —

Resptly,
Emma M. Chapin[7]

In the annals of the abolitionist crusade before the Civil War, William T. Allan ranks as one of the giants of the abolitionist movement.

Guy Beckley

The state of Michigan functioned as a kind of funnel through which fugitive slaves moved towards Canada. Freedom seekers coming from Iowa, Illinois, Wisconsin, Indiana, Ohio, and Western Pennsylvania moved across all parts of Michigan in significant numbers.

One of the most prominent Underground Railroad agents in Michigan was Guy Beckley, one of Weld's agents. His house in Ann Arbor, which still stands, was used on several occasions to harbor runaway slaves. When Beckley was lecturing in Michigan, he became familiar with other abolitionists who were willing to help usher fugitive slaves from one station to the next. While Beckley worked at his brother's dry goods store, he and Theodore Foster published an antislavery newspaper, the *Signal of Liberty* starting in 1841.[8] The following article that appeared in the May 12, 1841, issue of the abolitionist publication clearly outlines the editor's intention to aid freedom seekers:

> The number of colored people who are making their escape from the southern States are every day increasing, and their facilities for reaching the "Queen's dominions," were never so favorable as at present. From the number that have recently "landed" in Canada, one would be led to conclude that the "happiness and contentment," hitherto enjoyed by the sable sons of the south, has entirely passed away and a longing desire for the bliss of freedom seized their souls. Believing as we do that it is morally wrong to continue our fellow beings in involuntary servitude, it is with the utmost pleasure that we aid and assist them

in their flight from Southern kidnappers A few days since we had the rare pleasure, in connection with many of our friends in this place, of bestowing our "hospitalities upon six of our brethren, who tarried with us some sixteen hours to refresh themselves, on their journey to a "land of freedom." They were from twenty-one to thirty years of age — in good health and spirits, and apparently much delighted with the prospect of a new home, where the sound of the whip and clanking of chains will no longer grate upon their ear, and mangle and grill their limbs. They were sober, temperate, and gentlemanly in their appearance — discoursed with readiness on all subjects that had come under their observation — and with regard to general intelligence were far in advance of many white persons with whom we have discovered, whose opportunities for obtaining knowledge had been far superior to theirs. Before the reader's eye shall have traced these lines, they will all be in the possession of the RICH BOON OF FREEDOM in a Monarchial Government, having broken away from the southern prison house of this "home of the brave, and asylum for the oppressed of all nations." We bade them God speed in their magnanimous enterprise, and should be much rejoiced to learn that this system of colonization was becoming so general that the southern part of this confederacy would be under the necessity of granting emancipation to the slaves in order to obtain laborers for the cultivation of their soil. Let the people of this State arise in the greatness of their strength and give to the down trodden and neglected Americans the right of trial by jury, when claimed as fugitives, which will render them comparatively safe while passing through the peninsula state, to their destined place of freedom.[9]

One of the most famous UGRR travelers Beckley helped was Caroline Quarrls. In 1842, Quarrls left St. Louis and crossed the river to Alton, Illinois. Abolitionists there helped send her North to Milwaukee where she was later transported to Waukesha. In August, Quarrls was taken to other Wisconsin counties, and eventually she traveled around Chicago, through Indiana, and into Michigan. During her harrowing trip, she always managed to stay one step ahead of pursuing bounty hunters. Guy Beckley was one of the UGRR conductors in Michigan who helped her escape.[10] When he died in 1848, his death was a blow to the abolitionist movement in Michigan.

Jonathan Blanchard

Jonathan Blanchard's service as an American Anti-Slavery Society agent was impressive for he continued to labor for the national society under trying conditions in Pennsylvania after two colleagues working with him were forced to withdraw from the field. In 1837, after he concluded his service to the AASS, he enrolled at the Lane Seminary. Blanchard became a leading anti-slavery advocate in Cincinnati and a supporter of the Liberty Party. In 1846, he became the second president of Knox College in Illinois. His reputation as a bold, forthright abolitionist and a supporter of the temperance movement was well known to the founders of Gale's college. Almost immediately after his arrival in Western Illinois, President Blanchard helped aid the escape of a runaway slave who was passing through Galesburg. The following account of Blanchard's involvement in this affair is found in Chapman's *History of Knox County*:

> Bill Casey was another passenger over the Underground Railroad, but so closely pursued that he left the main line and worked his way as far as Galesburg himself...
>
> Bill Casey reached Galesburg Saturday night, and going to the residence of the colored lady, Susan Richardson, whose coming to the county is related above, he was admitted and kindly cared for. He was a miserable and affecting human being to look upon, having neither shoes nor hat and almost naked, with feet bleeding and swollen, and body bruised, besides being almost in a starving state, having had nothing with which to appease his hunger for several days. With five companions he had started from Missouri. They were pursued, and two or three of the number had been shot, and the others captured, and only by the rapidity of his flight through the woods with heavy undergrowth had he escaped. Sunday morning came, and "Aunt Sukey" locked her house and with her family as usual went to church, leaving Casey at her home. She knew, as she told us, "who to tell." Accordingly she soon made known to members of the Underground Railroad that a fugitive was at her house. They immediately visited him, and found him in a needy condition, and that he must have a pair of shoes before he could go father, as well as some clothing. So Messrs. Neeley, West and Blanchard began to prepare him for the journey. Of course he could not be taken to the store and have his shoes fitted there, but they had to bring them to him. His feet were so badly swollen that it was necessary for them to make three or four trips before they could find shoes that would fit or he could wear. After everything was fully arranged, Casey was put in charge of a conductor on the Underground Railroad and conveyed to the next station. In a year or two he returned to Galesburg and engaged in cutting timber northwest of town.[11]

Blanchard remained a steadfast loyalist to the abolitionist crusade and other reform movements throughout his presidency. A local newspaper said, "It is his nature to wage war. We find him at his favorite occupation in all the positions of life in which he has ever been placed,— the Church, the State, and Educational Institutions, forming no exception."[12] Blanchard allied himself to nearly every antislavery project in Illinois, helped establish antislavery churches around Galesburg and was in contact with known Underground Railroad operators in both Illinois and Iowa. He left Knox College in the late 1850s after a series of fundamental differences with George Washington Gale and in 1859 became the president of Wheaton College in Northern Illinois.[13]

W. L. Chaplin

Former American Anti-Slavery Society agent W. L. Chaplin was seriously involved in the work of Underground Railroad activities in the east. While serving as an agent for the New York Anti-Slavery Society, he came to be a close ally of UGRR conductor and abolitionist philanthropist Gerrit Smith. In 1841, while serving as an editor of the *Rochester American*, Chaplin openly invited the publication's readers to "assist runaway slaves who were making their way to Canada."[14] He generously committed much of his time raising money to be used to help free slaves.

Chaplin was the instigator of the notorious episode of the "Pearl." He contracted with a Philadelphia ship captain Daniel Drayton, to transport a few families to the North from Washington, D.C.; however, more than seventy-five enslaved people boarded the boat before it departed. Unfortunately, the escape was betrayed and the fugitives were taken from the ship in the Delaware River and returned to the Capital. Drayton was fined and imprisoned but Chaplin's culpability was not proved.[15]

In the summer of 1850, Chaplin became embroiled in a highly publicized UGRR affair that involved prominent Southern congressmen. On August 8, he was arrested in Rockville, Maryland, for helping two slaves escape who were the property of Robert Toombs and Alexander Stephens, both members of the United States House of Representatives from Georgia.[16] When Gerrit Smith heard this news, he sent Chaplin's fiancé and a Quaker abolitionist friend to the District of Columbia where they found Chaplin manacled, "sleeping on a bed of straw with a swollen and injured head."[17] Chaplin had been badly beaten when he was arrested. There was a dispute as to whether or not Chaplin had been arrested in Maryland or D.C., but authorities decided to imprison him in Washington. He remained in jail for six months and was finally released on bond. While Chaplin languished in jail, Gerrit Smith served as the treasurer of the Chaplin Fund and Smith provided the bulk of Chaplin's bail. Chaplin's abolitionist supporters, who had contributed money for his bail, thought he would return to the nation's capital for trial and they also believed he would financially reimburse them but he failed to do either.[18] His behavior following his forfeiture of bail left a bad taste in the mouth of many abolitionists who contributed to the Chaplin Fund. However, it seems to have been the case that after Chaplin was released from jail, his mind may have been "permanently altered and his health ruined."[19]

John Cross

Weld's Seventy included John Cross who was one of the nation's most openly self-confessed Underground Railroad operators. He made no attempt to be secretive about the aid he gave to freedom seekers. In western Illinois, he once accepted a ride home after church on a law officer's wagon and during the trip, told him he planned to "harbor, feed, and convey runaway slaves who were traveling through the area." His UGRR activities stretched from "Illinois, to Indiana and Michigan to the Detroit Gateway to Canada."[20] After moving to the Midwest, Cross "traveled between Illinois and Pennsylvania setting up an interstate freedom trail."[21] In 1842, he was a central figure in one of Illinois's most famous Underground Railroad incidents. This affair involved him with Galesburg's "Aunt Sukey" (Susan Richardson), her three children and another fugitive named Hannah. These five fugitives were captured in a cornfield on Cross's property in western Illinois. The matter took months to litigate in the courts and while most of the accused UGRR participants chose a passive course towards their prosecution, Cross decided to place his prosecutors in a most unpopular position.[22] He decided to exploit the charges brought against him after he moved to Bureau County:

In November of 1843 a writ for Cross's arrest had to be directed by the Knox County court to the sheriff of Bureau County, returnable at the next term in the spring of 1844. In April a deputy sheriff, John Long, arrested him, but could find no one to transport him to the authorities in Knox County. Cross, however, offered to take his own team, carrying the deputy along, for Cross had a preaching appointment at Osceola in Stark County the next day, and that was on the way to Knoxville where Cross was to be jailed. Long at first did not want the preacher to fill the appointment, explaining that the law did not allow him to let his prisoner deliver abolition lectures.... Cross's friends at Osceola insisted that he be allowed to preach, intimating that there might be trouble if the deputy tried to take his prisoner away, and the officer finally consented. The sermon aroused much sympathy for the man going to trial.

By the time the two men got to the Spoon River, Long was very nervous and excited, and when they saw a two men in the road leading down through the timber, the deputy was sure that the rescue was to be attempted. Cross knew better but told the deputy to get down out of sight so that if the men were friends of the abolitionist they would see him traveling alone and not think him a prisoner. Accordingly the officer lay down in the bottom of the wagon and Cross covered him with a buffalo robe and some horse blankets. When he passed the men on the road Cross spoke to them and then whipped up his horses to pass on in great speed. A little later he pretended to speak again to some imaginary persons and whipped his team into a gallop to get by them; this he did again and again. For about two miles over an extremely rough timber-bottom road the wagon rattled and creaked as it bounded over stumps and ragged ruts, while the sheriff's deputy under the blankets bounced more or less helplessly on the floor of the vehicle, bumping against the side of the box and cracking his head under the seat. Finally Cross halted his team and uncovered his victim and told him all danger was past. The officer, as Cross told it, arose, looked cautiously around him, examined his pistols, and said, "If they attacked me, I would have made a powerful resistance."[23]

When Cross had finished speaking at Oseola, he left with the sheriff for the Knox County seat in Knoxville. The law officer grew uneasy, however, sensing that Cross's friends might follow behind hoping to free him but no rescue attempt was made.

When his case came to trial Cross, to the judge's distress, insisted on being his own attorney.... This took the prosecutor by surprise, for he was not ready for trial, and he entered a *nolle prosequi*, thus depriving Cross of an opportunity for an anti-slavery lecture by way of an address to the jury.[24]

Cross later carried out his blatantly open Underground Railroad work in Lee County. He once bragged, that while living in northern Illinois, he escorted twelve fugitive slaves on a single trip:

John Cross, American Anti-Slavery Society agent and Underground Railroad operator (courtesy Wessington Springs [South Dakota] Carnegie Library and Templeton United Church of Christ).

The controversial and uncompromising John Cross eventually moved to Lee County and continued with vehemence his antislavery and Underground Railroad activity at Temperance Hill. "Rev. John Cross, a Presbyterian minister, lived at Temperance Hill and named the place Theoka, but for some reason it has outlived that name. Mr. Cross was a warm advocate for human freedom, a friend and fellow worker with Owen Lovejoy, and was imprisoned at Ottawa for his services as conductor on 'the under-ground railroad.' He made no secret of his work. He posted bills in Mr. Bliss's bar room side by side with Frink and Walker's stage route advertisement:—'free ride on the Underground Railroad,' and signed his name 'John Cross, Proprietor,' He had a pair of horses, one cream colored and the other bay, with which he took his passengers, who were flying from slavery to freedom, often gotten through from here to Chicago in a day, sometime having as many as four passengers. Palestine Grove being but about forty miles from the Mississippi River, it was easily reached by those who were sheltered and directed by other friends of the slave, who often helped them on their way to this point. These under-ground depots were stationed all along the way from 'Dixie's Land' and the station-agents were in communication with each other."[25]

In 1853, Cross and others helped organize and establish Wheaton College near Chicago where his former AASS comrade Jonathan Blanchard later became president. In 1857, Cross resettled in the southern Iowa town of Amity where he continued to serve the abolitionist cause.

Oliver Johnson

In 1887, Stephen K. Smith of Peru, New York, recorded recollections of his Underground Railroad activity. Included were references to Rowland T. Robinson, who Smith believed to be the principal operator in Ferrisburgh, Vermont. Smith said that "scores of slaves made their escape through him." Oliver Johnson, a prominent member of Weld's Seventy, wrote the following to Robinson in 1837 about a freedom seeker named "Simon:"

> I saw yesterday, in this township a stout man who ran away from Maryland. He is 28 years old, and appeared to me to be an honest, likely man. He says he was sold with several others to a soul-driver for $1,000; consequently he must have been considered very valuable. When he came here ... he was destitute of decent clothing, and unable to proceed, as he intended when he left Maryland, to Canada. A man in this place by the name of William C. Griffith, the son of a Friend, who has often rendered assistance to runaways kindly offered to keep him until spring. A reward of $200.00 has been offered for his apprehension, and it is not considered safe for him to remain here after winter has gone by ... I was so well pleased with his appearance, and with the account given of him by Griffith, that I could not help thinking he would be a good man for you to hire. Mr. Griffith says he is of a kind disposition, and knows how to do all most all kinds of farm work. He is used to teaming, and is very good to manage horses. He says that he could beat any man in the neighborhood where he lived, in Maryland, at mowing, cradling, or pitching. He has intended going to Canada in the spring, but says he would prefer to stay in the U.S., if he could be safe. I have no doubt he would be perfectly safe with you. Would you not like to have him go to you in the spring? I fear that, if he goes to Canada, he may fall into bad company; but if he is under your guardianship, I think he may become a useful man ... It will be a great way for him to walk, but not worse than going to Canada. He can be furnished with the names of abolitionists on whom to call upon the way, and I think may reach Vermont in safety.[26]

Robinson was known to hire fugitives to work for him until they had accumulated enough money to escape to Canada. He sent the following response to Johnson:

> Immediately after receiving your letter, I wrote to Wm. C. Griffith of Jenner, the man with whom Simon was living, telling him to send the man to you as soon as he could be got ready for the journey. I gave him such directions as will enable him to reach Philadelphia, where he will put himself under the direction of our friends, who will give him all needful information concerning the route to New York, at which last place he will be befriended by the "Committee of Vigilance," or by members of the Ex. Committee. I trust he will meet with no serious difficulty on the way. He appeared to me to be a man of considerable perseverance, and I trust he will not be discouraged though it is a long way to your residence.[27]

Oliver Johnson later became acquainted with one of America's most famous Underground Railroad conductors, Harriet Tubman. In 1886, Johnson recalled how impressed he was with Tubman's honesty, intelligence and modest disposition:

> During the period of my official connection with the anti-slavery office in New York, I saw her [Tubman] frequently, when she came there with the company of slaves whom she had successfully piloted way from the South; and often listened with wonder to the story of her adventures and her hair-breath escapes. She always told her tale with the modesty which showed how unconscious she was of having done anything more than her simple duty. No one who listened to her could doubt her perfect truthfulness and intensity ... her shrewdness in planning ... skill in avoiding arrest ... and willingness to endure hardship.[28]

James Milligan

In 1819, well before James Milligan became one of Weld's Seventy, he wrote:

> You may depend upon it the same God, who heard the groans of the Israelites hears and will free the Africans. What should Christians do? Should they strengthen the hands of the lordly despots, and heap calumnies upon the heavy yoke of the oppressed blacks? Rather, should they not echo the voice of the great Redeemer, urging our nation, in the name of consistency and humanity, piety and safety, to let the OPPRESSED GO FREE-BREAK EVERY YOKE?[29]

Milligan was a Reform Presbyterian minister in Vermont when he penned these words and was already advocating the immediate emancipation of slaves. He maintained of churches and governments that supported involuntary servitude that these institutions did not deserve the respect or allegiance of anyone. In short, he argued that God's law should reign supreme. Reform Presbyterians, also called Covenanters, believed Jesus Christ should be recognized as the head of state. They supported the abolition of slavery from the time their church was founded, became dedicated participants in the Underground Railroad and refused communion to known slaveholders.

Milligan was one of Weld's most radical AASS lecturers and became a close ally of the Garrison Wing of the Abolitionist Movement. In 1840, a few years after Milligan's service to the American Anti-Slavery Society had ended, he moved from Vermont to New Alexandria, Pennsylvania, and where he continued to help fugitive slaves escape northward. In 1847, he settled in Southern Illinois' Randolph County, where a Reform Presbyterian Church was already well established. His son sent the following letter to Underground Railroad historian Wilbur Siebert about his father's UGRR activities in Illinois:

> The Rev. James Milligan, D.D., formerly of Ryegate, Caledonia County, Vermont, after spending ten years in Alexandria, Westmoreland County, Pennsylvania, where he aided a few fugitive slaves from Virginia, to Gerrit Smith's home at Peterboro, N.Y., removed to Randolph County, Illinois, in 1847.

There he and the Rev. William Sloane and the Covenanter congregation kept a very large station for slaves escaping from Missouri. Scores at a time came to Sparta, Rev. James Milligan's location, and were harbored by him and his associates and even with guns, clubs and stone defended, until escorted to Elktown, the location of Rev. William Sloane. The latter's son, Dr. J.H.M. Sloane, then youthful but brave, and his comrades escorted them to the neighborhood of Nashville, Illinois, and by the regular trail northward. Nashville was about seventy miles from the Missouri border and about as far as the slave-owners cared to follow their runaways.

At Sparta, Coultersville, and Elktown there was an almost constant supply of fugitives and as constant an effort by armed, cursing bands of desperate men to secure them; but while the pursuit was hot and the encounters desperate, few of the fugitives were ever gotten from the aegis of the Hayes,' Moore's, Todd's, McLurkin's, Hood's, Sloane's, and Milligan's.

Dr. I. J. R. W. Sloane was born in Topsham, Vermont within twelve miles of my own birthplace. There we scarcely ever saw a negro but we heard the plea long and strong for emancipation.

Rev. J. S. T. Milligan[30]

One of the most noteworthy individuals mentioned in this letter, William Hayes, was a fellow Covenanter. Five years before Milligan arrived in Randolph County, Hayes had transported freedom seekers from Southern Illinois to Western Illinois. His uncle, Silvanus Ferris, had been one of the most important founders of the Abolitionist community of Galesburg in Knox County. Hayes handed the fugitives off to UGRR carrier Eli Wilson but the escapees were captured in eastern Knox County on the property of Milligan's former fellow Seventy's agent John Cross. After a protracted period of legal maneuvering, the aforementioned Susan Richardson and Hannah were freed but unfortunately, Susan's three children were returned to bondage.

John Rankin

Arguably, the most active Underground Railroad operator and member of the Seventy was John Rankin. In 1822, he moved from Kentucky to Ripley, Ohio, where he became a courageous UGRR operator. It was from Ripley, twelve years later, that Weld started his speaking tour across Ohio after staying at the Rankin home. In 1823, Rankin published *Letters on American Slavery*, a well-read antislavery text. In the mid 1820s, he constructed his house on the bluffs of the Ohio River and the residence came to be known as a safe haven for fugitive slaves. Over the course of the next four decades, he and his wife Jean aided hundreds of escaping slaves and they prided themselves on preventing bounty hunters from returning any of them to bondage. Harriet Beecher Stowe said she based much of her book *Uncle Tom's Cabin* on a story that involved the Rankin's giving aid to a fugitive slave woman and her child, who successfully crossed the icy Ohio River to safety and freedom. In 1841, the Rankin's and their sons fought off enemies who tried to burn their home and barn in the cover of the night.

Underground Railroad historian Wilbur Siebert gave this account of the Rankin's activities:

> It may have been a hundred and fifty feet northwest of the house a large barn was built, in which were horses, vehicles, harness, saddles and other farm equipment, also an ample cellar for concealing the fugitive slaves who could not be lodged in the upstairs rooms of the house. When the nine sons and four daughters of the household were all at home, there was scarcely room therein for transients. In 1828 Ripley College was founded by local citizens, with Mr. Rankin as president. It continued about twenty years. A few of the students, devoting themselves to their books by candle light at the gable windows of the Rankin house, provided beacons for slaves ready to cross the river....
>
> After the wayfarers had eaten and rested during the daylight, they were entrusted to a young Rankin to travel northward on horseback or in a conveyance. In times of danger young men of the village guarded the party. At first the trips were made twenty-one miles up to Sardinia, where there was a group of resourceful underground agents.[31]

In Ann Hagedorn's excellent history *Beyond the River*, she describes a horse drawn carriage taking John Rankin's coffin to the cemetery after his funeral service had concluded. It was followed "by a procession of men, women, and children who either had known John Rankin or had heard stories about him for all the years of their lives. Among them were the Settles family and other former slaves who had remained in Ripley or returned with their families years later."[32] The Rankin House still stands, as a monument to the dedicated service rendered to the antislavery movement by John and Jean Rankin.

James Thome

Arthur Thome, a Kentucky slaveholder, converted to abolitionism and emancipated his slaves in 1830. He started using his home as an Underground Railroad hideout, making it one of the few known UGRR shelters in the state. The Thome family's antislavery activities outraged their fellow Kentuckians, and eventually, the Thome's were driven from their house at gunpoint forcing them to leave the state. They resettled in Missouri.[33]

James Thome, Arthur's son, decided to enroll at the Lane Seminary and later became one of Weld's Seventy. In 1839, only three years after graduating from Oberlin's Theological Department, James was teaching rhetoric at Oberlin when he left the community abruptly. He had helped an elderly black woman escape from Kentucky but upon learning that he might be apprehended for giving her assistance, he fled from Ohio to avoid arrest. He took refuge in the East and remained in hiding for several months. In late August, he sent the following letter to Weld:

My Dear Bro. Weld,
    You will be surprised to learn that I have been obliged to flee from Oberlin and that my liberty is in jeopardy. A brief statement will make you acquainted with my present perilous situation. Last Spring, a short time before leaving Augusta for O[berlin], I was concerned in the escape of a slave woman, whose case was one of peculiar interest. She was a devotedly pious woman, between 45 and 50, had lived since my remembrance, and long before it, in Augusta. She was the property of two heirs, whom she had raised and served from their infancy. It was generally understood that her young masters intended to emancipate her when they reached their majority. This, one of them had already attained, and the other was on the eve of it, when their guardian-an uncle-determined to anticipate their movement by selling off the woman down the river. She providentially discovered this atrocious design in time to make her escape. She concealed herself in Augusta for a week or ten days. Her situation however was very precarious and was daily becoming more insecure. The certain prospect, if she continued in her place of concealment (which was nothing more than the garret of her own house), was that she would fall into the hands of her merciless pursuers, who all the while were on the hunt for her. In this crisis the case was brought to me (for the first time) for advice, by a few free colored women who were in the secret. Without hesitation I told them to urge her to make her escape across the river and push for Canada. After that I became exceedingly interested in the case, and with much prayer and a pondering of the consequences which might ensue to myself, I layed the train which eventuated in her rescue and safe arrival in Canada. Now to the point in question. At a monthly concert for the oppressed shortly after I reached O[berlin] I was called upon to say something, and without forethought I mentioned at the close of some remarks the case of this woman, and gave some of the particulars; and also intimated, though very indirectly, that I had something to do with it myself. The whole statement was made without a moment's reflection, and from the character of the meeting, being small and select, the tried friends of the slave, it gave me no uneasiness subsequently. One of the students, a youth from Boston, thinking it would make a fine story, wrote it off quite minutely and sent it to Bro. Southard, who to use Bro. Morgan's expression on the occasion, was *ass* enough to publish it in his Youth's Cabinet, *coupling my name in full* with it and not omitting to mention that *I was concerned in the transaction.* "As good luck would have it," the Youth's Cabinet is taken by several persons within seven miles of Augusta, and thus the whole affair was exposed. The other day to my utter surprise (for I did not before know any thing about the young man having written to Southard) I received a letter from my sister at home informing me that Augusta was in a blaze of excitement, and that if the slaveholders could get hold of me they would soon lodge me in state's Prison. My father thinks that it will never be safe for me to return to Augusta, and he warns me to be on my guard lest I be seized in Ohio and dragged away into Ky. This letter was written

on the first outbreak of the excitement. Knowing the state of feeling in Ky., and the vindictive character of the *guardian* above mentioned, I feel pretty confident that the most extreme measures which law will allow, will be pursued to secure and punish me. That application will be made to Governor Clark to demand me of the Gov. of this state, I have little doubt, and what the consequence will be is not hard to conjecture after the late specimens of base servility on the part of this State. It is the general opinion among my friends here that Gov. Shannon would instantly deliver me on demand of Gov. C. I went to Cleveland the other day purposely to get legal counsel in my emergency. S. J. Andrews, your friend, advised to me leave the state for a time, as he supposed that there were nine chances to one that the Gov. would deliver me on demand. He advises me to go to N. York. Gov. Seward he thinks may be relied upon in such a case. My friends generally advise this course. I have resolved to retreat from O. to some secluded place and there wait a few days, until I receive further intelligence from home; for it may be that the matter will be hushed up by the influence and efforts of my friends...

My dear brother, let me beg of you not to mention these things. The more quiet the matter is kept the better. My dear wife joins me in love to Angelina and yourself.

Affectionately and forever Yours —
James
August 27th, 1839[34]

Others

There were several other members of Weld's Seventy who attached themselves to the Underground Railroad throughout the North and in Canada. The Reverend John Monteith aided freedom seekers in the Michigan territory.[35] He later used his house in Elyria, Ohio, as a station for fugitive slaves. When Nathanial Colver was a clergyman in Detroit, he helped pilot fugitive slaves across the border to "Queen Victoria's Domain." A. T. Rankin, who helped establish both the Ohio and Indiana State Anti-Slavery Societies aided escaping slaves in Fort Wayne, Indiana. He was the pastor of the town's Presbyterian Church and his Underground Railroad efforts were supported in Fort Wayne by Baptist minister Daniel W. Burrough. In 1836, James G. Birney was found guilty of aiding a fugitive slave in Ohio. The verdict was later reversed. In Georgia, Vermont, Alvah Sabin kept a station. Sabin was one of the state's foremost antislavery politicians.[36] Theodore Weld's mentor, Charles Stuart, was involved with aiding fugitive slaves in Canada. While living in Amherstbury, Stuart established homes for fugitive slaves on his property and allowed them to grow crops on his land.[37]

Two of Weld's Seventy aided freedom seekers in both Wisconsin and Illinois. Ichabod Codding was a UGRR agent who ushered slaves to the home of John Hossack in Ottawa, Illinois. Codding and Hossack were once stoned by canal workers while transporting fugitives.[38] Codding also carried out work along Illinois' trail to freedom with the State's most famous Underground Railroad carrier, Owen Lovejoy.[39] When Hiram Foote was living in Janesville, Wisconsin, he was a Congregationalist minister. On one occasion, he harbored a fugitive slave who had been shot in the leg by his pursuers. When the escaping slave was again able to travel, he was disguised and sent to Canada. In Kansas, former AASS agent Augustus Wattles published the *Herald of Freedom*. Wattles became involved with the Underground Railroad when John Brown brought eleven slaves to his home. Wattles aided the fugitive slaves but criticized Brown for using violent tactics while supporting their escape.

In Pennsylvania, one of the state's most prominent abolitionists, James Miller McKim, was an active Underground Railroad agent. He was connected to the UGRR operation in Philadelphia where he was known for careful and cautious planning. Shortly before the Civil War, McKim stated that the Underground Railroad restored "stolen men to liberty." In Ohio, Marius Robinson, after recovering from his severe beating as an AASS lecturer, became a dedicated UGRR agent. He and his wife used their farm as an Underground Railroad headquarters in Putnam County.[40]

In addition, other members of Weld's band supported the movement of freedom seekers. They included David Thurston in Maine, Charles C. Burleigh in Pennsylvania and Hiram Wilson in Canada.[41]

Conclusion

By the mid–1820s, the men who, nearly fifty years earlier had organized the American Revolution and who later had helped establish a new American Republic were either very old or had died. Consequently, a new generation of Americans was stepping forward to fill leadership positions that would take the United States onward. This second generation of Americans included men and women who were not content to simply ride the crest of what their fore-fathers had established, but instead believed that the country could be molded into an even more perfect union. By the third decade of the nineteenth century, many of these people attached themselves to a growing number of social reform movements. These reformers were inspired by moral idealism and nur-tured by genuine optimism. During this era, by far the most important reform movement was the antislavery crusade. The existence of human bondage, in a nation that prided itself on the principles of liberty and justice for all, com-pelled many people, most of whom were Northerners, to insist that the insti-tution of slavery must be struck down. The buying and selling of human beings, they said, was simply not tolerable.

Between 1834 and 1840, the American Anti-Slavery Society commis-sioned numerous agents to work under the auspicious of the national organ-ization. The AASS was established in 1833, and by May of 1835, it had hired nine agents, but by the spring of 1837 that number had swelled into the mid-60s. The agents' primary strategy was to engage the slavery issue by means of constant agitation. A few of these agents were given special assignments, four were asked to address the special needs of free blacks living in northern states and in Canada, and two were sent to the West Indies to investigate and report upon the impact of British emancipation. The vast majority of agents, however, were given the task of helping to organize state and local antislavery societies, soliciting and collecting funds for the operation of the national soci-ety, and by delivering speeches, attempting to raise the consciousness of the general populous regarding the need to support the immediate emancipation of slaves in the United States. One must remember that a large percentage of Americans then did not know how to read, so most of what they learned came by word of mouth. Although every Northern state from Maine to Indiana was influenced by this campaign, remarkable success was achieved in Massachusetts, New York, Ohio and Rhode Island.

The agents, for the most part, were remarkably effective orators. Over time, their reputations as powerful speakers preceded them, which encouraged large crowds to assemble. Another factor in attracting audiences was the appeal of a theatrical performance. The speakers, usually articulate and fluent, were dramatic figures. They tended to be extroverts who spoke with great energy and they exercised their ability to influence others by their skill at oratory. Like great actors on a stage, they often entertained crowds with enthusiasm and charisma. Those listeners vehemently opposed to their abolitionist advocacy were, of course, not impressed. In fact, as these adversaries witnessed audiences being swayed by abolitionist agents, they often resorted to violence against the lecturers. But mob violence perpetrated against abolitionists often had the effect of creating sympathy for them and in some cases, actually converted to the antislavery cause those who had previously been indifferent to the plight of slaves.

In January of 1833, fewer than fifty antislavery organizations existed in Northern states but by 1837, more than 1,000 of these societies had been created. By the end of 1837, James G. Birney, by then the chief operating officer of the American Anti-Slavery Society, estimated that well over 100,000 individuals held membership in the AASS. By 1840, more than 2,000 abolitionist societies had been organized across the north with a membership that conservatively exceeded 150,000 people. There can be little doubt that the striking increase in the number of antislavery organizations by the end of the 1830s was primarily due to the tireless efforts of American Anti-Slavery Society agents and the savvy administrative efforts of the society's executive committee.

Theodore Dwight Weld stands out as one of the leading figures associated with abolitionism throughout the 1830s. His inclination to avoid self-promotion and his desire to carry out his work in relative anonymity explains why he is not nearly as well-known as one might expect, given the significant contributions he made to the antislavery crusade. As a public orator, he held audiences spellbound. His executive committee colleagues were extremely impressed with his thoroughness as an administrator when they worked with him at the national society's central office in Manhattan. As a recruiter of the society's agents, he seemed to have possessed a sixth sense for determining who would be able to withstand the rigorous demands of the antislavery lecture circuit. Those who observed him as an instructor of newly commissioned agents were awestruck at his effective teaching techniques. Weld was, according to his friend, the poet John Greenleaf Whittier, a man of "marvelous eloquence, which in the early days of antislavery, shamed the church and silenced the mob."

In 1884, Whittier wrote these lines into an album for one of Theodore Weld's grandsons:

> What shall I wish him? Strength and health
> May be abused, and so may wealth.
> Even fame itself may come to be
> But wearying notoriety.
> What better can I ask than this?—
> A life of brave unselfishness,
> Wisdom for council, eloquence
> For Freedom's need, for Truth's defense,
> The championship of all that's good,
> The manliest faith in womenhood,
> The steadfast friendship changing not
> With change of time or place or lot,
> Hatred of sin, but not the less
> A heart of pitying tenderness
> And charity, that, suffering long,
> Shames the wrong-doer from his wrong:
> One wish expresses all — that he
> May even as his grandsire be!

In the annals of American abolitionists, Theodore Dwight Weld was second to none in giving strength, direction, and personal example to the antislavery cause, and by doing so, he helped redirect the moral compass of the American ship of state. As a leading proselytizer of emancipation, Weld helped encourage a debate in the North about the slavery issue that drew in thousands of individuals who had never before engaged the subject. If one definition of being a hero is the willingness to take risks in an effort to achieve an ideal, then Weld and each agent who belonged to the Seventy were heroes.

The achievements of Weld's Seventy and other antislavery crusaders in the 1830s were truly remarkable. This new breed of abolitionists had learned from the failures of their antislavery predecessors. They made it clear that they did not fear their opposition and they skillfully utilized their pens and tongues by announcing themselves as Champions of Liberty. American Anti-Slavery Society agents somehow managed to sustain themselves on meager financial recompense and though loathed by the majority of their fellow citizens, they conducted their work energized by believing in their principles and following the dictates of conscience. Sometimes the things they said shocked their listeners. Occasionally, they intentionally provoked those assembled to hear them and frequently, they pleaded with people to shake off their lethargy and join the abolitionist crusade as kindred spirits. The overwhelming majority of the agents Weld recruited were clergymen who deeply believed that slavery was a sin and genuinely felt that they were acting in concert with Christ's teachings. Motivated by their religious beliefs, some of these clergymen clearly believed that it was their destiny to have been selected as heralds of abolition.

Gradually, Weld and his fellow agents influenced a considerable number of Americans to reject the existence of slavery in the United States, helped others take positions on the slavery issue contrary to the interests of slave owners, and convinced a significant group of their fellow countrymen to realize that slaves would need to be emancipated at sometime in the future. These agents, at the very least, were successful at exciting a widespread uneasiness about slavery that had not beforehand existed across the land. In many cases the risks they took while carrying out this work took a toll on their health and general well being; some lost close friendships and family ties forever. All of them endured poisonous attacks on their character from the public press and many AASS agents made personal sacrifices that forced them to live on the edge of poverty. Nearly every segment of American society accused them of potentially destroying the Union. At that time, most Americans believed that blacks were inferior to whites and they therefore had accepted the notion that slavery was an acceptable institution.

One of the unanticipated consequences of this antislavery effort was the effect it had on spurring forward the women's rights movement. When female abolitionists started delivering antislavery lectures in the late 1830s, they received harsh criticism for speaking in public. In addition, women were told by many antislavery men not to seek leadership positions in the American Anti-Slavery Society. This helped awaken many women and some men to the fact that remarkable similarities existed between the denial of all rights to American slaves and the denial of most rights to American women. Because of this realization, a good number of women who had joined the antislavery campaign in the 1830s attended the women's rights convention in Seneca Falls, New York, in 1848.

There was a time when abolitionists were generally criticized by most historians as a self-serving group of troublesome fanatics who put the overall well-being of the nation aside in order to satisfy their own self-assured agendas. Fortunately, that point of view has mostly faded away, replaced by a broader, more sympathetic and even-handed scholarship. The greater comprehension of the full humanity of all Americans, indeed all people, has no doubt influenced historians' approach to this topic.

It is not necessary to spend time dwelling upon the question of who was the most important individual associated with the abolitionist cause or what part of the antislavery movement ranks as its most important branch. In the ultimate scheme of things, making this kind of assessment is impossible. But the work of Theodore Weld and his band of brothers and sisters surely ranks among the most important contributions to the abolitionist movement in America.

Appendix A:
Anti-Slavery Songs and Poems

Songs

Anti-slavery songs played an important role in the abolitionist movement. Abolitionist musical arrangements were sung before or at the conclusion of anti-slavery meetings. Religious music had long been used for the purpose of moral edification, but these pieces were for the most part protest songs. In the nineteenth century, women were beginning to be allowed to give public musical performances. In 1836, Maria Weston Chapman published *Songs of the Free and Hymns of Christian Freedom*. Chapman explained that the book of songs was written for people "who are laboring for the freedom of the American slave" and intended to give "strength afforded by poetry and music." A committed abolitionist, she traveled throughout the state of Massachusetts helping to organize female anti-slavery societies. Weston, who was sometimes referred to as "Garrison's lieutenant," often helped edit *The Liberator*. Her grandson, William J. Chapman, said she "reminded me of a gladiator." In 1843, Jairus Lincoln's *Anti-Slavery Melodies* were published, and the following year, George W. Clark's *Liberty Minstrel* was released. Below are four selections taken from Maria Weston Chapman's 1836 abolitionist songs.

PRAYER FOR THE REMOVAL OF PREJUDICE

Oh! Hear the wailing cry;
The wretched slave complains,
His brother's hand deep wrong inflicts,
And binds in galling chains.

* * *

With scoffs that brother sees,
Those chains his brother bind,

And draws the more debasing cords
Around the immortal mind.

* * *

Oh! Melt those flinty hearts,
Strong prejudice remove,
And teach thy paler children, Lord
Thee sable sons to love

CONVERSION

Awake my people! Saith our God
Our brothers' blood the land profanes
Ye been beneath the oppressor's rod —
He binds your spirits in his chain.

* * *

With breaking heart and tortured nerve,
Your brother drains the accursed cup!
Now in the name of Him ye serve —

The living God of Hosts — come up!

* * *

While faith each fervent spirit fills
Arise with hope and triumph crowned!
Shout freedom through your hundred
  hills
Till banded hosts come surging round!

* * *

Our God! We come at thy commands —
Thy people offer willingly!

No swords are in our peaceful hands —
From wrath and doubt our hearts are
  free.

* * *

Vowed to the cause of awful truth
As erst our pilgrim fathers came
With mind and matron, age and youth
We throng round freedom's kindling
  flame.

THE DUTY OF REBUKE

It is good to mourn for those
Crushed down by slavery's iron hand
And feel, while numbering o'r their woes
Strength for the just and true to stand?

* * *

It is good to say to those,
Who claim a right in humankind
Mercy and justice are your foes
And certain triumph shall they find?

* * *

It is not good to say to those
Who call not robbery a wrong,
Within whose breast no pity glowes
Can ye indeed to God belong?

* * *

It is not good to say to all,
Arise for the forsaken slave,
Upon your God for courage call
And in *His* strength go forth and save?

* * *

Lord! This is all we seek to do;
Grant us thy grace to do it well,
Grant us thy glory to pursue,
And fondly of thy truth to tell.

* * *

What then shall harm us? In the end
Each sorrow shall a good appear,
And every trial thou shalt send
But bring our jubilee more near.

MONTHLY CONCERT OF PRAYER FOR EMANCIPATION

Oh, God of freedom! Bless this night,
The steadfast hearts that toil as one
Till thy sure law of truth and right
Alike in heaven and earth be done.

* * *

A piercing voice of grief and wrong
Goes upward from the groaning earth
Oh true and holy Lord! How long?
In majesty and might come forth!

* * *

Yet Lord, remembering mercy too,
Behold the oppressor in his sin;
Make all his actions just and true,
Renew his wayward heart within.

* * *

From thee let righteous purpose flow,
And find in every heart its home,
Till truth and judgment reign below
And here, on earth, the kingdom come.

Poems

When the American Anti-Slavery Society convened in Philadelphia to establish the national organization in December of 1833, John Greenleaf Whittier, at 25, was one of the youngest delegates in attendance. Thereafter, he dedicated himself to abolitionism, and he is remembered as the movement's gifted poet. Below are three of his anti-slavery poems. Later in his life, Whittier indicated that he had written his anti-slavery poems to send "alarm signals [and to] trumpet calls to action."[1] The first was written for a meeting of the American Anti-Slavery Society in 1834.

HYMN

O Thou, whose presence went before
  Our fathers in their weary way,
As with Thy chosen moved of yore
  The fire by night, the cloud by day!

When from each temple of the free,
  A nation's song ascends to Heaven
Most Holy Father! unto Thee
  May not our humble prayers be given?

They children all, though hue and form
  Are varied in Thine own good will,
With Thy own holy breathings warm,
  And fashioned in Thine image still.

We thank Thee, Father! hill and plain
  Around us wave their fruits once more,
And clustered vine, and blossomed grain,
  Are bending round each cottage door.

And peace is here; and hope and love
  Are round us as a mantle thrown,
And unto Thee, supreme above,
  The knee of prayer is bowed alone.

But oh, for those this day can bring,
  As unto us, no joyful thrill;
For those who, under Freedom's wing,
  Are bound in Slavery's fetters still:

For those to whom Thy written word
  Of light and love is never given;
For those whose ears have never heard
  The promise and the hope of heaven!

For broken heart, and clouded mind,
  Whereon no human mercies fall;
Oh, be Thy gracious love inclined,
  Who, as a Father, pitiest all!

And grant, O Father! that the time
  Of Earth's deliverance may be near,
When every land and tongue and clime
  The message of Thy love shall hear;

When, smitten as with fire from heaven,
  The captive's chain shall sink in dust,
And to his fettered soul be given
  The glorious freedom of the just![2]

The poem below was written by Whittier in 1835. No other anti-slavery poem composed by Whittier better communicates his indignation about the evils of slavery.

THE HUNTERS OF MEN

Have ye heard of our hunting, o'er
  mountain and glen,
Through cane-brake and forest,— the
  hunting of men?
The lords of our land to this hunting
  have gone,
As the fox-hunter follows the sound of
  the horn;
Hark! The cheer and the hallo! the crack
  of the whip,
And the yell of the hound as he fastens
  his grip!
All blithe are our hunters, and noble
  their match,
Though hundreds are caught, there are
  millions to catch.
So speed to their hunting, o'er mountain
  and glen,

Through cane-brake and forest,— the
  hunting of men!

Gay luck to our hunters! how nobly they
  ride
In the glow of their zeal, and the strength
  of their pride!
The priest with his cassock flung back on
  the wind,
Just screening the politic statement behind;
The saint and the sinner, with cursing
  and prayer,
The drunk and the sober, ride merrily
  there.
And woman, kind woman, wife, widow,
  and maid,
For the good of the hunted, is lending
  her aid:

Her foot's in the stirrup, her hand on the rein,
How blithely she rides to the hunting of men!
Oh goodly and grand is our hunting to see,
In this "land of the brave and this home of the free."
Priest, warrior, and statesman, from Georgia to Maine,
All mounting the saddle, all grasping the rein;
Right merrily hunting the black man, whose sin
Is the curl of his hair and the hue of his skin!
Woe, now, to the hunted who turns him at bay!
Will our hunters be turned from their purpose and prey?
Will their hearts fail within them? their nerves tremble, when
All roughly they ride to the hunting of men?

Ho! alms for our hunters! all weary and faint,
Wax the curse of the sinner and prayer of the saint.
The horn is wound faintly, the echoes are still,
Over cane-brake and river, and forest and hill.

Haste, alms for our hunters! the hunted once more
Have turned from their flight with their backs to the shore:
What right have they here in the home of the white,
Shadowed o'er by our banner of Freedom and Right?
Ho! alms for the hunters! or never again
Will they ride in their pomp to the hunting of men!

Alms, alms for our hunters! why will ye delay,
When their pride and their glory are melting away?
The parson has turned; for, on charge of his own,
Who goeth a warfare, or hunting, alone?
The politic statesman looks back with a sigh,
There is doubt in his heart, there is fear in his eye.
Oh, haste, lest that doubting and fear shall prevail,
And the head of his steed take the place of the tail.
Oh, haste, ere he leave us! for who will ride then,
For pleasure or gain, to the hunting of men?[3]

The following poem about a mother's children sold away to another slaveholder was composed by Whittier in 1838.

THE FAREWELL

Of a Virginia slave mother to her daughters sold into Southern bondage.

GONE, gone,— sold and gone,
To the rice-swamp dank and lone.
Where the slave-whip ceaseless swings,
Where the noisome insect stings,
Where the fever demon strews
Poison with the falling dews,
Where the sickly sunbeams glare
Through the hot and misty air;
Gone, gone — sold and gone,
To the rice-swamp dank and lone,
From Virginia's hills and waters;

Woe is me, my stolen daughters!

Gone, gone — sold and gone,
To the rice-swamp dank and lone.
There no mother's eye is near them,
There no mother's ear can hear them;
Never, when the torturing lash
Seams their back with many a gash,
Shall a mother's kindness bless them,
Or a mother's arms caress them.
Gone, gone — sold and gone,

To the rice-swamp dank and lone,
From Virginia's hills and waters;
Woe is me, my stolen daughters!

Gone, gone — sold and gone,
To the rice-swamp dank and lone.
Oh, when weary, sad, and slow,
From the fields at night they go,
Faint with toil, and racked with pain,
To their cheerless homes again,
There no brother's voice shall greet them;
There no father's welcome meet them.

Gone, gone — sold and gone,
To the rice-swamp dank and lone,
From Virginia's hills and waters;
Woe is me, my stolen daughters!

Gone, gone — sold and gone,
To the rice-swamp dank and lone.
From the tree whose shadow lay
On their childhood's place of play;
From the cool spring where they drank;
Rock, and hill, and rivulet bank;
From the solemn house of prayer,
And the holy counsels there.

Gone, gone — sold and gone,
To the rice-swamp dank and lone,
From Virginia's hills and waters;
Woe is me, my stolen daughters!

Gone, gone — sold and gone,
To the rice-swamp dank and lone;
Toiling through the weary day,
And at night the spoiler's prey.
Oh, that they had earlier died,
Sleeping calmly, side by side,
Where the tyrant's power is o'er,
And the fetter galls no more!

Gone, gone — sold and gone,
To the rice-swamp dank and lone,
From Virginia's hills and waters;
Woe is me, my stolen daughters!

Gone, gone — sold and gone,
To the rice-swamp dank and lone.
By the holy love He beareth;
By the bruised reed He spareth;
Oh, may He, to whom alone
All their cruel wrongs are known,
Still their hope and refuge prove,
With more than a mother's love.

Gone, gone — sold and gone,
To the rice-swamp dank and lone,
From Virginia's hills and waters;
Woe is me, my stolen daughters![4]

Appendix B: Correspondence

In the winter of 1834, Theodore Dwight Weld was given his commission by the American Anti-Slavery Society. Below is a copy of the commission he received.

COMMISSION OF THE AMERICAN ANTI-SLAVERY SOCIETY TO WELD

Dear Sir,

You are hereby appointed and commissioned, by the Executive Committee of the <u>American Anti-Slavery Society</u>, instituted at Philadelphia in 1833, as their Agent, for the space of three months commencing with the 22d day of February, 1834, in the State of Ohio and elsewhere as the Committee may direct.

The Society was formed for the purpose of awakening the attention of our whole community to the character of American Slavery, and presenting the claims and urging the rights of the colored people of the United States; so as to promote, in the most efficient manner, the immediate abolition of Slavery, and the restoration of our colored brethren to their equal rights as citizens.

For a more definite statement of the objects of your agency, and the methods of its prosecution, the Committee refer you to their printed "Particular Instructions," communicated to you herewith; a full acquaintance and compliance with which, according to your ability, you will, on accepting this commission, consider as indispensable.

The Committee welcome you as a fellow -laborer in this blessed and responsible work; the success of which will depend, in no small degree, under God, on the results of your efforts. Their ardent desires for your success will continually attend you; you will have their sympathy in trial; and nothing, they trust, will be wanting, on their part, for your encouragement and aid.

They commend you to the kindness and cooperation of all who love Zion; praying that the presence of God may be with you, cheering your heart, sustaining you in your arduous labors, and making them a means of speedy liberation of all the oppressed.

Given at the Society's Office, No. 130 Nassau-street, New-York, the twentieth day of February in the year of our Lord eighteen hundred and thirty-four.

Arthur Tappan
Chairman of the Executive Committee

Attest,
E. Wright, Jr.
Secretary of Domestic Correspondence

In addition to sending Weld the national society's commission, Elizer Wright, Jr., also included some "particular instructions" for him to adhere to while he conducted his work. The first part of these instructions discussed the "general principles" of the American Anti-Slavery Society, "set forth" in the Declaration of Sentiments. Wright told the new agent to speak against "compensation to slaveholders," and Weld was also advised to emphasize "the sin of slavery." The last two-thirds of Wright's instructions were very specific. What follows are excerpts from that part of Wright's correspondence:

You will make yourself familiar with FACTS; for they chiefly influence reflecting minds. Be careful to use only facts that are well authenticated, and always state them with the precision of a witness under oath. You cannot do our cause a greater injury than by overstating facts. Clarkson's "Thoughts," and Stuart's "West India Question," are Magazines of facts respecting the safety and benefit of immediate emancipation. Mrs. Child's Book, Stroud's Slave Laws, Paxton's and Rankin's Letters, D. L. Child's Address, are good authorities respecting the character of American slavery. The African Repository and Garrison's Thoughts will show the whole subject of expatriation.

The field marked out by the Committee for your agency is [to be filled in]

The Committee expects you to confine your labors to that field, unless some special circumstances call you elsewhere. And in such case you will confer with the Committee before changing your field, if time will allow, And if not, we wish immediate notice of the fact. In traversing your field, you will generally find it wise to visit first several prominent places in it, particularly those where it is known our cause has friends. In going to a place, you will naturally call upon those who are friendly to our objects, and take advice from them. Also call on ministers of the gospel and other leading characters, and labor specially to enlighten them and secure their favor and influence. Ministers are the hinges of community, and ought to be moved, if possible. If they can be gained, much is gained. But if not, you will not be discouraged; and if not plainly inexpedient, attempt to obtain a house of worship; or if none can be had, some other convenient place — and hold a public meeting, where you can present our cause, its facts, arguments and appeals, to as many people as you can collect, by notices in pulpits and newspapers, and other proper means.

Form Auxiliary Societies, both male and female, in every place where it is practicable. Even if such societies are very small at the outset, they may be much good as centres of light, and means of future access to the people. Encourage them to raise funds and apply them in purchasing and circulating anti-slavery publications gratuitously; particularly the Anti-Slavery Reporter, of which you will keep specimens with you, and which can always be had of the Society at $2.00 per 100. You are at liberty, with due discretion, to recommend other publications, *so far* as they advocate our views of immediate abolition. We hold ourselves responsible only for our own.

You are not to take up collections in your public meetings, as the practice often prevents persons from attending, whom it might be desirable to reach. Let this be stated in the public notice of the meeting. If you find individuals friendly to our views, who are able to give us money, you will make special personal application, and urge upon them the duty of liberally supporting this cause. You can also give notice of some place where those disposed can give their donations. Generally, it is best to invite them to do this the *next morning*.

We shall expect you to write frequently to the Secretary for Domestic Correspondence, and give minute accounts of your proceedings and success. If you receive money for the Society, you will transmit it, *by mail*, WITHOUT DELAY, to the Treasurer.

Always keep us advised, if possible, of the place where letters may reach you...

Eliza Wright, Jr., closed this correspondence by expressing the following to Weld:

> We will only remind you, that the Society is but the almoner of the public — that the silver and gold are the Lord's — that the amount as yet set apart by his people for promoting this particular object is small — our work is great and our resources limited — and we therefore trust that you will not fail to use a faithful economy in regard to the expenses of traveling, and reduce them as low as you can without impairing your usefulness.[1]

Although the Grimke sisters were not salaried agents of the American Anti-Slavery Society, the following letter sent to Weld by Angelina Grimke on August 27, 1837, clearly indicates both women thought of themselves as agents. This correspondence falls within the timeframe of the sisters' controversial series of abolitionist lectures delivered in the East, at which time they were conducting the very same kind of work as other AASS agents who had attended Weld's New York convention. She is speaking of the negative reaction among fellow abolitionists to women's lecturing to mixed audiences.

Dear Brother

> Wilt thou be pleased to tell us whether our names ever have stood on the list of Agents to the Am. A. S. S'y? We tho't *they did*, and have received the Emancipator, etc. without paying any subscription for them, supposing we were so considered. Had we better pay for them now? Didst thou not tell us that thou hadst enrolled our names?
>
> Today has been a day of much trial as I have tho't of *our* being the ostensible cause of the Clerical movement: and the query has arisen am *I* in my right place and doing my appropriate work? Was it *right* for us to come to Massachusetts? I expect to meet with trials, *personal* trials and I (vainly perhaps) *think* I could have borne THEM, but all this unsettlement and complaint among the *friends* of the cause is so unexpected that I don't know how to bear it. My only consolation is the hope that it will drive us nearer to Him who alone can guide and sustain. O! how precious to feel that I came out of faith, in simple obedience to what I believed was my Father's will, *not mine* own.
>
> We understand that brother Whittier means to send thee the letter I wrote you a week since. Sister begs thee to give it to her as we have no copy and she wants to preserve it. Farewell. When it is well with thee and thou art permitted to hold converse with Jesus then remember to ask a blessing; only DIRECTION for us in the untrodden path we are, we humbly trust, called to walk in.
>
> Thine for the poor and the outcast
> E. Ge-[2]

The letter below, written by Weld on either September 1 or October 1 of 1837, is a response to the Grimkes about their status as agents. Although Weld maintains in this letter that the sisters were not officially agents, this in no way negates the fact that they were members of the "Seventy." What follows is the first part of that letter:

My dear sisters,

> I have just received a letter from Angelina, written I know not when — as there is no date — and sent, as far as I can learn, in a box of books from the anti slavery office in Boston, but even this is not certain. Nevertheless a letter is a letter, whatever doubt [one] may have over its date or transmission; and a letter from *you* I am always glad to get, even tho,' as in this case, I get an ear boxing with it.
> A sound thrashing by the way sticks to the memory and often pins there a whole-

some truth which might slide off in a moment but for the smarting. I know of nobody better qualified to testify on such a point than *I* am. Experience is a great schoolmaster, and in my case the *birch* was the instrument; for surely till I got into my "teens" the most frequent and the *deepest* impressions made on my heart were thro' my *back*. But I utterly forgot!! You dont believe in "*physical force*" as I learn by H. C. W[right]s "Domestic Scene," so this illustration is lost upon you.

But to this letter. You ask "have our names ever stood on the list of agents to the Am. A. S. Soc?" "Didst thou not tell us that thou hadst enrolled our names"? Answer, they stand on the list of those who receive publications gratuitously, and so do those of some others who are doing much for the cause, but yet not *agents*. You wish me to state what is the *exact relation* which you sustain in the Executive Committee, and in what sense have considered you their agents if at all. Answer, your exact position with reference to them never has been, if I understand it, that of *their agents*. 1. You are in no respect supported by their funds and never have been. 2. You are in no respect *under their control* and never have been. They have never claimed or exercised any authority over you. They have never *directed* your labors nor marked out any *field* , nor even given you any *advice*. The[y] have made neither suggestion nor hint as to your operations, time, place, measures, spirit, matter or manner. Further the Executive Committee has never framed any vote of any sort respecting either of you. *They never appointed you their agents.* You never had any commission from them and all their *agents*, whether *travelling* or *local, temporary,* or *permanent,* have been *appointed by vote*, and have been officially certified of that appointment by the secretary and have received *printed* commissions. I find by examining the records of the Executive Committee that *nothing* of this sort has transpired respecting you. How then I ask can you be called the agents of the Am. A. S. Society?

I confess I had supposed till I inspected the records today to get the facts, that the Exec. Com had *by vote* made some sort of recognition of you as *cooperators* in the general movement, tho' *not* as their appointed agents; but I find that they have never acted *at all in the premises.*

When you have been spoken of as *agents* of the A. A. S. Soc. by us in New York, it has been in the sense of *helpers* in the great cause, cooperators, devoting your time to its advancement, as heartily coinciding with us all in *sentiment* on the subject and occasionally conferring with us as individuals, etc. But perhaps you will say, we have received their periodicals and a set of their publications gratuitously; and is not that some sort of recognition of us as agents? Answer, so have scores of others who were never agents of the society and some of them not even *abolitionists* at the time.

The fact that you are making the promotion of the anti slavery cause your daily business and devoting your time to it makes you in the highest and best sense of the word *agents,* tho *not* the agents *of* the Executive Com[mittee] nor *of* the Am. Or any other Society, but *your own* agents *for* the cause.[3]

On November 28, 1838, Weld drafted a letter to Gerrit Smith about his plans to publish *Slavery As It Is, the Testimony of a Thousand Witnesses*. Below are excerpts from this correspondence that describe how Weld planned to assemble the book:

Dear Brother Smith

The Executive Committee of the A. A. S. Society have resolved to publish a series of tracts refuting the main objections to abolition sentiments. The demand for such tracts from all quarters is urgent. The first of the series will consist mainly of facts and testimony as to the actual condition of the Slaves. Showing that they are overworked, underfed, have insufficient sleep, live in miserable huts, generally without floors, and with a single apartment in which both sexes are herded promiscuous; that their clothing serves neither purposes of comfort nor common decency; that barbarous cruelties are inflicted upon them, such as terrible lacerations with the whip and paddle, fastening upon them iron collars, yokes, chains, horns and bells, branding them with hot irons, knocking out their teeth, maiming and killing them.

The pamphlet will be filled mostly with the testimony of eye witnesses, with their names and residences. In this way the credence of millions will be secured who are now slow of heart to believe, and would never credit *anonymous* testimony.

A multitude of such facts never yet published, facts that would thrill the land with horror, are now in the possession of abolitionists, or can with little trouble be gathered from the immediate circle of their acquaintance.

Shall the facts lie hushed any longer, when from one end of heaven to the other, myriad voices are crying "O Earth, Earth, cover not their blood." The old falsehood, that the slave is *kindly treated*, shallow and stupid as it is, has lullabied to sleep four-fifths of the free north and west; but with God's blessing this sleep shall not be unto death. Give facts a voice, and cries of blood shall ring till deaf ears tingle.

Many such facts, endorsed by unimpeachable eye-witnesses, are now in our possession, and the committee earnestly desire all such as can be certified to as *actually witnessed* by individuals whose statements can be relied on.

Now dear brother, suffer us to look to you for some help in this matter. If you have ever witnessed cruelties inflicted on the slaves, or severe privations suffered by them, or if any abolitionists or others in your place to whose trustworthiness you can testify, have witnessed such enormities, and will furnish them, will you write out the facts, and immediately forward them by mail. In case you state facts on the authority of others, give the name and residence of your informant, and other circumstances concerning him which may with the public add to the credibility of his or her testimony, such as his or her profession or calling, title if any, membership in any religious society, the hold of any office of trust, etc. The importance of great care and accuracy in all such details as well as in the subject matter of the testimony both for the sake of the truth itself, and for securing the full credence of a gainsaying generation, cannot be too highly appreciated.[4]

Appendix C: Reminiscences

Hiram Foote and the Gravel Debate

In 1834, at the Lane Seminary in Cincinnati, Theodore Weld organized a two and a half week student debate about slavery.[1] Many of these student seminarians later became leading figures in the abolitionist movement. Had it not been for the student debates at the Lane Seminary, the abolitionist movement might well have moved in a different direction.

Why had Weld, in February of 1834, suggested student anti-slavery debates as a way to generate such enthusiasm among Lane classmates? Where had Weld gotten the idea that the kind of debates he orchestrated at the Cincinnati seminary would work so well? The answer to this can be traced back to something that happened in June of 1833 at the Oneida Institute in Whitesboro, New York, where Weld was a student. This was the "Gravel Debate."[2] Shortly after the Gravel Debate occurred, Oneida Institute students established the first anti-slavery society of any kind in the state of New York.[3]

George Washington Gale established the Oneida Institute in 1827. The Reverend John Frost was Gale's right hand man while establishing the school, and he later helped raise funds for the Institute. Gale is remembered as a leading figure in the second Great Awakening that swept across New York in the 1820s and 1830s. Almost immediately after Weld enrolled at Gale's manual labor school, he emerged as a popular figure with the majority of his fellow students. They admired his work ethic, enterprising spirit, and leadership qualities. Nearly all of Weld's classmates at the Oneida Institute were idealistic young men who were willing to deal with the hardships of flooded fields, small living quarters, and demanding physical work. In June of 1833, about the time Weld was preparing to leave New York and enroll at Lane, the issue of emancipating slaves came to a head at Oneida. In the April 28, 1870 issue of the *Advanced Supplement*, former Oneida Institute student H. L. Hammond[4] gave a detailed account of exactly when, where, and why this took place. He also identified the young man who was responsible for what happened. Hammond wrote the following article:

THE GRAVEL DEBATE
AN ANTI SLAVERY REMINISCENCE
BY REV. H. L. HAMMOND

In June, 1833, the students of Oneida Institute were "warned out" to work on the road. The Institute was a Manual Labor School, in Whitesboro, near Utica, N.Y.

161

Most of the students were poor, and as they were accustomed to work, and money was not easily obtained for paying their road tax, they reported themselves in a body to the pathmaster for actual service. He sent them, with some of the citizens, down to the Sauquoit Creek, to shovel gravel. The teams were too few to keep the vigorous shovelers busy all the time; and as it was an all pervading sentiment of that institution, that no moment should ever be left unoccupied, and that everything in heaven and earth, and under the earth, needed a new discussion, they extemporized a debating society there on the gravel. One of the citizens was appointed chairman, and then they inquired what should be discussed. The right of the slaves to receive their freedom without going to Africa, was proposed. "Who'll argue for the nigger?" was sneeringly asked. Surprising as this question is now, it was natural enough then. So great an authority as Paley had declared, "immediate emancipation will ruin the slaves as well as their masters." Those who hoped for the abolition of slavery, looked for it through some gradual process of Colonization. "The fanatic," Wm. Lloyd Garrison, had begun to publish on the subject, but few thought of heeding him.

One of those students, however, had seen in the reading room a few numbers of *The Liberator*, and also the first annual report of the New England Anti Slavery Society, written by Garrison, and had become convinced that the "fanatic" was telling the truth. His indignation was roused by the heartless inquiry, which assumed that the poor oppressed slave had none to plead his cause, and he boldly stepped forth and answered, "I will!" Some thought he was in fun, and laughed; others, that he had not counted the cost. "You'll be alone," it was said. When they discovered that he was in earnest, two or three others, out of sympathy with one whom they loved and respected, and pity for the weaker side, volunteered to stand with him, though they remarked, "we have nothing to say in the affirmative."

But the lone student was stronger than they imagined. All his energies were roused, and he spoke with a power that astonished both citizens and students. His argument was very plain and simple. "Slavery is a sin. All sin should be repented of. There is no repentance without forsaking the sin. There is no gradual repenting. It must be immediate. Therefore the poor slave has an immediate right to his liberty. Nor have we any right to compel him to cross the ocean to find liberty." For those who predicted that massacre and rapine would follow emancipation, he had these facts: In Guadoloupe, in 1794, 85,000 slaves were set free, where there were only 13,000 of the slaveholding class, and no disaster followed. Similar facts in Columbia, Mexico, Cape Colony, and even in St. Domingo, were cited. This last was turning the tables, for "the horrors of St. Domingo" was a watch cry rung through all possible changes by the opponents of emancipation. When it came to be known that those "horrors" sprung from the effort to reduce freed slaves again to bondage, the guns were effectually turned. He further argued that it was contrary to man's nature to take revenge for *ceasing* to do him wrong. When called on for proof, he recalled, just as the village bell was ringing for noon: "Go to the reading room, and in the *Liberator*, and first report of the New England Anti-Slavery Society, you will find all I have said confirmed." After dinner, the reading room was thronged, and happy was he who could get hold of a *Liberator*.

The discussion begun on the gravel, was transferred to all the debating societies of the institution, and was carried on earnestly for three months. The result was the formation of an anti-slavery society, comprising more than half of the students, and an opposition colonization society, aided, at first, by the influence of nearly all the teachers. Yet the anti-slavery society, like the house of David, waxed stronger and stronger, while the colonization society, like the house of Saul, waxed weaker and weaker, till its extinction in a year or two.

The second article of the Constitution read thus:

"The object of this Society shall be to endeavor by all means sanctioned by law, humanity and religion, to effect the *immediate* abolition of slavery in the United States *without expatriation*; to improve the character and condition of the free people of color; to inform and correct public opinion in relation of their situation and rights, and obtain for them civil and political rights and privileges equal with those of the whites."

After a lapse of thirty-seven years, the country has just reached the position taken by those students! Only three of the first officers of that society, are alive to witness the triumph of their principles, viz: Rev. HIRAM FOOTE, of Janesville, (Wis.,) the first President, -*the same man who stood alone in the Gravel Debate*,- and Rev. PHI-LANDER BARBOUR and Mr. WM SMITH, of Boston. This was the third of the modern anti-slavery societies of the country. The first was formed at Boston, and the second at Western Reserve College, Hudson, O. When this was organized, Wendell Phillips had never spoken in public, Fred Douglas had not escaped from slavery, the Lovejoys were unknown, Gerrit Smith was with tongue and pen and princely wealth aiding the Colonization Society, Lane Seminary had not discussed the question, Oberlin had scarcely found its home in the woods.[5]

The first object of purpose stated in the Preamble and Constitution of the Lane Student Anti-Slavery Society paraphrases the Oneida Institute Anti-Slavery Society's object of purpose. The Lane Constitution stated:

1st. *Object.* Our object is the immediate emancipation of the whole colored race within the United States: The emancipation of the slave from the oppression of the master, the emancipation of the free colored man from the oppression of public sentiment, and the elevation of both to an intellectual, moral, and political equality with the whites.[6]

On September 20, 1866, only ten months after passage of the Thirteenth Amendment abolishing slavery in the United States, Hiram Foote wrote a letter to Weld.[7] Foote recalled the time years earlier when the two men had entered "Old Oneida." Midway through this correspondence, Foote recounted what he remembered about introducing the concept of immediate emancipation to his fellow students at the school:

I will name to you a fact that but few know — Soon after the publication of the 1st Annual Report of the New England Anti Slavery Soc. in Jan. 1833 a copy came to our reading room at Oneida Institute — several numbers of Mr Garrison's Liberator also hung upon our files — I read those documents & immediately embraced the views therein set forth — I proclaimed them to the students & at my first public discussion I stood alone — It was while working at the road, embracing intervals when there was nothing to do, we had it all the forenoon; one against forty — I had so thoroughly digested what I had read that nearly half those present embraced my views & we, forty strong, others coming in soon after *formed the first Anti Slavery Soc ever organized in the state of N. York* & I was appointed their Pres.[8]

We know that Weld left the Oneida area for Cincinnati sometime in June of 1833.[9] Because the Gravel Debate about slavery in New York took place in June, Weld surely must have been aware of its impact on the Oneida Institute student body, although it is unclear how familiar he was with the details. Equally important, in regard to the influence of the Gravel Debate on the later debates about slavery at Lane, was the significant number of Oneida Institute students, including Hiram Foote, who enrolled at the seminary after Weld moved to Cincinnati. By 1834, twenty-four former Oneida seminarians were studying at Lane, and nine of these men later became members of Weld's Seventy.[10]

Distinguished historian of abolition Dwight L. Dumond maintains in his book *Anti-Slavery Origins of the Civil War in the United States* that Theodore Weld, though opposed to slavery, was not advocating immediate emancipation of slaves, as late as July, 1832.[11] We do know, however, that by the winter of 1834, Weld had embraced "immediatism." The first important student debate about the emancipation of slaves in the United States really occurred in upstate New York along Sauquoit Creek in the summer of 1833, and the consequence was that over the course of the next several months, Weld and his friends from the Oneida Institute came to the conclusion that the enslaved should be freed with haste. Knowing about the Gravel Debates does not diminish the importance of the Lane Debates, but instead amplifies their importance and allows us to interpret them by giving them context.

Charles C. Burleigh

In 1883, R. C. Smedley wrote *A History of the Underground Railroad in Chester and Neighboring Counties of Pennsylvania.* In his book, Smedley included an account of the effect Charles C. Burleigh had on abolitionism in Chester County, Pennsylvania. Burleigh's impact on the citizens in this part of the state was immediate and powerful:

The real earnestness and activity of Chester county abolitionism had its date with the advent of Charles C. Burleigh, who, about the year 1835, appeared as a lecturer in the neighborhood of Kennett Square.

There being at that time no railroad or stage facilities by which he could be accommodated, and being a remarkable walker, this gifted orator left Philadelphia for Dr. Fussell's, one mile east of the village of Kennett Square, traveling on foot over bad roads, the whole distance. Arriving at this destination in the evening, he learned that the doctor and his wife had already departed to attend a discussion on the subject of Phrenology, in the village. Tired as he was and supperless, our friend immediately followed, and soon overtook and passed the doctor and his wife in their carriage. Being excessively muddy with travel, this young athlete did not present an extraordinarily attractive exterior. The first impulse of the kind doctor had been to invite the stranger he saw passing to a seat in his carriage, but a glance at his boots, and a thought of the wife by his side checked the impulse, and the wayfarer was allowed to pass on. When they reached the place of meeting, he was already there, and during the debate which followed he modestly asked permission to speak, exhibiting such an amount of knowledge, extent of research, profundity of thought, and such oratorical and logical powers as to astonish and captivate his hearers. Dr. Fussell used often to tell the story of how he was cheated of doing a kindness to Charles C. Burleigh, by allowing himself to be governed by a pair of muddy boots.

At this meeting, all were so delighted that Charles C. Burleigh had only to express the wish to have appointed and announced a meeting on the subject of slavery. This meeting was largely attended, for the fame of the speaker had gone abroad. Here he pictured slavery and liberty in such clear contrast, and depicted the Christian duty of man to his fellow men in such glowing colors, embellished by the sublime rhetoric of which he was master, that the latent sense of justice and the anti-slavery emotions were stirred up in the hearts of the good people of Kennett, and organization and agitation were at once instituted. From that time onward until emancipation was effected, Kennett Square was noted among those who were slow to accept the movement, as the "hot-bed of abolitionism" while the earnest sympathizers with the negro in bondage, in this and in other States, found here kind-hearted, able, and intelligent men and women to aid in the cause, ever ready to assist with their money and their labor, and in whose homes they always had a hearty welcome. It was the cynosure alike of the fugitive and his friends...

On one occasion, Charles C. Burleigh was arrested in Oxford and sent to jail in West Chester. He was in custody of a constable passing through Unionville, when word was sent to Simon Barnard, who immediately started, although the roads were deep with mud. He arrived there just as the door of the jail was about to close upon Burleigh, and took him out of custody on bail.

Burleigh deeming his mission at Oxford unfinished, repeated his offence by preaching abolition and selling his tracts there on the next Sunday. He was re-arrested, and on the evening of a bitter cold day, he and the Oxford constable drove up to Simon Barnard's comfortable house, nearly perished — both nearly frozen. The ludicrous part of the scene was keenly relished by Simon, who used to say that instead of the constable taking Burleigh to jail, Burleigh was conducting the frozen officer to the house of his friend, where they were both kindly treated to a warm supper, lodging and breakfast; not only they but their horses. Next morning they departed, and Simon humorously remarked afterward that he was left in doubt as to whether the constable took Burleigh, or Burleigh took the constable.[12]

Burleigh worked for the American Anti-Slavery Society until mid summer 1837, and two years later, he resumed lecturing in Pennsylvania when he became an agent of the Pennsylvania State Anti-Slavery Society.

James G. Birney

James G. Birney's printing press was wrecked by a group of antiabolitionist vandals in Cincinnati on July 12, 1836. They also destroyed all of the issues of his next publication of the *Philanthropist*. The next day, the following handbill appeared in the city:

ABOLITIONISTS BEWARE
The Citizens of Cincinnati, embracing every class, interested in the prosperity of the City, satisfied that the business of the place is receiving a vital stab from the wicked and misguided operations of the abolitionists, are resolved to arrest their course. The destruction of their Press on the night of the 12th instant, may be taken as a warning. As there are some worthy citizens engaged in the unholy cause of annoying our southern neighbors, they are appealed to, to pause before they bring things to a crisis. If an attempt is made to re-establish their press, it will be viewed as an act of defiance to an already outraged community, and on their own heads be the results which follow.

Every kind of expostulation and remonstrance has been resorted to in vain — longer patience would be criminal. The plan is matured to eradicate an evil which every citizen feels is undermining his business and property.[13]

James G. Birney and his fellow members of the Cincinnati Anti-Slavery Society refused to be intimidated. On July 15, Birney reissued his *Philanthropist*.

Random Reflections

In 1885, towards the end of his life, Henry B. Stanton wrote *Random Reflections*. This short booklet discussed various aspects of his life, including his education, political involvements, travels abroad, observations about noted public figures, experiences as a writer for and editor of newspapers, and various other topics. Below are some of his reflections regarding his activities as an abolitionist:

In 1834, I went to Danville, Ky., to obtain a letter from Mr. Birney giving his reasons for joining the anti-Slavery Society. It was a remarkably able document and had a large circulation. He had been a slave-holder, belonged to one of the first Kentucky families, and was a profound lawyer. He was the father of Major General David B. Birney who commanded a corps in the Army of the Potomac in the War of the Rebellion, where he fought in defence of his father's principles. He died in the war. Mr. Birney was the first Liberty-Party candidate for President. He was a wise, upright, far-seeing patriot.

ANTI-SLAVERY

I attended the Anniversary of the American Anti-Slavery Society in New York, in 1834, and there encountered the first of my two hundred mobs. We had a great anti-Slavery debate at the [Lane] Seminary and formed a society during that fall. Pro-Slavery Trustees required that we should dissolve it. We refused to do so. They then passed arbitrary rules in respect to discussion and even conversation on the subject of slavery at the Seminary. A goodly portion of us, who were not to be thus throttled, left. It was a heavy blow to the Seminary, which hardly regained its feet for the next six years. I was on the Committee that issued an address in vindication of our course. It produced a profound impression. In the early spring of 1835, Mr. Birney and myself went east on an anti-Slavery Mission. We spoke at Philadelphia and New York. I then held meetings at Providence, R. I., Boston, Mass., and Concord, N.H., intending to return west and pursue my studies. On my return to New York I received a commission as General Agent of the American Anti-Slavery Society. I immediately entered upon the work which occupied so large a share of my active life.

I shall deal as summarily as possible with this subject. When I entered upon my life-work, Slavery had the State and Church by the throat; and though the Abolitionists advocated peaceful measures for the emancipation of the bondmen, they were everywhere at the mercy of mobs. For the dozen years following the fall of 1834, I was in the field. I was several years in the Executive Committee and Secretary of the American Anti-Slavery Society, and as such, I addressed millions of men and women in every northern State, from Indiana to Maine, in Kentucky, Maryland, and Delaware, and in England, Scotland, Ireland, and France. I appeared before ten Legislative Committees, and addressed the first committee of the kind in the country — that of the Senate and House of Massachusetts, in February, 1837, in support of John Quincy Adams' course in Congress. The Hon. S. G Goodrich — better known as Peter Parley — was a member of the Committee. I spoke for two days in the Hall of the Representatives in Boston, and at the close, joint resolutions were passed by the Legislature in favor of the abolition of slavery in the District of Columbia, and John Quincy Adams' course in Congress was approved. Three hundred thousand copies of my speech on that occasion were distributed.

I subsequently addressed Committees of the Massachusetts Legislature against the annexation of Texas, eliciting reports in accord with my arguments.

MOBS

Vice-President Wilson, in the "Rise and Fall of the Slave Power," is my authority for saying that I was mobbed at least 200 times. In 1835, I went into the town of East

Greenwich, R.I., and was the guest of Judge Brown, a gentleman of high standing. My anti-Slavery meeting was advertised. A constable arrived at Judge Brown's, and I was served with a warrant warning me out of town as a vagrant without visible means of support, and therefore liable to become a town charge. Judge Brown gave bail for me, and I held the meeting, and invited the constable to hear me. In those days it was the practice to get signatures to the anti-Slavery roll. The first name signed was that of the constable who had served the warrant. I viewed the capture of that constable as a great achievement.

We resorted to odd expedients to get in anti-Slavery speeches. The temperance cause was popular. In 1835, in Rhode Island, I agreed to address an audience an hour and a half on Temperance, if they would then let me speak an hour and a half on Slavery. On the next Sabbath the compact was faithfully fulfilled on both sides in the presence of a large concourse.

MOB IN PROVIDENCE

In 1836, I was outrageously treated while attempting to speak to a meeting in a Methodist Church at Providence. The mills of the gods ground slowly, but they did not stop. I addressed an immense Frémont out-door meeting at Providence in 1856. In respect to Slavery I dealt with it far more severely than in 1836. There were plenty of Governors on the platform, and Bishop Clark, of that diocese, was at my right hand. A man on the platform, bedecked with orders, was Chief Marshal. His enthusiasm in repeatedly calling for cheers bothered me while speaking. After I had finished, I asked who that chief Marshal was, and my friend, laughing, said: "Don't you remember that, in 1836, when you were delivering an anti-Slavery address in the Methodist Church here, a howling mob kept rushing up the aisles, shaking their fists at you and yelling, and they finally broke up the meeting? Well, he was the leader of the mob, and now he is making amends."

CHURCH BURNING

The respectable scoundrels who encouraged these crimes against society had no regard for the kind of edifices their vulgar tools assailed. I delivered one evening an address in a beautiful little church in Livingston Co., N.Y. I cannot now recall the name of the town where I spoke. The next morning the church was a heap of ashes. Pro-Slavery incendiaries had set it on fire during the night.

MOB IN PORTLAND

In Portland, in 1838, an anti-Slavery Convention sat for four days in the old Quaker meetinghouse. Gen. Samuel Fesseden, a leading member of the Bar of Maine, presided, but not all his influence could deter the mob. The meeting-house was utterly riddled. At length the best men of Portland said, "this won't do." The poet John Neal organized about 200 special constables, and leading them himself, put the mob down. Years afterward, meeting Gen. Fesseden's son, Senator William Pitt Fesseden, in Washington City, I eulogized his father's behavior in 1838. He asked, "Do you recollect that on one of those evenings a young man took your arm as you walked out of the meeting to go through the outside mob and said, "I will accompany you to your lodgings and share the peril with you? I am that person."[14]

Milford, New Hampshire, Congregational Church

A significant number of Weld's Seventy were clergymen before they became American Anti-Slavery Society agents and many of them returned to the pulpit when their service to the national society was concluded. The churches that employed these former agents as ministers were, not surprisingly, greatly influenced by their anti-slavery advocacy. One such pastor was former AASS agent Abner Warner who became the minister of the Milford New Hampshire Congregational Church in 1839. He was described by one local historian as follows:

> Abner Warner, a very noble and eloquent man, left a lasting mark on this community. He valiantly espoused the cause of freedom, while he held aloft the banner of the cross...Warner, from the day he entered the pulpit of the Congregational church, in February, 1839, until the day he left it, near the close of the year 1846, with the approbation of his congregation ceased not to cry aloud, with a pathos and an eloquence that few men could command, against the accursed institution of human bondage, we are compelled to say as impartial historians, that the offence of the Congregational church in Milford consisted in nothing worse than an unwillingness to break loose from ecclesiastical fellowship with churches apologizing for, or approving, this barbarous institution whose death blow was struck by the early abolitionists.[15]

There were, of course, members of the Milford Congregational Church who opposed efforts to use the Congregationalists's building to support the abolitionist cause:

> Not a few members of the churches were among the warmest friends of the slave. Conspicuous among this class were Dea. Freeman Crosby and his brother, Capt. Fredrick Crosby, of the Congregational church. One Nathaniel Coggin during the early days of discussion attempted to prevent the holding of a free-soil meeting in the Congregational church edifice by surreptitiously obtaining the keys and nailing the windows and doors, and going out of town with the key to the only unbarred door of the meeting-house. The members of the parish rose as one man, broke open the doors, and the meeting was held. From the day of this meeting to the day of his decease, the man who undertook in this way to close the doors of the church against an appeal for human bondage was known as Key Coggin.[16]

In 1841, the Milford Congregational Church passed the following resolution:

> *Resolved,* that we believe slaveholding to be contrary to the spirit of the Gospel, and that it threatens the peace, purity, and permanence of the religious institutions of the land...
> *Resolved,* That we ... protest against the course, wherever pursued, of receiving into the treasury of the Lord the avails of unpaid labor — the price of slaves, and the souls of men.[17]

In 1842, at the church's annual Thanksgiving dinner Warner said during his sermon:

> No, the soil of the pilgrims shall not be trod by human hounds that hunt for the panting fugitive slave. We will resist the aggression of the Lords of rice-tierce and cotton bales not with violence and blood but with the burning righteous public opinion that better than cold-steel and bristling bayonets will keep off the enemies of the race.[18]

A newspaper story about Warner that appeared in the *Milford Mirror* in 1843 described him thus:

> [Warner was] a man to be held, being free from the fear of man, and having, as it were, the word of the Lord shut up in his bosom, — he must speak that he might be

refreshed. If man would act in conformity with his preaching — laying aside all malice and guile, hypocrisy, and evil speaking... there would be joy in heaven and on earth there would be goodwill to man.[19]

In 1846, Warner resigned his position as the pastor of the Milford Congregational Church due to poor health. One hundred and two individuals joined the church during the years that he was the minister. Before the Civil War began, the citizens of Milford invited several famous abolitionists to speak in their churches and town hall. The lecturers included Henry Ward Beecher, Frederick Douglass, Wendell Phillips, Parker Pillsbury, and Abby Foster.

Whittier Recalls the Establishment of the American Anti-Slavery Society

Forty-one years after the American Anti-Slavery Society was established, John Greenleaf Whittier put down a recollection of what he recalled about the society's organizational meeting. The following is taken from that reminiscence:

Committees were chosen to draft a constitution for a national Anti-Slavery Society, nominate a list of officers, and prepare a declaration of principles to be signed by the members. Dr. A. L. Cox of New York, while these committees were absent, read something from my pen eulogistic of William Lloyd Garrison; and Lewis Tappan and Amos A. Phelps, a Congregational clergyman of Boston, afterwards one of the most devoted laborers in the cause, followed in generous commendation of the zeal, courage, and devotion of the young pioneer. The president, after calling James McCrummell, one of the two or three colored members of the convention, to the chair, made some eloquent remarks upon those editors who had ventured to advocate emancipation. At the close of his speech a young man rose to speak, whose appearance at once arrested my attention.

I think I have never seen a finer face and figure; and his manner, words, and bearing were in keeping. "Who is he?" I asked of one of the Pennsylvania delegates. "Robert Purvis, of this city, a colored man," was the answer. He began by uttering his heart-felt thanks to the delegates who had convened for the deliverance of his people.

He spoke of Garrison in terms of warmest eulogy, as one who had stirred the heart of the nation, broken the tomb-like slumber of the Church, and compelled it to listen to the story of the slave's wrongs. He closed by declaring that the friends of colored Americans would not be forgotten. "Their memories," he said, "will be cherished when pyramids and monuments shall have crumbled in dust. The flood of time, which is sweeping away the refuge of lies, is bearing on the advocates of our cause to a glorious immortality."

The committee on the constitution made their report, which after discussion was adopted. It disclaimed any right or intention of interfering, otherwise than by persuasion and Christian expostulation, with slavery as it existed in the States, but affirming the duty of Congress to abolish it in the District of Columbia and Territories, and to put an end to the domestic slave-trade.

A list of officers of the new society was then chosen: Arthur Tappan, of New York, president, and Elizur Wright, Jr., William Lloyd Garrison, and A. L. Cox, secretaries. Among the vice-presidents was Dr. Lord, of Dartmouth College, then professedly in favor of emancipation, but who afterwards turned a moral somersault, a self-inversion which left him ever after on his head instead of his feet. He became a querulous advocate of slavery as a divine institution, and denounced woe upon the abolitionists for interfering with the will and purpose of the Creator. As the cause of freedom gained ground, the poor man's heart failed him, and his hope for Church and State grew fainter and fainter. A sad prophet of the evangel of slavery, he testified in the unwilling ears of an unbelieving generation, and died at last, despairing of a world which seemed determined that Canaan should no longer be cursed, nor Onesimus sent back to Philemon. The committee on the declaration of principles, of which I was a member, held a long session discussing the proper scope and tenor of the document. But little progress being made, it was finally decided to [entrust] the matter to a sub-committee, consisting of William L. Garrison, S. J. May, and myself; and, after a brief consultation and comparison of each other's views the drafting of the important paper was assigned to the former gentleman.

We agreed to meet him at his lodgings in the house of a colored friend early the next morning. It was still dark when we climbed up to his room, and the lamp was still burning by the light of which he was writing the last sentence of the declaration. We read it carefully, made a few verbal changes, and submitted it to the large committee, who unanimously agreed to report it to the convention.

The paper was read to the convention by Dr. Atlee, chairman of the committee, and listened to with the profoundest interest...

The reading of the [Declaration of Sentiments] was followed by a discussion which lasted several hours. A member of the Society of Friends moved its immediate adoption. "We have," he said, "all given it our assent: every heart here responds to it. It is a doctrine of Friends that these strong and deep impressions should be heeded." The convention, nevertheless, deemed it important to go over the declaration carefully, paragraph by paragraph. During the discussion one of the spectators asked leave to say a few words.

A beautiful and graceful woman, in the prime of life, with a face beneath her plain cap as finely intellectual as that of Madame Roland, offered some wise and valuable suggestions, in a clear, sweet voice, the charm of which I have never forgotten. It was Lucretia Mott, of Philadelphia. The president courteously thanked her, and encouraged her to take a part in the discussion. On the morning of the last day of our session the declaration, with its few verbal amendments, carefully engrossed on parchment, was brought before the convention. Samuel J. May rose to read it for the last time.

His sweet, persuasive voice faltered with the intensity of his emotions as he repeated the solemn pledges of the concluding paragraphs. After a season of silence, David Thurston, of Maine, rose as his name was called by one of the secretaries, and affixed his name to the document. One after another passed up to the platform, signed, and retired in silence. All felt the deep responsibility of the occasion: the shadow and forecast of a lifelong struggle rested upon every countenance.

Our work as a convention was now done. President Green arose to make the concluding address. The circumstances under which it was uttered may have lent it an impressiveness not its own; but, as I now recall it, it seems to me the most powerful and eloquent speech to which I have ever listened. He passed in review the work that had been done, the constitution of the new society, the declaration of sentiments, and the union and earnestness which had marked the proceedings. His closing words will never be forgotten by those who heard them:—

"Brethren, it has been good to be here. In this hallowed atmosphere I have been revived and refreshed. This brief interview has more than repaid me for all that I have ever suffered. I have here met congenial minds. I have rejoiced in sympathies delightful to the soul. Heart has beat responsive to heart, and the holy work of seeking to benefit the outraged and despised has proved the most blessed employment.

"But now we must retire from these balmy influences, and breathe another atmosphere. The chill hoar frost will be upon us. The storm and tempest will rise, and the waves of persecution will dash against our souls. Let us be prepared for the worst. Let us fasten ourselves to the throne of God as with hooks of steel. If we cling not to him, our names to that document will be but as dust.

"Let us court no applause, indulge in no spirit of vain boasting. Let us be assured that our only hope in grappling with the bony monster is in an Arm that is stronger than ours. Let us fix our gaze on God, and walk in the light of his countenance. If our cause be just,—and we know it is,—his omnipotence is pledged to its triumph. Let this cause be entwined around the very fibers of our hearts. Let our hearts grow to it, so that nothing but death can sunder the bond."

He ceased, and then, amidst a silence broken only by the deep-drawn breath of emotion in the assembly, lifted up his voice in a prayer to Almighty God, full of fervor and feeling, imploring his blessing and sanctification upon the convention and its labors. And with the solemnity of this supplication in our hearts we clasped hands in farewell, and went forth each man to his place of duty, not knowing the things that should befall us as individuals, but with a confidence never shaken by abuse and persecution in the certain triumph of our cause.[20]

Appendix D: Tributes

Although tributes to the recently dead are sometimes fulsome, exaggerated, and laced with hyperbole, at other times they also do in fact convey much about the essence of the deceased. The following tributes convey all of the elements listed above but are worthy expressions of the individuals they praise.

Arthur Tappan

The following tribute, written by Joshua Leavitt, appeared in the New York *Independent* shortly after the death of Arthur Tappan:

The vulnerable Christian philanthropist, whose name has been, at one time, a word of power to all who love Christ's cause and, at another, the song of the negro-haters throughout the country, as the representative of justice and mercy to the oppressed, has been gathered to his fathers in peace and honor at the ripe age of fourscore. Mr. Tappan died at New Haven, on Sunday, July 23 [1865], and was buried on Tuesday, in the cemetery of that place. Reserving for another occasion the fuller account which we hope to give of his life, and the services he rendered to his generation and to the cause of Christ in the world, we now only express the first emotions that arise at the event when we say that this world has parted with one of the truest Christians it ever knew. Sincerity as pure as crystal, and integrity as true as the beams of the morning, were the leading traits of his character. What he said, he believed; and what he saw to be right, he did. Those who differed from him most widely, and those who were most displeased by his action, felt and confessed that he was conscientious in his opinions, and honest in his conduct, to a degree never surpassed. He had no classification of principles or duties, by their times or relations. Hs piety was for every day, and his religion controlled his bargains as it did his devotions. A Christian indeed, he was a Christian everywhere, and in all his relations. He would no more wrong his closet in devotion than he would cheat a customer in trade. He believed the evangelical system of doctrine as honestly as the Decalogue, and practiced the duties of the second table as diligently as the first. He was a good man in whatever circumstances you tried him, and from whatever point of view you observed him. His character honored alike his profession as a Christian, his calling as a merchant, his position as a member of society. He was thought to be severe in judgment, but it was only because he judged others as he did himself, and he could not modify the decision, because he knew the law could not bend. He could not compromise in duty, because he could not alter the truth, which he believed because it was true. His whole life was eminently uniform and consistent, because it was wholly and always governed by one principle — the law of God. The life of such a man is a profitable study for all survivors, and its history needs to be written by one who is in full sympathy with the principles which governed him, and the objects for which he lived. His life consisted in what he believed and what he did- not in loud sentiments or florid imaginations. It had no lack of the essentials of faith and action, and he never sought for it the adornments of fancy or the excitements of overwrought emotion. Undoubting belief, unhesitating submission, unremitting obedience, made up a religion which he was resolved to live by, and which he was not afraid to die by. The life of which it could be said in youth that he never told a lie is completed and rounded out with a consistency as perfect as the circle of the sky.

There is, probably, no man living whose influence upon the destinies of the country is equal to his. Our great system of benevolent institutions owes its expansion and power, in a great degree, to his influence. His example inspired the merchants of New York with the principle of enlarged benevolence, leading them to give their hundreds, and thousands and tens of thousands where before they were accustomed to think it a great matter if they gave their tens or fifties. His wise counsels and energetic determination, and munificent donation of five or six thousand dollars in 1825, decided the formation and destiny of the American Tract Society, and gave it the strong and steady career on which it has advanced for so many years. His thoughtful mind planned the great enterprise of the American Bible Society, of giving a Bible to every family in the United States, and his pledge of ten thousand dollars rendered it impossible but that the work should be undertaken — and done. Many others might be named of the great social movements of the last forty years, which owed their being or their power to his comprehensiveness of vision, sagacity of forethought, or largeness of liberality. Hardly any one can be named which did not become what it was through his agency and influence. It was a large heart, gifted with most extensive foresight, guiding a singularly effective will.

In the slavery agitation, its beginning, its extent, its power, its results, it may be said, without a question, that Arthur Tappan was the pivotal centre of the whole movement. He supported the Colonization Society for some years, because he believed it would aid in the overthrow of slavery, and only abandoned it when he became fully convinced that it was formed and was managed mainly in the interest of slavery, and for the purpose of strengthening the system by removing its chief dangers. His decision and generosity released Mr. Garrison from his imprisonment at Baltimore, and placed him in a position to commence the publication of the *Liberator*. The formation of the Anti-Slavery Society in New York, to be guided by those principles of religion and patriotism to which his own soul held glad allegiance, hinged upon him, both for its conception and execution. For years his contribution to its treasury were its main reliance, amounting for successive years to at least one-fourth of its yearly income. His generous response at that very juncture saved the *Liberator* from pending and instant suppression. And, in addition, he gave money and stirred up men to effort, right and left, to an extent which no earthly registry has recorded. In the darkest hours of mobs, and obloquy, and threatened assassination, he never quailed nor changed his course, nor doubted as to duties or results, but pressed right on, with steady step, toward the end which he was sure must come. For seven years he was the hinge on which a great nation turned to its new destiny. And he never let go, nor relaxed his energy, until he had seen the country so thoroughly aroused and so far permeated in all its ranks with the anti-slavery spirit as to make the final issue no longer doubtful, except as a question of time. He has been graciously permitted to remain among us until the great abomination has received its death-blow, and then departed in peace, to enter into the joy of his Lord. Well done, good and faithful servant! Thou has been faithful above many, be thou ruler over higher interests in a world yet more exalted![1]

Lewis Tappan

John Greenleaf Whittier wrote the following tribute to Arthur Tappan's brother, Lewis, following his death in 1873. Although Arthur Tappan and Lewis Tappan were both dedicated supporters of the abolitionist movement, Lewis was more prominently involved with the strategies developed and the operational organization of the anti-slavery crusade:

One after another, those foremost in the antislavery conflict of the last half-century are rapidly passing away. The grave has just closed over all that was mortal of Salmon P. Chase, the kingliest of men, a statesman second to no other in our history, too great and pure for the Presidency, yet leaving behind him a record which any incumbent of that station might envy, — and now the telegraph brings us the tidings of the death of Lewis Tappan, of Brooklyn, so long and so honorably identified with the anti-slavery cause, and with every philanthropic and Christian enterprise. He was a native of Massachusetts, born at Northampton in 1788, of Puritan lineage, — one of a family remarkable for integrity, decision of character, and intellectual ability. At the very outset, in company with his brother Arthur, he devoted his time, talents, wealth and social position to the righteous but unpopular cause of Emancipation, and became, in consequence, a mark for the persecution which followed such devotion.. His business was crippled, his name cast out as evil, his dwelling sacked, and his furniture dragged into the street and burned. Yet he never, in the darkest hour, faltered or hesitated for a moment. He knew he was right, and that the end would justify him; one of the cheerfullest of men, he was strong where others were weak, hopeful where others despaired. He was wise in counsel, and prompt in action; like Tennyson's Sir Galahad,

"His strength was as the strength of ten,
Because his heart was pure."

I met him for the first time forty years ago, at the convention which formed the American Anti-Slavery Society, where I chanced to sit by him as one of the secretaries. Myself young and inexperienced, I remember how profoundly I was impressed by his cool self-possession, clearness of perception, and wonderful executive ability. Had he devoted himself to party politics with half the zeal which he manifested in behalf of those who had no votes to give and no honors to bestow, he could have reached the highest offices in the land. He chose his course, knowing all that he renounced, and he chose it wisely. He never, at least, regretted it.

And now, at the ripe age of eighty-five years, the brave old man has passed onward to the higher life, having outlived here all hatred, abuse, and misrepresentation, having seen the great work of Emancipation completed, and white men and black men equal before the law. I saw him for the last time three years ago, when he was preparing his valuable biography of his beloved brother Arthur. Age had begun to tell upon his constitution, but his intellectual force was not abated. The old, pleasant laugh and playful humor remained. He looked forward to the close of life hopefully, even cheerfully, as he called to mind the dear friends who had passed on before him, to await his coming.

Of the sixty-three signers of the Anti-Slavery Declaration at the Philadelphia Convention in 1833, probably not more than eight or ten are now living.

"As clouds that rake the mountain summits,
As waves that know no guiding hand,
So swift has brother followed brother
From sunshine to the sunless land."

Yet it is a noteworthy fact that the oldest member of that convention, David Thurston, D.D., of Maine, lived to see the slaves emancipated, and to mingle his voice of thanksgiving with the bells that rang in the day of universal freedom.[2]

James G. Birney

The following tribute was written by Samuel J. May in honor of James G. Birney. The excerpts below are primarily in reference to Birney's early life and his conversion from supporting colonization to becoming an adherent of immediate emancipation:

A Tribute to James G. Birney

One generation has passed away since James G. Birney attempted to show that the enslaving of men, as an institution could not be safely tolerated in a republican government. There were peculiarities in his history that make his case eminently an illustration, in the treatment exhibited toward him, of the powerful and almost irresistible influence that slaveholders had acquired in society, in the church, in politics, and in the control of the government in the Northern as well as Southern States. They will also show that such opposition as he elicited, was not excited by anything unacceptable, in himself, personally, but was owing to the fact that he announced truths, for which the public mind was *not then prepared*.

It is the purpose of this article, by brief allusion to an incident occurring in the career of James G. Birney, to illustrate the remarkable hold slavery possessed upon the regards of the people of the United States, and how difficult has been the task to diminish the deference almost universally entertained for it.

In order to show that the treatment exhibited toward him as a public man, was an expression of the influence of slavery, it will be necessary to make some reference to his antecedents, and social position.

James G. Birney was a native of Kentucky. His father, through application to business, and by contracts with the government, for furnishing supplies to the army, during the war of 1812, had acquired a large estate. Woodland residence, in the vicinity of Danville, had celebrity as one of the most attractive sites in the State. Having only two children, he spared no expense in their education. His daughter married John J. Marshall, an eminent lawyer at Frankfort, and afterwards, for many years, Chancellor at Louisville, Kentucky.

The early education of the son was under the tutorage of Mr. Priestly. Subsequently he was transferred to Transylvania University at Lexington, Ky., thence to Nassau Hall, at Princeton, N.J. At this latter institution, James G. Birney was graduated in 1910, being regarded as one of the most proficient linguists of his class. To accomplish him in the study of the law, he was entered as a student in the law office of Mr. Dallas, of Philadelphia, where he spent two years.

After traveling extensively, he entered upon the practice of the law at Danville, his native place. Within the following two years he was elected a member of the Legislature of Kentucky.

His marriage to Miss McDowell, allied him to a large connection, both in Kentucky and Virginia.

He soon after removed to Huntsville, Alabama, where he gained an enviable

position in his profession, and enjoyed the fruits of a lucrative practice. He was
elected Solicitor General for the State, and was offered a seat upon the Bench. His
partner, in the law, for several years, was the Hon. Arthur F. Hopkins, subsequently
Judge of the Supreme Court of Alabama, and United States Senator from the same
State.

When John Q. Adams was nominated for the Presidency in 1828, James G. Birney
was selected by the Whig party of Alabama as one of the Presidential Electors for that
State.

Having made a profession of religion, he became an active member of the Presbyterian Church, and exerted an extensive influence as an elder in that denomination,
the more so, perhaps, from having been previously regarded as altogether a man of
the world.

By inheritance and purchase, he became the owner of slaves, and had a cotton
plantation carried on under his direction.

After his mind became engaged upon the subject of slavery as a question of morals,
he was solicited by the American Colonization Society, to accept the superintendency
of its interests in a district composed of the States of Tennessee, Alabama, Mississippi, Arkansas and Louisiana. While thus engaged he was treated with every manifestation of popular favor. When traveling through the district a free passage,
accompanied by every courtesy was tendered him upon all public conveyances. Funds
were placed in his hands, for the purpose of fitting out a vessel to sail from New
Orleans freighted with Colonists for Liberia. He had, by these opportunities, abundant means of forming an opinion as to the future effect of colonization upon the
permanency of slavery.

At the earnest entreaty of his aged father, he returned to Kentucky, to be near him
during the declining years. Here at his native place, he was offered the Professorship
of Belles Letters and Political Economy, in Centre College.... This he declined chiefly
for the reason, that he was then interesting himself in organizing into an association,
those in Kentucky who were in favor of gradual emancipation. Having known Henry
Clay from boyhood, he sought in several interviews, his co-operation, but although
receiving expression of sympathy from him in private conversation, he failed to
obtain any avowal publicly in favor of the plan.

Upon giving the subject longer and more mature consideration, his mind reached
the conclusion, that the doctrine of immediate emancipation was the only adequate
remedy for the system of slavery.

No sooner had he adopted this conviction, that he had all the slaves upon his farm,
and in his household assembled, and informed them that he had executed deeds of
manumission, for each and all of them, that they would be recorded, and the bonds
required filed, so that they would no longer be slaves but freemen and free women.
He further informed them, that from that time, to so many as preferred to remain
with him, he would pay wages for their services and they would be regarded and
treated as hired persons.

He then called upon a clergyman present, to ask to the blessing of God upon the
act. Hereupon the entire household, white and black, knelt in worship, and the sobs
and responses! of the negroes made indeed an impressive scene.

Coming, at the same time, to the conclusion, that colonization was inadequate as a
remedy for slavery, he resigned his position as Vice-President of the State Society, and
in a letter to the Secretary, gave his reasons at length for doing so. This concluding
paragraph of that letter is as follows:

"Permit me, in conclusion, to say that the views submitted in this communication,
are entertained after long and very circumspect examination of the main subject to

which they apply. Born in the midst of a slaveholding community — accustomed to the services of slaves from my infancy — reared under an exposure to all the prejudices that slavery begets — and being myself heretofore, from early life, a slaveholder — my efforts at mental liberation were commenced in the very lowest and grossest atmosphere. Fearing the reality, as well as the imputation of enthusiasm, each ascent that my mind made to a higher and purer moral and intellectual region, I used, as a *stand point* to survey deliberately all the tract I had left. When I remembered how calmly and dispassionately my mind has proceeded from one truth connected with this subject to another still higher, — that the opinions I have embraced are those to which such minds and hearts as Wilberforce's and Clarkson's yielded their full assent — that they are the opinions of the disinterested and excellent of our own country; I feel well satisfied that my conclusions are not the fruits of enthusiasm. When I recur to my own observation through a life already of more that forty years — of the anti-republican tendency of slavery — and take up our most solemn State paper, and there see that all men are created equal, and have a right that is alienable to life, liberty and the pursuit of happiness; I feel a settled conviction of mind *that Slavery, as it exists among us*, is opposed to the very essence of our government, and that by prolonging it, we are *living down* the foundation principles of our happy institutions."

"But one word more. The views contained in this letter are my own, and they have been the result of my own reading, observation and thought. I am a member of no antislavery society, nor have I any acquaintance, either personally or by literary correspondence, with any of Northern abolitionists. No one, besides myself, is committed to any thing I have said..."

Speaking of the effect of such action, in his own case, he says:

"My own manumitted slaves, at the end of the first year of their employment on wages, will have used but half the amount they are entitled to receive. They have not fallen into disorderly or vagrant habits, but have manifested, at least the younger ones, an increased desire for knowledge and for attendance on the sabbath schools, and the common ministrations of the sanctuary."

May continued with the following from the Address of General John C. Frémont:

What to-day is the position of the men, who for the past thirty years, have worked to bring our practice into conformity with the principles of the government? And who in the struggle against established and powerful interests, have accepted political disability and humiliated lives? Have any of those been put in governing places, where their proved fidelity, would guarantee the direct execution of what is to-day the nearly unanimous will of the people? Certainly not yet. So far the virtue of Reformers is its own reward. While yet living their mantles have fallen upon the shoulders of others to whom you have given high position, but they are still laboring in narrow paths, — broadening, to be sure, and brightening, — for the rough ground is passed and the sun of victory is already rising. We give deep sympathy and honor to the men who in the interests of civilization, separated themselves from mankind to penetrate the chill solitudes of the arctic regions. Their names remain an added constellation in polar skies. But we know that bitter skies and winter winds are not so unkind as man's ingratitude. And why then, do we withhold sympathy and honor from these men who have unflinchingly trod their isolated path of self appointed duty — accepting political and social excommunication — these heroes of the moral solitudes.

— *From address of Gen Frémont, Feb. 29th, 1864, N.Y.*

Treatment in a Slave State.

Feeling, that unless such views were general accepted, the true glory, of his country must be eclipsed by the growing magnitude of slavery, he determined to devote himself to their dissemination in the midst of those whom they were designed to influence. He did not seek to go North where the risk might be less, but to discuss the subject with slaveholders whom he wished to persuade to act as he had. He bought press and type for the publication of a paper at Danville, Ky. He made a contract with the printer of the weekly newspaper at that place, to publish under his editorial control, a paper to be called *The Philanthropist*. He issued a prospectus in which occurs the following paragraph:

"Those who have investigated the subject of slavery, with one consent declare, if something effectual be not done without any delay, it will become, in a short time unmanageable, and in the end *overwhelming*. In our condition, to do nothing, would show an unpardonable lack of manhood. Something effectual ought to be — for as yet it *can* be done. With the *sin* of slavery its evils may be terminated, our land may be blessed of God; raised, cleansed from defilement, and without a single remaining blood spot, stand clothed in the majesty of her free principles, the rebuke of tyrants, the refuge of the oppressed."

When the fact became known that Mr. Birney had freed his slaves, it was regarded by neighboring slaveholders as satisfactory evidence of his earnestness, and there was immediately an entire change of feeling toward him. It was altogether allowable for him while he held slaves, to say what he pleased upon the subject, but the moment his theory was converted into practice, he was regarded as a dangerous member of society.

Learning that he had provided press and type, and engaged a printer to give publicity of his views, slaveholders assembled in mass meeting in the town of his residence, and pledged themselves to use every means in their power, whether peaceable or violent to prevent their publication. Having known him from childhood, they felt assured that he did not lack the courage necessary to carry out his plans. The meeting appointed a committee to address him a letter of remonstrance. This they did on the 12th of July, 1835. The following extract shows the spirit by which they were actuated:

"We address you now in the calmness and candor that should characterize law abiding men, as willing to avoid violence, as they are determined to meet extremity, and advise you of the peril that must and inevitably will attend the execution of your purpose. We propose to you to postpone the setting up of your press, and the publication of your paper, until application can be had to the Legislature, who will, by a positive law, set rules for your observance, or by a refusal to act, admonish us of our duty. We admonish you, sir, as citizens of the same neighborhood, as members of the same society in which you live and move, and for whose harmony and quiet we feel the most sincere solicitude, to beware how you make an experiment here, which no American slaveholding community has found itself able to bear."

Mr. Birney replied, refusing in respectful yet dignified and decided terms, to comply with their request. He suggested that it would have been far more becoming, and more like the spirit of law abiding men, had they abstained entirely from the threat that a resort might be had to violence, to prevent the exercise of one of the most precious rights of an American, — a right, which, however, it might be violated in the destruction of his property, or cloven down in the abuse of his person, can never for a moment be surrendered. He, therefore, after giving his reason, concluded:

"However desirous I may be of obliging you, as citizens and neighbors, I cannot accede to your proposition."

The Committee finding him determined to persevere, succeeded through bribery, and by exciting his apprehensions of personal danger, in inducing the printer to violate his contract, by refusing to print the paper.

When the report reached Alabama that Mr. Birney had freed his slaves, various devices were resorted to for the purpose of dishonoring him, and showing their contempt for such a heresy.

The Supreme Court of Alabama, being at that time in session, a member of the bar moved the Court, that the name of James G. Birney be expunged from the roll of attorneys of that Court, as unworthy to remain there longer. And although Judge Hopkins, his former partner and bosom friend, was the President Judge, he had not courage to say aught in objection, or to express a word in extenuation, and ordered the motion to be granted.

While he was resident in Alabama, the University of that State was organized upon an endowment of remarkable liberality. On account of his reputation as a classical scholar, and the interest he had uniformly shown in the cause of education, Mr. Birney was commissioned by the Trustees to visit the New England States and form the acquaintance of literary men, with the view of selecting competent professors for the several departments of the University. He did so, and the President and Professors of that institution were elected to their several posts, chiefly upon his recommendation. He had frequently attended upon examinations and taken an active part in promoting its welfare, being a member of the Board of Trustees. The literary societies connected with it, had chosen him as one of their honorary members. But no sooner did they hear that he had given liberty to slaves, than they hastened to pass resolution declaring him unworthy of such membership, and expelled him.

In Northern Alabama a large meeting was held about the same time, for the purpose of denouncing Mr. Birney. They appointed a vigilance committee to inflict blows and death upon the objects of the vengeance, wherever they may lay their lawless hands upon them. Of this committee, more than one-third were described as professed Christians, belonging to three of the leading denominations in our country, one of whom was a Baptist minister.

This committee took special pains to communicate these proceedings to Mr. Birney. The following is an extract from the answer which he published and sent them:

"In this reply, which after no hurried reflection, I have thought proper to make to your proceedings, I shall take but little time in noticing what was done that was strictly personal to myself. I will stop only long enough to remind you — especially that portion of you who profess to be followers of Christ — of the unjust impression you have attempted to make on those to whom I am a stranger, by associating me, in your proceedings arduous in its duties, and to a conscientious mind, beset with difficulties and temptations. To the generousness of my practice the bar will testify, and with parties and witnesses bear record to my exemptions from the petty tricks and advantages which bring the profession into disrepute. Knowing me by an acquaintance of many years, as you did, in my profession — as a member of the church — as a citizen — you have tried to produce an impression you knew to be unjust and injurious. As Christians, and as gentlemen, now that you have had time for reflection, you should be sorry for it, and ashamed of it.

His Treatment in a Free State

The foregoing incidents tend to show what kind of treatment slaveholders were disposed to manifest to one who left their ranks, and how they regarded conduct, designed practically, to exemplify the teachings of the Declaration of Independence. His reception by men of the North will now be adverted to.

Having lost his printer, in his native State, rendering it impracticable to carry out his design as to the publication of his views there, he concluded to seek the protection of the constitution of the free State of Ohio, which guarantees to her citizens, freedom of speech and of the press. He removed his residence to Cincinnati.[3]

Appendix E: Declaration of Sentiments and the Constitution of the Society

Declaration of Sentiments

ADOPTED AT THE FORMATION OF SAID SOCIETY, IN PHILADELPHIA, ON THE 4TH DAY OF DECEMBER, 1833.

The Convention, assembled in the city of Philadelphia, to organize a National Anti-Slavery Society, promptly seize the opportunity to promulgate the following DECLARATION OF SENTIMENTS, as cherished by them, in relation to the enslavement of one sixth portion of the American people.

More than fifty-seven years have elapsed since a band of patriots convened in this place to devise measures for the deliverance of this country from a foreign yoke. The corner-stone upon which they founded the TEMPLE OF FREEDOM was broadly this — "that all men are created equal; that they are endowed by their Creator with certain inalienable rights; that among these are life, LIBERTY, and the pursuit of happiness." At the sound of their trumpet-call, three millions of people rose up as from the sleep of death, and rushed to the strife of blood; deeming it more glorious to die instantly as freemen, then desirable to live one hour as slaves. They were few in number — poor in resources; but the honest conviction that TRUTH, JUSTICE, and RIGHT were on their side, made them invincible.

We have met together for the achievement of an enterprise without which that of our fathers is incomplete, and which, for its magnitude, solemnity, and probable results upon the destiny of the world, as far transcends theirs as moral truth does physical force.

In purity of motive, in earnest of zeal, in decision of purpose, in intrepidity of action, in steadfastness of faith, in sincerity of spirit, we would not be inferior to them.

Their principles led them to wage war against their oppressors, and to spill human blood like water, in order to be free. *Ours* forbid the doing of evil that good may come, and lead us to reject, and to entreat the oppressed to reject, the use of all carnal weapons for deliverance from bondage; relying solely upon those which are spiritual and mighty through God to the pulling down of strongholds.

Their measures were physical resistance — the marshalling in arms — the hostile array — the mortal encounter. Ours shall be such only as the opposition of moral purity to moral corruption — the destruction of error by the potency of truth — the

180

overthrow of prejudice by the power of love — and the abolition of slavery by the spirit of repentance.

Their grievances, great as they were, were trifling in comparison with the wrongs and suffering of those for whom we plead. Our fathers were never slaves — never bought and sold like cattle — never shut out from the light of knowledge and religion — never subjected to the lash of brutal taskmasters. But those, for whose emancipation we are striving — constituting, at the present time, at least one sixth part of our countrymen — are recognized by the law, and treated by their fellow-beings, as marketable commodities, as goods and chattels, as brute beasts; are plundered daily of the fruits of their toil, without redress — really enjoying no constitutional nor legal protection from licentious and murderous outrages upon their persons; are ruthlessly torn asunder — the tender babe from the arms of its frantic mother — the heart-broken wife from her weeping husband — at the caprice or pleasure of irresponsible tyrants. For the crime of having a dark complexion, they suffer the pangs of hunger, the infliction of stripes, and the ignominy of brutal servitude. They are kept in heathenish darkness by laws expressly enacted to make their instruction a criminal offense.

These are the prominent circumstances in the condition of more than two millions of our people, the proof of which may be found in thousands of indisputable facts, and in the laws of the slaveholding States.

Hence we maintain, that in view of the civil and religious privileges of this nation, the guilt of its oppression is unequalled by any other on the face of the earth; and, therefore,

That it is bound to repent instantly, to undo the heavy burdens, to break every yoke, and to let the oppressed go free.

We further maintain, that no man has a right to enslave or imbrute his brother — to hold or acknowledge him, for one moment, as a piece of merchandize — to keep back his hire by fraud — or to brutalize his mind by denying him the means of intellectual, social, and moral improvement.

The right to enjoy liberty is inalienable. To invade it is to usurp the prerogative of Jehovah. Every man has a right to his own body — to the products of his own labor — to the protection of law, and to the common advantages of society. It is piracy to buy or steal a native African, and subject him to servitude. Surely that sin is as great to enslave an AMERICAN as an AFRICAN.

Therefore, we believe and affirm, That there is no difference, *in principle*, between the African slave-trade and American slavery.

That every American citizen who retains a human being in involuntary bondage as his property, is, according to Scripture (Ex.xxi.16) a MAN-STEALER.

That the slaves ought instantly to be set free, and brought under the protection of law.

That if they lived from the time of Pharaoh down to the present period, and had been entailed through successive generations, their right to be free could never have been alienated, but their claims would have constantly risen in solemnity.

That all those laws which are now in force admitting the right of slavery, are therefore before God utterly null and void; being an audacious usurpation of the Divine prerogative, a daring infringement on the law of nature, a base overthrow of the very foundations of the social compact, a complete extinction of all the relations, endearments, and obligations of mankind, and a presumptuous transgression of all the holy commandments; and that, therefore, they ought instantly to be abrogated.

We further believe and affirm — That all persons of color who possess the qualifications which are demanded of others, ought to be admitted forthwith to the enjoyment of the same privileges, and the exercise of the same prerogatives, as others; and that the paths of preferment, of wealth, and of intelligence, should be opened as widely to them as to persons of a white complexion.

We maintain that no compensation should be given to the planters emancipating the slaves —

Because it would be a surrender of the great fundamental principle that man cannot hold property in man;

Because SLAVERY IS A CRIME, AND THEREFORE IS NOT AN ARTICLE TO BE SOLD;

Because the holders of slaves are not the just proprietors of what they claim; freeing the slaves is not depriving them of property, but restoring it to its rightful owners; it is not wronging the master, but righting the slave — restoring him to himself;

Because immediate and general emancipation would only destroy nominal, not real property; it would not amputate or break a bone of the slaves; but, by infusing motives into their breasts, would make them doubly valuable to the masters as free laborers; and

Because, if compensation is to be given at all, it should be given to the outraged and guiltless slaves, and not to those who have plundered and abused them.

We regard as delusive, cruel, and dangerous, any scheme of expatriation which pretends to aid, either directly or indirectly, in the emancipation of the slaves, or to be a substitute for the immediate and total abolition of slavery.

We fully and unanimously recognize the sovereignty of each State to legislate exclusively on the subject of the slavery which is tolerated within its limits; we conclude that Congress, *under the present national compact*, has no right to interfere with any Slave States in relation to this momentous subject.

But we maintain that Congress has a right, and is solemnly bound, to suppress the domestic slave-trade between the several States, and to abolish slavery in those portions of our territory which the Constitution has placed under its exclusive jurisdiction.

We also maintain that there are, at the present time, the highest obligations resting upon the people of the free States to remove slavery by moral and political action, as prescribed in the Constitution of the United States. They are now living under a pledge of their tremendous physical force, to fasten the galling fetters of tyranny upon the limbs of millions in the Southern States; they are liable to be called at any moment to suppress a general insurrection of slaves; they authorize the slave-owner to vote for three-fifths of his slaves as property, and thus enable him to perpetuate his oppression; they support a standing army at the South for its protection; and they seize the slave who has escaped into their territories, and send him back to be tortured by an enraged master or a brutal driver. This relation to slavery is criminal and full of danger; IT MUST BE BROKEN UP.

These are our views and principles — these our designs and measures. With entire confidence in the overruling justice of God, we plant ourselves upon the Declaration of our Independence and the truths of Divine Revelation, as upon the Everlasting Rock.

We shall organize Anti-Slavery Societies, if possible, in every city, town, and village in our land.

We shall send forth agents to lift up the voice of remonstrance, of warning, of entreaty, and rebuke.

We shall circulate, unsparingly and extensively, anti-slavery tracts and periodicals.

We shall enlist the pulpit and the press in the cause of the suffering and the dumb.

We shall aim at a purification of the churches from all participation in the guilt of slavery.

We shall encourage the labor of freemen rather than that of slaves, by giving a preference to their productions; and

We shall spare no exertions nor means to bring the whole nation to speedy repentance.

Our trust for victory is solely in God. *We* may be personally defeated, but our principles, never. TRUTH, JUSTICE, REASON, HUMANITY, must and will gloriously triumph. Already a host is coming up to the help of the Lord against the mighty, and the prospect before us is full of encouragement.

Submitting this DECLARATION to the candid examination of the people of this country, and of the friends of liberty throughout the world, we hereby affix our signatures to it; pledging ourselves that, under the guidance and by the help of Almighty God, we will do all that in us lies, consistently with this Declaration of our principles, to overthrow the most execrable system of slavery that has ever been witnessed upon earth — to deliver our land from its deadliest curse — to wipe out the foulest stain which rests upon our national escutcheon — and to secure to the colored population of the United States all the rights and privileges which belong to them as men and as Americans — come what may to our persons, our interests, or our reputation — whether we live to witness the triumph of LIBERTY, JUSTICE, and HUMANITY, or perish untimely as martyrs in this great, benevolent, and holy cause.

Done at Philadelphia, the 6th day of December, A.D. 1833.

Maine.
DAVID THURSTON,
NATHAN WINSLOW,
JOSEPH SOUTHWICK,
JAMES FREDERIC OTIS,
ISAAC WINSLOW.

New Hampshire.
DAVID CAMPBELL.

Vermont.
ORSON S. MURRAY.

Massachusetts.
DANIEL S. SOUTHMAYD,
EFFINGHAM I. CAPRON,
JOSHUA COFFIN,
AMOS S. PHELPS,
JOHN G. WHITTIER,
HORACE P. WAKEFIELD,
JAMES G. BARBADOES,
DAVID T. KIMBALL, JR.,
DANIEL E. JEWETT,
JOHN R. CAMBELL,
NATHANIEL SOUTHARD,
ARNOLD BUFFUM,
WILLIAM L. GARRISON.

Rhode Island.
JOHN PRENTICE,
GEORGE W. BENSON,
RAY POTTER.

Connecticut
SAMUEL J. MAY,
ALPHEUS KINGSLEY,
EDWIN A. STILLMAN,

SIMEON S. JOCELYN,
ROBERT B. HALL.

New York.
BERIAH GREEN, JR.,
LEWIS TAPPAN,
JOHN RANKIN,
WILLIAM GREEN, JR.,
ABRAM L. COX,
WILLIAM GOODELL
ELIZUR WRIGHT, JR.,
CHARLES W. DENISON,
JOHN FROST.

New Jersey.
JOHNATHAN PARKHURST,
CHALKLEY GILLINGHAM,
JOHN M'CULLOUGH,
JAMES WHITE.

Pennsylvania.
EVAN LEWIS,
EDWIN A. ATLEE,
ROBERT PURVIS,
JAS M'CRUMMILL,
THOMAS SHIPLEY,
BARTH'W FUSSELL,
DAVID JONES,
ENOCH MACK,
J.M. M'KIM,
AARON VICKERS,
JAMES LOUGHEAD,
EDWIN P. ATLEE,
THOMAS WHITSON,

JOHN R. SLEEPER,   JOHN M. STERLING,
JOHN SHARP, JR.,   MILTON SUTLIFF,
JAMES MOTT.   LEVI SUTLIFF.
Ohio.

Constitution of the Society

FORMED IN PHILADELPHIA, DECEMBER 4TH, 1833

WHEREAS the Most High God "hath made of one blood all nations of men to dwell on all the face of the earth," and hath commanded them to love their neighbors as themselves; and whereas, our National existence is based upon this principle, as recognized in the Declaration of Independence, "that all mankind are created equal, and that they are endowed by their creator with certain inalienable rights, among which are life, liberty, and pursuit of happiness;" and whereas, after the lapse of nearly sixty years, since the faith and honor of the American people were pledged to this avowal, before Almighty God and the World, nearly one-sixth part of the nation are held in bondage by their fellow-citizens; and whereas, Slavery is contrary to the principles of natural justice, of our republican form of government, and of the Christian religion, and is destructive of the prosperity of the country, while it is endangering the peace, union, and liberties of the States; and whereas, we believe it is the duty and interest of the masters immediately to emancipate their slaves, and that no scheme of expatriation, either voluntary or by compulsion, can remove this great and increasing evil; and whereas, we believe that it is practicable, by appeals to the consciences, hearts, and interests of the people, to awaken a public sentiment throughout the nation that will be opposed to the continuance of Slavery at any part of the Republic, and by effecting the speedy abolition of Slavery, prevent a general convulsion; and whereas, we believe we owe it to the oppressed, to our fellow-citizens who hold slaves, to our whole country, to posterity, and to God, to do all that is lawfully in our power to bring about the extinction of Slavery, we do hereby agree, with a prayerful reliance on the Divine aid, to form ourselves into a Society, to be governed by the following Constitution:—

ARTICLE I.

This Society shall be called the AMERICAN ANTI-SLAVERY SOCIETY.

ARTICLE II.

The object of this Society is the entire abolition of Slavery in the United States. It shall aim to convince all our fellow citizens, by arguments addressed to their understandings and consciences, that Slaveholding is a heinous crime in the sight of God, and that the duty, safety, and best interests of all concerned, require its *immediate abandonment*, without expatriation. The Society will also endeavor, in a constitutional way, to influence Congress to put an end to the domestic Slave trade, and to abolish Slavery in all those portions of our common country which come under its control, especially in the District of Columbia,—and likewise to prevent the extension of it to any State that may be hereafter admitted to the Union.

ARTICLE III.

This Society shall aim to elevate the character and condition of the people of color, by encouraging their intellectual, moral, and religious improvement, and by removing public prejudice, that thus they may, according to their intellectual and moral worth, share an equality with the whites, of civil and religious privileges; but this

Society will never, in any way, countenance the oppressed in vindicating their rights by resorting to physical force.

ARTICLE IV.

Any person who consents to the principles of this constitution, who contributes to the funds of this Society, and is not a Slaveholder, may be a member of this Society, and shall be entitled to vote at the meetings.

ARTICLE V.

The officers of this Society shall be a President, Vice-Presidents, a Recording Secretary, Corresponding Secretaries, a Treasurer, and an Executive Committee of not less than five nor more than twelve members.

ARTICLE VI.

The Executive Committee shall have power to enact their own by-laws, fill any vacancy in their body and in the offices of Secretary and Treasurer, employ agents, determine what compensation shall be paid to agents, and to the Corresponding Secretaries, direct the Treasurer in the application of all moneys, and call special meetings of the Society. They shall make arrangements for all meetings of the Society, make an annual written report of their doings, the expenditures and funds of the Society, and shall hold stated meetings, and adopt the most energetic measures in their power to advance the objects of the Society. They may, if they shall see fit, appoint a Board of Assistant Managers, composed of not less than three nor more than seven persons residing in New York City or its vicinity, whose duty it shall be to render such assistance to the Committee in conducting the affairs of the Society as the exigencies of the cause may require. To this Board they may from time to time confide such of their own powers as they may deem necessary to the efficient conduct of the Society's business. The Board shall keep a record of its proceedings, and furnish a copy of the same for the information of the Committee, as often as may be required.

ARTICLE VII.

The President shall preside at all meetings of the Society, or, in his absence, one of the Vice-Presidents, or, in their absence, a President *pro tem.* The Corresponding Secretaries shall conduct the correspondence of the Society. The Recording Secretary shall notify all meetings of the Society, and of the Executive Committee, and shall keep records of the same in separate books. The Treasurer shall collect the subscriptions, make payments at the direction of the Executive Committee, and present a written and audited account to accompany the annual report.

ARTICLE VIII.

The Annual Meeting of the Society shall be held each year at such time and place as the Executive Committee may direct, and when the accounts of the Treasurer shall be presented, the annual report read, appropriate addresses delivered, the officers chosen, and such other business transacted as shall be deemed expedient.

ARTICLE IX.

Any Anti-Slavery Society or Association, founded on the same principles, may become auxiliary to this Society. The officers of each Auxiliary Society shall be *ex officio* members of the Parent Institution, and shall be entitled to deliberate and vote in the transactions of its concerns.

ARTICLE X.

This Constitution may be amended, at any annual meeting of the Society, by a vote of two-thirds of the members present, provided the amendments proposed have been previously submitted, in writing, to the Executive Committee.

An Appeal on Behalf of the Oberlin Institute in Aid of the Abolition of Slavery in the United States of America

Theodore Weld took great pride in his association with the "Oberlin Institute" and the school's forthright advocacy against slavery. In 1839, in an effort to help Oberlin raise money, he wrote an appeal that eventually brought in nearly thirty thousand dollars for the school. Excerpts from Weld's "Appeal" follow:

The Institution on behalf of which the present application is made, is situated in the northern part of Ohio, near the head of the great valley of the Mississippi. It has a Charter with University privileges, and originated in the following circumstances:-

The Students at Lane Seminary, (a Theological College,) at Cincinnati, in Ohio, in 1834, having become interested in the Abolition controversy, held a protracted discussion among themselves on the subject, and after three days solemn debate, came to a resolution condemnatory of Slavery as incompatible with the spirit and precepts of Christianity. They formed an Abolition Society, and took means to acquaint themselves more thoroughly with the real nature of the slave system, and of the obligations which devolved on them in relation to it. These measures gave great offense to the Heads of the College, who authoritatively interposed to prevent any further discussion of the subject. The young men were prohibited from making it the topic of conversation, "on ordinary occasions and elsewhere," and on remonstrance, were given to understand that their continuance in the Seminary, was dependent on their yielding an unqualified submission to this injunction. The heads of College were positive, and it was left for the students either to sacrifice their duty to God and remain; or to maintain it and leave. They nobly chose the latter, and the result was that about forty of the most pious and talented, were thus compelled to quit Lane Seminary. Such a body of young men who so conscientiously maintained their principles at the expense of their prospects in life, was hailed with joy by the abolitionists, for it at once supplied them with a number of most zealous advocates.

It now became necessary to establish an Institution, in which the rights of conscience and of the Christian religion should be maintained, and in which the coloured person could be taught, and where they would be in all respects treated as a man and a brother.

A tract of 500 acres, in the midst of a forest, was obtained; and thither this noble band repaired, and commenced cutting down the timber and clearing the land; and so ardent were they in this cause, that they freely submitted to all the hardships incident to these new circumstances, and persevered in their labour during the Winter season of 1834 and 1835.

Thus commenced the present Institution, which consists of a brick building 111 feet long, and 42 feet wide; containing ninety-two rooms, including a Hall and a Library, with nine other buildings chiefly of wood, and a barn. There are about 200 acres of land partially cleared, and brought into cultivation. A practical farmer superintends the cultivation; the labour is performed by the Students for the support, maintenance, and general good of the Institution.

In all its features this Institution is opposed to Slavery; and is a practical and standing exhibition of the great doctrine of immediate emancipation, producing its legitimate and beneficent results; youth are admitted to all its privileges, without regard to colour, or nation, and there is a department for the instruction of females. It is thoroughly evangelical in its spirit and character, is free from all sectarian partialities, discards the prejudice of caste in its various and disgraceful forms, and has already become a terror to the slave-holder, and a shield and a solace to the victim of the white man's tyranny. By uniting the youth of all colours in the same course of Academical training, it furnishes a practical method of elevating the African race, of abolishing the tyranny of caste, and of opening an effectual door through which the black and the free-coloured man may attain the rights of citizenship, and the blessings of a quiet and protected home. It compromises a Preparatory, Collegiate, and Theological department, and at present, numbers above 450 Students with twenty-six Professors and Teachers. This Institution is the great nursery of teachers for the coloured people in the United States and Canada, in the latter of which are 10,000 refugees from American bondage. It is an admirable school for the training of Anti-Slavery Lecturers and Preachers,— a class of men long demanded and now called for more urgently than ever by the state of the Abolition controversy, and the increasing horrors of the American slave system. Several of the Students have already entered on this arduous and self-denying field of labour, others are looking forward to the same holy calling. Twelve have gone to the West Indies as missionaries and teachers of the emancipated negroes, ten are on their way to the oppressed Aborigines in the Western parts of America, and twenty are engaged among the coloured fugitives in Canada.

During the annual vacations, the students and professors have traversed extensively the States of Ohio, Michigan, Indiana, and the Western parts of New York and Pennsylvania. Wherever they have gone, drooping liberty has revived and gained strength.

With the noble exception of the Oneida Institute in the State of New York, which in the midst of persecution has stood erect and pre-eminently true to the slave, mighty in its free testimony and terrible to the oppressor, the Institution of Oberlin is the only one in the United States in which the black and coloured student finds a home, where he is fully and joyfully regarded as a man and a brother.

The stand which has been taken at Oberlin against Slavery, and the prejudice respecting colour, has excited not only the bitter hostility of the upholders of Slavery, but also of a large proportion of the professing church. Another cause of offense is, that at this Institution a plan of manual daily labour is adopted, shared in alike by the white as well as the coloured man. The founders of this Institution consider this plan most important to the health, industry, energetic habits, independence of character, good morals, and economy of the students...

The necessities of the Institution are now so pressing, that its operations must inevitably cease, if effectual relief be not speedily afforded. The Professors, their families, and the Students, have often been reduced to such straits, even for their daily food, that from week to week they have not known from whence the next providential supply would come. Thus far, through the kind care of Him whose eyes are over all his works, when to human view the last resource was cut off, and no earthly alternative remained, their daily wants have been supplied, and their hearts strengthened, to wait in the patience of hope, and to look to God for a like supply on the morrow...

JOHN KEEP and WILLIAM DAVIS, are now in this country, for the purpose of bringing the claims of the Institution before the benevolent, to whose confidence, prayers, sympathies, and benefactions they are affectionately commended in a document, signed by —

ARTHUR TAPPAN, LA ROY SUNDERLAND, JAMES G. BIRNEY, JOHN G. WHITTIER, JAMES FORTEN, JOSEPH SOUTHWICK, THANKFUL SOUTHWICK, ELLIS GREY LORING, CHARLES FOLLEN, HENRY B. STANTON, SAMUEL J. MAY, WILLIAM L. GARRISON, HENRY GREW, JAMES C. FULLER, ANGELINA D. WELD, SARAH M. GRIMKE, THEODORE D. WELD, JAMES MCCUNE SMITH, LEWIS TAPPAN, JOSHUA LEAVITT, GERRIT SMITH, CHARLES W. GARDNER, SAMUEL E. CORNISH, DAVID LEE CHILD, MARIA W. CHAPMAN, MARY S. PARKER, WENDELL PHILLIPS, HENRY G. CHAPMAN, AMASA WALKER, FRAN-

CIS JACKSON, ROBERT PURVIS, ALVAN STEWART, PETER WILLIAMS, JOSHUA R. GIDDINGS, E. C. DELAVAN...

On a review of the whole circumstances of the Oberlin Institute, its origin, history, and tendency, the conviction must be deeply felt, that it is pre-eminently adapted to compass the benevolent and Christian object of its founders; that it is friendly alike to the elevation of an oppressed people, and the emancipation of the American churches from their vassalage to the spirit of this world, and that it is strongly commended to the friends of the slave and the coloured free man, and, indeed, to all who are concerned for the welfare of their species, and the purity of the church of Christ.

Appendix F: Officers of the Society, 1833–1840

Name	Residence(s)	Office(s)	Date(s)
Aaron, Samuel		Vice-President	1839–40
Adair, William A.	Pittsburgh, PA	Manager	1837–40
Adams, E. M.	NY	Manager	1836–37
Adams, William	Pawtucket, RI	Manager	1837–40
Aldis, Asa	St. Albans, VT	Manager	1835–37
Allan, William T.	Huntsville, AL	Manager	1834–37
Allen, William	Buffalo, NY	Manager	1833–37
Andrews, Samuel C.	OH	Vice-President	1838–39
Appleton, James	Portland, ME	Vice-President	1839–40
Arthur, William	Williston, VT	Manager	1833–36
Atlee, Edwin, P.	Philadelphia, PA	Vice-President	1833–36
		Manager	1833–37
Bailey, Kiah	Hardwich, VT	Manager	1837–39
Ballard, James	Bennington, VT	Vice-President	1834–35
		Manager	1835–37
Bancroft, William W.	Granville, OH	Manager	1836–40
Barbadoes, James G.	Boston, MA	Manager	1833–35
	RI	Manager	1835–36
Barber, Edward	Middlebury, VT	Manager	1838–40
Barnaby, James	W. Harwich, MA	Vice-President	1833–40
Bascom, Elisha	Shoreham, VT	Manager	1833–37
Bassett, William	Boston, MA	Manager	1839–40
Bates, Merrit	Swanton, VT	Manager	1839–40
Beecher, Edward	Jacksonville, IL	Manager	1838–40
Beman, Jehiel C.	CT	Manager	1837–39
Benedict, Seth W.	New York, NY	Manager	1839–40
Benson, George	Brooklyn, CT	Vice-President	1834–35
Benson, George W.	Providence, RI	Manager	1833–40
	Brooklyn, CT		1837–40
Benton, Andrew	St. Louis, MO	Manager	1834–46
Birchard, Matthew W.	VT	Vice-President	1833–35
Birney, James G.	KY	Manager	1835–36
	KY	Vice-President	1835–36

189

Name	Residence(s)	Office(s)	Date(s)
	Cincinnati, OH	Vice-President	1836–38
	New York, NY	Exec. Comm.	1838–40
	New York, NY	Corres. Secretary	1838–40
Blain, John	Pawtucket, RI	Vice-President	1834–37
Blaisdell, James, J.	Lebanon, NH	Manager	1839–40
Blaisdell, Timothy K.	Haverhill, NH	Manager	1838–39
Bleeker, Leonard	New York, NY	Vice-President	1834–35
Bourne, George	NY	Manager	1833–39
Brainerd, Lawrence	St. Albans, VT	Manager	1833–39
Brewster, Henry	LeRoy, NY	Manager	1837–40
Brown, David P.	Philadelphia, PA	Vice-President	1834–35
Brown, James C.	Putnam, OH	Manager	1838–39
Brown, Moses	Providence, RI	Vice-President	1833–34
Bruce, Robert	Pittsburgh, PA	Vice-President	1833–35
Buchanan, James M.	IL	Manager	1837–40
Buffum, Arnold	MA	Manager	1833–37
	Philadelphia, PA	Manager	1835–37
		Vice-President	1834–36
Buffum, William	Providence, RI	Manager	1837–40
Bush, Oren N.	Rochester, NY	Manager	1839–40
Butler, J.	VT	Manager	1833–34
Buzby, Samuel	DE	Manager	1839–40
Cady, Josiah	Providence, RI	Manager	1833–37
		Vice-President	1837–38
Cambell, Amos	Acworth, NH	Manager	1833–37
Camp, David M.	Swanton, VT	Manager	1837–40
Capron, Effingham L.	Uxbridge, MA	Vice-President	1833–36
Carey, George	Cincinnati, OH	Manager	1837–40
Cassey, Joseph	Philadelphia, PA	Manager	1834–37
Chaplin, William L.	Farmington, NY	Manager	1839–40
Cheever, George B.	Salem, MA	Manager	1835–37
Child, David L.	Boston, MA	Manager	1833–40
Clark, John G.	S. Kingston, RI	Manager	1836–40
Clarke, Augustine	Danville, VT	Manager	1833–36
Clarke, Peleg C.	Coventry, RI	Vice-President	1838–40
Cleveland, John P.	Detroit, MI	Manager	1837–40
Coates, Lindley	Lancaster Co., PA	Manger	1833–40
Coffin, Joshua	Tyngsborough, PA	Manager	1834–37
Collins, Amos M.	Hartford, CT	Manager	1835–37
Cook, James	NJ	Manager	1836–40
Copeland, Melvin	Hartford, CT	Manager	1837–39
Cornish, Samuel E.		Manager	1834–37
Cowles, Henry	Oberlin, OH	Manager	1834–36
Cowles, Horace	Farmington, CT	Manager	1833–40
Cox, Abraham	New York, NY	Rec. Secretary	1833–36
Cox, Samuel H.	New York, NY	Corres. Secretary	1834–35
		Exec. Comm.	1834–40
Crandall, Phineas	Fall River, MA	Manager	1834–36 1839–40
Crothers, Samuel	Greenfield, OH	Vice-President	1833–37
Cushing, Henry	Providence, RI	Vice-President	1833–37

Name	Residence(s)	Office(s)	Date(s)
Cushman, John P.	Troy, NY	Manager	1835–37
Cutler, Calvin	Windham, NH	Vice-President	1833–35
		Manager	1835–40
Davis, Gustavus F.	Hartford, CT	Vice-President	1834–36
Dean, James E.	New Haven, CT	Manager	1835–37
Delevan, Edward C.	Ballston Ctre, NY	Manager	1837–39
Denison, Charles W.	NY	Manager	1833–37
			1839–40
	DE	Manager	1837–39
Dickey, James H.	IL	Manager	1836–37
			1839–40
Dickinson, James T.	Durham, CT	Manager	1833–34
Dickson, John	W. Bloomfield, NY	Manager	1835–37
Dimond, Isaac M.	New York, NY	Manager	1833–34
Dodge, William B.	Salem, MA	Manager	1834–37
Dole, Ebenezer	Hallowell, ME	Vice-President	1833–35
Dole, S. F.	Middletown, CT	Manager	1833–35
Donald, Samuel	IN	Manager	1839–40
Donaldson, William	Cincinnati, OH	Manager	1838–40
Dougherty, Alexander M.	Newark, NJ	Manager	1838–40
Dowling, John	Newport, RI	Vice-President	1834–35
Dowling, Thomas	Catskill, NY	Manager	1835–39
Drury, Asa	Granville, OH	Manager	1835–39
Duffield, George	Detroit, MI	Vice-President	1834–35
Dunbar, Duncan	New York, NY	Exec. Comm.	1837–40
Eames, James H.	Providence, RI	Vice-President	1836–40
Earle, Thomas	Philadelphia, PA	Manager	1839–40
Elles, Oliver J.	W. Cornwall, VT	Manager	1835–37
			1837–39
Esten, George W.	Boonton, NJ	Manager	1837–39
Farmer, John	Concord, NH	Manager	1837–39
Farnsworth, Amos	Groton, MA	Manager	1837–40
Farnsworth, Benjamin	Providence, RI	Manager	1835–36
Ferris, Benjamin	Wilmington, DE	Vice-President	1833–34
Ferris, Zeba	DE	Vice-President	1838–40
Fessenden, Samuel	Portland, ME	Vice-President	1833–39
		Manager	1839–40
Field, Issac	Iowa Territory	Manager	1839–40
Field, Nathaniel	Jeffersonville, IN	Vice-President	1835–39
Fitch, Eleazer T.	New Haven, CT	Vice-President	1833–35
Fletcher, Leonard	Chester Co., PA	Manager	1838–40
Follen, Charles	Cambridge, MA	Vice-President	1834–35
			1836–37
		Exec. Comm.	1837–38
Forten, James, Sr.	Philadelphia, PA	Vice-President	1834–35
		Manager	1835–40
Frost, Daniel, Jr.	NY	Manager	1837–39
Frost, John	Whitesborough, NY	Vice-President	1834–35
Fuller, James C.	Skeneateles, NY	Manager	1839–40
Fussell, Bartholomew	Kennet, PA	Manager	1833–37
Gale, George W.	Galesburgh, IL	Manager	1837–40

Name	*Residence(s)*	*Office(s)*	*Date(s)*
Galusha, Elon	Perry, NY	Manager	1837–40
Gardiner, Charles W.	Philadelphia, PA	Manager	1839–40
Garrison, William	Boston, MA	Corres. Secretary	1833–34
		Manager	1834–40
Gayley, Samuel M.	Wilmington, DE	Manager	1838–40
Gazzam, J. P.	Pittsburgh, PA	Manager	1837–40
Gibbons, Henry	Wilmington, DE	Manager	1839–40
Gibbons, James S.	Philadelphia, PA	Manager	1834–35
	New York, NY	Exec. Comm.	1839–40
Gibbons, William	Wilmington, DE	Vice-President	1834–37
Gilleland, James	Red Oak, OH	Manager	1839–40
Goodell, William	NY	Manager	1833–39
Graham, J. T.	PA	Manager	1836–37
Graves, Frederick W.	Alton, IL	Manager	1838–39
Green, Beriah	Whitesboro, NY	Vice-President	1833–37
		Manager	1837–40
Green, William, Jr.	New York, NY	Treasurer	1833–36
		Exec. Comm.	1834–35
		Manager	1835–37
Greene, Henry K.	Charlestown, MA	Vice-President	1834–35
Greenleaf, Patrick H.	Portland, ME	Manager	1833–36
Grimes, John		Manager	1839–40
Grosvenor, Cyrus P.		Vice-President	1834–35
		Manager	1839–40
Hale, Josiah W.	Brandon, VT	Manager	1839–40
Halsey, Job F.	Allegheny City, PA	Manager	1833–35
	MO	Manager	1835–37
Harrison, Marcus	Decatur, MI	Manager	1838–40
Hastings, Charles	Detroit, MI	Manager	1839–40
Hastings, Erotas P.	Detroit, MI	Vice-President	1833–36
		Manager	1836–37
Hawley, Orestes K.	Austinburgh, OH	Manager	1833–37
Higgins, James W.	Jersey City, NJ	Manager	1839–40
Hill, Moses	ME	Manager	1839–40
Himes, Stephen D.	Sandy Hill, NY	Manager	1833–36
Hoit, Daniel	Sandwich, NH	Manager	1836–40
Hollister, David S.	Wisconsin, Territory	Manager	1837–40
Howells, Henry C.	Zanesville, OH	Manager	1833–37
Hussey, Samuel F.	Portland, ME	Vice-President	1833–35
Hutchins, Samuel	Norridgework, ME	Manager	1839–40
Ide, Jacob	W. Medway, MA	Manager	1833–37
Ives, Eli	New Haven, CT	Vice-President	1833–38
Jackson, Francis	Boston, MA	Vice-President	1837–40
Jackson, William	Philadelphia, PA	Vice-President	1833–36
Janes, D. P.	New London, CT	Manager	1839–40
Janney, Joseph	Washington, DC	Vice-President	1834–38
Jay, William	Bedford, NY	Corres. Secretary	1835–38
		Exec. Comm.	1836–37
Jenckes, John	Providence, PA	Manager	1836–37
Jenkins, Huron	DE	Manager	1838–40
Jennings, Jonathan	DE	Manager	1837–38

Name	Residence(s)	Office(s)	Date(s)
Jessup, William	Montrose, PA	Manager	1838–40
Jocelyn, Simeon S.	New Haven, CT	Vice-President	1834–35
		Manager	1835–40
		Exec. Comm.	1835–40
Johnson, Nathan	New Bedford, MA	Manager	1839–40
Johnson, Nathaniel E.	New York, NY	Manager	1839–40
Jones, William R.	MD	Vice-President	1834–35
Kanouse, Peter	Boontoon, NJ	Manager	1835–38
Kellogg, Spenser	Utica, NJ	Vice-President	1834–35
Kennedy, James M.	KY	Vice-President	1836–37
Kent, George	Concord, NH	Vice-President	1837–40
Kimball, David T.	Ipswich, MA	Manager	1833–37
Kimball, George	IL	Manager	1837–38
King, Leicester	Warren, OH	Manager	1837–39
		Vice-President	1839–40
Kingsley, Alpeus	Norwich, OH	Manager	1833–37
Kirkland, William	MI	Manager	1837–40
Kittridge, Ingalls	Beverly, MA	Manager	1834–37
Knapp, Chauncey, L.	Montpelier, VT	Manager	1837–40
Knapp, Isaac	Boston, MA	Manager	1833–37
Lansing, Dirck C.	New York, NY	Vice-President	1833–35
Leavitt, Harvey F.	Vergennes, VT	Manager	1837–40
Leavitt, Joshua	New York, NY	Manager	1833–37
		Exec. Comm.	1834–40
		Rec. Secretary	1838–40
LeMoyne, Francis J.	Washington, PA	Manager	1837–40
Lewis, Evan	Philadelphia, PA	Vice-President	1833–35
Lines, Charles B.	New Haven, CT	Manager	1836–37
Lord, Nathan	Hanover, NH	Manager	1833–34
Loring, Ellis G.	Boston, MA	Manager	1833–40
Lovejoy, Owen	Princeton, IL	Manager	1838–40
Luca, Alexander, C.	New Haven, CT	Manager	1839–40
Ludlow, Henry G.	New York, NY	Manager	1834–37
Ludlow, James G.	Cincinnati, OH	Manager	1837–40
Lundy, Benjamin	PA	Manager	1833–34
			1837–38
	IL	Manager	1838–40
	PA	Vice-President	1834–35
Lyman, Huntington	New Orleans, LA	Manager	1834–35
Mack, Enoch	Dover, NH	Manager	1833–37
Mahan, Asa	OH	Vice-President	1834–35
Marriott, Charles	Athens, NY	Manager	1834–38
May, Samuel J.	S Scituate, MA	Vice-President	1833–35
		Manager	1835–40
McCrummell, James	Philadelphia, PA	Manager	1833–37
Middleton, Jonathan	New York, NY	Manager	1835–37
Miller, Jonathan P.	Montpelier, VT	Manager	1834–37
Milligan, James	Rygate, VT	Manager	1834–37
Monthieth, John	Elyria, OH	Manager	1833–37
Morgan, John	Cincinnati, OH	Vice-President	1834–35
Morrow, James	Jefferson Co., IN	Vice-President	1839–40

Name	Residence(s)	Office(s)	Date(s)
Mott, James	Philadelphia, PA	Vice-President	1834–35
Munsell, Luke	KY	Manager	1835–37
	Marion Co., IN	Manager	1837–40
Murray, Orson S.	Orwell, VT	Manager	1834–40
Neall, Daniel, Jr.	Philadelphia, PA	Manager	1838–40
Needles, John	Baltimore, MD	Vice-President	1838–40
Nelson, David	Quincy, IL	Vice-President	1836–40
Nevin, John W.	Allegheny Co., PA	Manager	1835–37
Newcomb, Harvey	Pittsburgh, PA	Manager	1836–37
Newton, Calvin	Thomaston, ME	Manager	1833–40
Norton, John T.	Farmington, CT	Vice-President	1838–40
Oakes, William	Ipswich, MA	Manager	1834–37
Osgood, Samuel	Springfield, MA	Manager	1837–40
Parkhurst, Jonathan	Essex Co., NJ	Manager	1833–40
Parrish, Isaac	Philadelphia, PA	Manager	1834–37
Peloubet, Chabrier	Bloomfield, NJ	Manager	1839–40
Pennock, Abraham L.	Haverford, PA	Vice-President	1835–40
Perkins, Jared	Nashua, NH	Manager	1839–40
Perry, Gardiner B.	E. Bradford, MA	Vice-President	1834–35
Perry, John M.	Mendon, MA	Manager	1833–36
Pettengill, Moses	Newburyport, MA	Manager	1834–37
Phelps, Amos A.	Boston, MA	Manager	1834–35
		Vice-President	1834–35
		Exec. Comm.	1836–38
		Rec. Secretary	1836–40
Phillips, Wendell	Boston, MA	Manager	1838–40
Phoenix, Samuel F.	Wisconsin, Territory	Manager	1835–37
Pomeroy, Swan L.	Bangor, ME	Vice-President	1834–35
		Manager	1836–39
Pond, Samuel	Bucksport, ME	Manager	1837–40
Porter, Arthur L.	Detroit, MI	Manager	1837–40
Porter, Benjamin	Marblehead, MA	Manager	1834–37
Potter, Anson	Cranston, RI	Vice-President	1834–35
Potter, Ray	Pawtucket, RI	Manager	1833–37
Prentice, John	Providence, RI	Manager	1833–37
Preston, Jonas	PA	Vice-President	1833–34
Purvis, Robert	Philadelphia, PA	Manager	1833–40
Quincy, Edmund	Dedham, MA	Manager	1838–40
Rand, Asa	Lowell, MA	Vice-President	1833–35
Randall, Daniel B.	Hallowell, ME	Manager	1839–40
Rankin, John	New York, NY	Vice-President	1833–35
		Exec. Comm.	1834–40
		Treasurer	1836–40
Rankin, John	Ripley, OH	Manager	1835–38
			1839–40
Reed, George B.	Deep River, CT	Manager	1836–37
			1839–40
Reid, William W.	Rochester, NY	Manager	1834–37
Roberts, Daniel	Manchester, VT	Manager	1839–40
Robinson, Rowland T.	N. Ferrisburg, VT	Vice-President	1835–40
Rockwell, Reuben	Colebrook, CT	Manager	1836–37

Name	Residence(s)	Office(s)	Date(s)
Rogers, Nathaniel P.	Concord, NH	Manager	1837–40
Root, David	Dover, NH	Manager	1835–40
Rush, Christopher	New York, NY	Manager	1834–37
Russell, Philemon R.	W. Boylston, MA	Manager	1833–37
Sailer, John	Michigan City, IN	Manager	1837–40
Sawyer, Leicester A.	New Haven, CT	Manager	1837–40
Scott, James	Providence, RI	Manager	1834–36
Scott, Orange	Lowell, MA	Manager	1838–40
Sewall, Charles	MA	Manager	1834–37
Sewall, Samuel	Boston, MA	Manager	1833–37
Shadd, Abraham	Chester Co., PA	Manager	1833–37
Sharp, George	Stratford, CT	Manager	1836–37
Shepard, George B.	Hallowell, ME	Manager	1833–37
			1838–40
Shipley, Thomas	Philadelphia, PA	Manager	1833–35
Sleeper, Reuben	Mountmorris, NY	Manager	1839–40
Smith, Gerrit	Peterboro, NY	Vice-President	1836–40
Smith, Israel	Bainbridge, NY	Manager	1835–36
Smith, James W.	NY	Vice-President	1834–35
Smith, Samuel	DE	Vice-President	1837–38
Smyth, William	Brunswick, ME	Manager	1835–37
Southmayd, Daniel S.	Lowell, MA	Manager	1833–34
Southwick, Edward	Augusta, ME	Manager	1839–40
Southwick, Joseph	ME	Vice-President	1833–35
Spaulding, Timothy	LaPorte Co., IN	Manager	1838–40
Spencer, Thomas	Salem, MA	Manager	1834–35
Stanton, Benjamin	Marlboro, OH	Manager	1837–40
Stanton, Henry B.	Cincinnati, OH	Manager	1834–38
	New York, NY	Corres. Secretary	1838–40
		Exec. Comm.	1838–40
Sterling, John M.	Cleveland, OH	Manager	1833–40
Stern, Nathaniel	PA	Manager	1837–40
Stewart, Alvan	Utica, NY	Vice-President	1834–35
		Manager	1837–40
Stewart, Robert	Ross Co., OH	Manager	1835–40
Stewart, William	IL	Manager	1837–39
Stocking, Samuel	NY	Vice-President	1834–35
Storrs, George	NH	Manager	1835–36
		Vice-President	1835–37
Storrs, Nathan	Milwaukee, WI	Manager	1839–40
Stow, Baron	Boston, MA	Vice-President	1834–36
Stuart, Robert	Detroit, MI	Vice-President	1839–40
Sunderland, LaRoy	MA	Manager	1833–36
	NY	Manager	1836–37
Sweet, Samuel N.	Adams, NY	Manager	1834–35
Tappan, Arthur	New York, NY	Manager	1833–37
		Exec. Comm.	1833–40
Tapping, Lewis	Iowa Territory	Manager	1839–40
Thatcher, Moses	N. Wrentham, MA	Manager	1833–37
Thomas, N. P.	Whippany, NY	Manager	1838–40
Thome, Arthur	Augusta, KY	Vice-President	1839–40

Name	Residence(s)	Office(s)	Date(s)
Thome, James A.	Augusta, KY	Vice-President	1839–40
Thompson, E. N.	CT	Manager	1835–36
Thurston, David	Winthrop, ME	Manager	1833–40
Turner, Asa, Jr.	Quincy, IL	Manager	1837–39
	IA	Manager	1839–40
Tuttle, Uriel	Torrington, CT	Manager	1839–40
Twining, William	Madison, IN	Manager	1837–40
Van Vliet, Peter	Iowa Territory	Vice-President	1839–40
Vashon, John B.	Pittsburgh, PA	Manager	1833–37
Vose, Richard H.	Augusta, ME	Manager	1833–37
Walker, Amasa	Boston, MA	Manager	1837–40
Ward, George	Plymouth, MA	Manager	1833–37
Warren, James	OH	Manager	1833–34
Watkins, William	Baltimore, MD	Vice-President	1834–35
Weeks, William R.	Newark, NJ	Vice-President	1834–39
Weld, Theodore	OH	Manager	1833–35
	New York, NY	Corres. Secretary	1839–40
Wells, Eleazer M.	Boston, MA	Vice-President	1833–35
Wells, Samuel	Whitesboro, NY	Manager	1839–40
Wells, Woolsey	Akron, OH	Manager	1834–36
Welton, Alonzo	NJ	Manager	1838–39
Wess, Samuel	PA	Manager	1839–40
Whipple, Charles K.	Boston, MA	Manager	1836–37
Whipple, George	Oberlin, OH	Manager	1839–40
Whitcomb, James	MI	Manager	1837–39
White, James	Essex Co., NJ	Manager	1833–40
Whitman, Isaac	Bangor, ME	Manager	1833–34
Whitson, Thomas	Coopersville, PA	Manager	1833–37
Whittier, John G.	Haverhill, MA	Manager	1833–38
		Manager	1838–40
Williams, Herbert	LaPorte Co., IN	Manager	1837–40
Williams, Peter	New York, NY	Manager	1833–36
		Exec. Comm.	1834–35
Williams, Samuel	Pittsburgh, PA	Manager	1833–37
Williams, Thomas	Providence, RI	Manager	1833–34
Wilson, J. R.	Coldenham, NJ	Vice-President	1834–35
Wilson, James	Keene, NH	Manager	1833–36
Winslow, Nathan	Portland, ME	Manager	1834–40
Worth, Edmund	Fisherville, NH	Manager	1839–40
Wright, Elizur, Jr.		Vice-President	1833–35
		Secretary	1833–39
Wright, Peter	Philadelphia, PA	Manager	1837–40
Wright, Richard S.	Schnectady, NY	Manager	1834–40
Wright, Theodore S.	New York, NY	Manager	1834–40
		Exec. Comm.	1834–40[32]

Notes

Introduction

1. Howard Zinn, *A People's History of the United States 1492–Present* (New York: Harper Perennial, 1995), 97.

2. James Brewer Stewart, *Abolitionist Politics and the Coming of the Civil War* (Amherst: University of Massachusetts Press, 2008), 8.

3. Lewis Tappan, *The Life of Arthur Tappan* (Cambridge: Hurd and Houghton, 1871; New York: Argo, 1970), 177. Citations are to the Argo edition.

4. William Lee Miller, *Arguing about Slavery* (New York: Alfred A. Knopf, 1996), 39.

5. Martin Duberman, *The Antislavery Vanguard: New Essays on the Abolitionists* (NJ: Princeton University Press, 1965), 422.

6. Ibid., 177.

7. Paul Goodman, *Of One Blood: Abolitionism and the Origins of Racial Equality* (Berkeley: University of California Press, 1998), 143.

8. Frederick Marryat, *A Diary in America: with Remarks on Its Institutions* (New York: Alfred A. Knopf, 1962), 282–289.

Chapter 1

1. Lewis Tappan and his brother Arthur were partners in a New York mercantile house, and after they began importing silk in 1826, they accumulated sizable wealth. In the 1840s, they founded a commercial credit rating company, and Lewis later established a mercantile agency that eventually became part of the Dun & Bradstreet Company. The brothers supported numerous reform movements but were particularly interested in abolitionism. They generously funded the American Anti-Slavery Society.

2. George Bourne, after arriving in America from England, became a minister in South River, Virginia, in 1814. In 1816 he issued *The Book and Slavery Irreconcilable*. The Presbyterian Church severely chastised Bourne for publishing this work. He left Virginia, moved to Pennsylvania, and joined the Dutch Reformed Church. Bourne continued to be a committed abolitionist until his death.

3. Joshua Levitt, after completing his undergraduate education at Yale, went on to graduate from the school's theological seminary. He became editor of the *Seaman's Friend*, an evangelical periodical, and then became a traveling agent for the American Temperance Society. In 1831 he was made editor of the *New York Evangelist* that regularly reported stories about the abolitionist movement. In 1837 the AASS hired him as editor of *The Emancipator*. Levitt was also instrumental in establishing the Liberty Party.

4. Simeon Jocelyn was a Yale graduate who helped Lewis Tappan plan a college for blacks that was never launched due to the hostility of New Haven citizens. A man of limited ability, Jocelyn was remembered for his abundant kindness. After serving on the executive committee of the AASS, he devoted the rest of his life to the ministry.

5. William Goodell was the editor of *The Emancipator* who, after helping to establish the AASS, became an agent of the national society in 1834. He later became actively involved with the estab-

lishment of the Liberty Party. Goodell wrote for and helped edit *The Genesis of Temperance, The Emancipator, The Friend of Man,* and *The Radical Abolitionist.* He was also involved with several other reforms, including temperance and antigambling. In 1834 he briefly served as an AASS agent.

6. Dwight L. Dumond, *Antislavery: The Crusade for Freedom in America* (Ann Arbor: University of Michigan Press, 1961), 175.

7. Louis Filler, *The Crusade Against Slavery, 1830–1860* (New York: Harper & Row, 1960), 175.

8. Jesse Macy, *The Anti-Slavery Crusade* (New Haven: Yale University Press, 1920), 31.

9. George M. Frederickson, *William Lloyd Garrison* (Englewood Cliffs, NJ: Prentice-Hall, 1968), 1–2.

10. Benjamin P. Thomas, *Theodore Weld: Crusader for Freedom* (New Brunswick, NJ: Rutgers University Press, 1950), 51.

11. Lucretia Mott was a feminist and abolitionist who helped establish the Pennsylvania Female Anti-Slavery Society. In 1840 she was denied the right to be recognized at the World Anti-Slavery Convention in London, which motivated her to be a champion of women's rights. Mott and Elizabeth Cady Stanton helped organize the Women's Rights Convention in Seneca Falls, New York, in 1848.

12. John L. Myers, "The Agency System of the Anti-Slavery Movement, 1832–1837, and its Antecedents in Other Benevolent and Reform Societies" (PhD dissertation, University of Michigan, 1961), 137.

13. Ibid.

14. Merton L. Dillon, *The Abolitionists: The Growth of a Dissenting Minority* (DeKalb: Northern Illinois University Press, 1974), 71.

15. Fergus M. Bordewich, *Bound for Canaan: The Underground Railroad and the War for the Soul of America* (New York: HarperCollins, 2005), 144.

16. Hermann R. Muelder, *Fighters for Freedom: A History of Anti-Slavery Activities of Men and Women Associated with Knox College* (New York: Columbia University Press, 1959), 33.

17. The abolitionist movement recommended not buying or using commodities produced from slave labor because to do so supported the institution of human bondage. In 1839, in Philadelphia, the American Free Produce Association was organized to help distribute free goods. Similar associations were also established in Ohio and Indiana.

18. Henry Mayer, *All on Fire: William Lloyd Garrison and the Abolition of Slavery* (New York: St. Martin's Press, 1998), 174–176.

19. Myers, "Agency System," 137.

20. Dumond, *Crusade for Freedom,* 178.

21. When Lovejoy was murdered in Illinois, it was considered an outrage by people across the Prairie State and by thousands of Americans throughout the North who had been indifferent to the antislavery cause. Lovejoy was born in Maine and moved to St. Louis, where he began publishing the *Observer,* a Presbyterian weekly. He faced hostility in Missouri from antiabolitionists and moved to Alton, where he continued to print his antislavery newspaper until his death. His brother Owen, Illinois' most famous Underground Railroad operator, was elected to Congress in the mid–1850s, where he was an outspoken antislavery advocate in the House of Representatives. The Executive Committee of the AASS put out a special issue of *Human Rights* detailing the events surrounding the martyr's death.

22. If William Lloyd Garrison was the antislavery movement's primary agitator and Theodore Dwight Weld was the movement's conscience, then poet John Greenleaf Whittier was the eloquent voice of abolitionism. Following his participation in the establishment of the AASS, Whittier briefly served in the Massachusetts legislature. In 1842 he ran for Congress on the Liberty Party ticket. He helped edit antislavery publications and was corresponding secretary of the *National Era* from 1847 to 1849. Whittier's powerful antislavery poems were an inspiration to the antislavery cause. He was an ineffective agent for the AASS, however, because his gentle nature did not lend itself to confrontational public presentations.

23. James Brewer Stewart, *Holy Warriors: The Abolitionists and American Slavery* (New York: Hill & Wang, 1976), 72–73.

24. Leonard L. Richards, *"Gentlemen of Property and Standing": Anti-Abolition Mobs in Jacksonian America* (New York: Oxford University Press, 1970), 77.

25. Ibid., 85.

26. Bertram Wyatt-Brown, *Lewis Tappan and His Evangelical War Against Slavery* (Cleveland, OH: Press of Case Western Reserve University, 1969), 114.

27. Dumond, *Crusade for Freedom*, 179.

28. Robert William Fogel, *Without Consent or Contract: The Rise and Fall of American Slavery* (New York: W. W. Norton, 1989), 264–265.

29. Hermann Muelder, 60.

30. Henry H. Simms, *Emotions at High Tide: Abolition as a Controversial Factor, 1830–1845* (Richmond: William Bird Press, 1960), 39.

31. John R. McKivigan, *The War against Proslavery Religion: Abolitionism and the Northern Churches, 1830–1865* (Ithaca, NY: Cornell University Press, 1984), 37–38.

32. Bernard Mandel, *Labor: Free and Slave, Workingmen and the Anti-Slavery Movement in the United States* (New York: Associated Authors, 1955), 69.

33. McKivigan, 52.

34. Frederick I. Kuhns, *The American Home Missionary Society in Relation to the Antislavery Controversy in the Old Northwest* (Ann Arbor, MI: Edwards Brothers, 1959), 1.

35. Ibid., 112–113.

36. Lawrence Lader, *The Bold Brahmins: New England's War Against Slavery, 1831–1863* (Westport, CT: Greenwood Press, 1973), 40.

37. John F. Hume, *Abolitionists* (New York: G. P. Putnam's Sons, 1905), 33.

38. Stewart, 46.

39. Edward Magdol, *The Antislavery Rank and File: A Social Profile of the Abolitionists' Constituency* (Westport, CT: Greenwood Press, 1986), 12.

40. Gilbert H. Barnes, *The Antislavery Impulse, 1830–1844* (New York: D. Appleton-Century, 1933), 98.

41. Duberman, 248.

42. Fogel, 257–258.

43. Gordon S. Wood, *Empire of Liberty: A History of the Early Republic, 1789–1815* (New York: Oxford University Press, 2009), 340.

44. Daniel Okrent, *Last Call: The Rise and Fall of Prohibition* (New York: Scribner, 2010), 8.

45. Wood, 339.

46. Donald Yacovone, *Samuel Joseph May and the Dilemmas of the Liberal Persuasion, 1797–1871* (Philadelphia: Temple University Press, 1991), 30–32.

47. Okrent, 42.

48. Ibid., 7.

49. See Myers, "Agency System," chapters 1–4.

50. In 1807 Great Britain outlawed the slave trade, but it did not stop English sea captains from continuing the practice of trading in slaves. In 1823 the first antislavery society was established in England with Great Britain's two most famous abolitionist advocates, Thomas Clarkson and William Wilberforce, among its members. Clarkson gathered volumes of information about the slave trade and spent most of his life agitating against slavery. Wilberforce was elected to Parliament in 1785 and spent years there fighting tirelessly against slavery and the slave trade. He died shortly before Parliament passed the Abolition Act of 1833.

51. Adam Hochschild, *Bury the Chains, Prophets and Rebels in the Fight to Free an Empire's Slaves* (New York: First Mariner, 2005), 347.

52. Ira Berlin, *The Making of African America* (New York: Viking Penguin, 2010), 98.

53. Dwight L. Dumond, *Antislavery Origins of the Civil War in the United States* (Ann Arbor: University of Michigan Press, 1959), 11.

54. Richards, 22.

55. Tappan, 129.

56. Duberman, 419.

57. Hume, 108.

58. Myers, "Agency System," 134.

59. Dumond, *Crusade for Freedom*, 172–173.

60. Dorothy Sterling, *We Are Your Sisters: Black Women in the Nineteenth Century* (New York: W. W. Norton, 1984), 113.

61. Beth Salerno, *Sister Societies: Women's Antislavery Organizations in Antebellum America* (DeKalb: Northern Illinois University Press, 2005), 26–28.

62. Ibid., 36.

63. Ibid., 45–46.

64. Dorothy Sterling, *Turning the World Upside Down: The Anti-Slavery Convention of American*

Women, Held in New York, May 9–12, 1837 (New York: The Feminist Press at the City University of New York, 1987), 3–4.

65. Larry Ceplair, *The Public Years of Sarah and Angelina Grimke: Selected Writings, 1835–1839* (New York: Columbia University Press, 1989), 86.

66. Margaret Washington, *Sojourner Truth's America* (Urbana: University of Illinois Press, 2009), 355.

67. Gilbert H. Barnes and Dwight L. Dumond, eds., *Letters of Theodore Dwight Weld, Angelina Grimke Weld, and Sarah Grimke, 1822–1844*, vols. 1–2 (New York: D. Appleton-Century, 1934), 574.

68. Ibid., 180.

69. Louis Ruchames, *The Abolitionists: A Collection of their Writings* (New York: G. P. Putnam's Sons, 1963), 110.

70. Northern newspaper stories sometimes conveyed the extent to which Southerners grew to be callously blasé about the psychological pain they inflicted on their bondsmen. The following story that appeared in the *New York Tribune* (n.d.) is a good example: "She was a fine looking woman about 25 years old with three beautiful children....One of these traders asked her what was the matter with her eyes? Wiping away the tears, she replied, 'I s'pose I have been crying.'—'Why do you cry?'—'Because I have left my man behind, and his master won't let him come along.'—'Oh, if I buy you, I will furnish you with a better husband, or man as you call him, than your old one.'—'I don't want any better and won't have any other as long as he lives.'—'Oh, but you will though, if I buy you.'"

71. Bordewich, 225.

72. Wyatt-Brown, 113.

73. Myers, "Agency System," 367–373.

74. Barnes and Dumond, *Letters*, 147.

75. J. G. Randall, *The Civil War and Reconstruction* (1937; repr., Boston: D. C. Heath, 1953), 101.

76. Barnes and Dumond, *Letters*, 54–55.

77. Dumond, *Crusade for Freedom*, 177.

78. Lawrence B. Goodheart, *Abolitionist, Actuary, Atheist: Elizur Wright and the Reform Impulse* (Kent, OH: Kent State University Press, 1990), 74.

79. Mayer, 177.

80. Fogel, 265.

81. Frederickson, 175.

82. Ernest G. Bormann, *Forerunners of Black Power* (Englewood Cliffs, NJ: Prentice Hall, 1971), 18–21.

83. Dumond, *Crusade for Freedom*, 218.

84. Dillon, *Dissenting Minority*, 117.

85. A superior account of ivory and its connection to slavery can be found in *Complicity: How the North Promoted and Profited from Slavery* by Anne Farrow, Joel Lang, and Jenifer Frank (see bibliography).

86. Lewis Perry and Michael Fellman, eds., *Antislavery Reconsidered: New Perspectives on the Abolitionists* (Baton Rouge: Louisiana State University Press, 1979), 112.

87. Ibid., 104–105.

88. Dillon, *Dissenting Minority*, 128.

89. *Third Annual Report of the American Anti-Slavery Society: With the Speeches Delivered at the Anniversary Meeting, Held in the City of New-York on the 10th May, 1835, and the Minutes of the Meetings of the Society for Business* (New York: William S. Door, 1836).

90. Lacy K. Ford, *Deliver Us from Evil: The Slavery Question in the Old South* (New York: Oxford University Press, 2009), 481–482.

91. Bordewich, 161.

92. John W. Blassingame, *The Slave Community: Plantation Life in the Antebellum South* (New York: Oxford University Press, 1979), 233–234.

93. The American Anti-Slavery Society's agents' expenditures more than doubled after the spring of 1836. The financial records of the national society in May of 1836 reported at the organization's annual meeting that $7,628.40 had been spent during the previous twelve months on agents' salaries and travel expenses. But at the society's meeting one year later (1837), the treasurer's report indicated that $15,725.11 was spent on the agents' wages and expenditures for travel.

94. John L. Myers, "The Major Effort of National Anti-Slavery Agents in New York State, 1836–1837," *New York History: Quarterly Journal of the New York State Historical Association* 46 (April 1965): 162.

95. John R. McKivigan and Stanley Harrold, eds., *Antislavery Violence: Sectional, Racial, and Cultural Conflict in Antebellum America* (Knoxville: University of Tennessee Press, 1999), 113.

96. David Ruggles was an African American printer. He established *Mirror of Liberty* in 1838, and he also wrote scores of articles and numerous pamphlets. Ruggles believed that newspapers were a crucial tool to bringing about the end of slavery.

97. Robert Purvis was born to a half-black, half-white woman; his father was white. When his father died, he inherited substantial wealth. Purvis helped establish the AASS, was an active Underground Railroad operator, and strong supporter of women's rights. He was a proponent of enlisting black soldiers into the Union Army during the Civil War.

98. Sterling, *We Are Your Sisters*, 70.

99. Nathaniel W. Stephenson, *Texas and the Mexican War: A Chronicle of the Winning of the Southwest* (New Haven: Yale University Press, 1921), 104–105.

100. Mayer, 221–222.

101. Stephenson, 103.

102. Mandel, 115.

103. Macy, 40.

104. Ibid., 46.

105. Carol E. Mull, *The Underground Railroad in Michigan* (Jefferson, NC: McFarland, 2010), 55.

106. Bordewich, 162.

107. Stacey M. Robertson, *Parker Pillsbury: Radical Abolitionist, Male Feminist* (Ithaca, NY: Cornell University Press, 2000), 19.

108. Barnes and Dumond, *Letters*, 93.

109. Ibid., 174.

110. Dillon, *Dissenting Minority*, 129–130.

111. Ibid., 93, 148; Filler, 141.

112. Fogel, 279.

113. John L. Myers, "Organization of 'The Seventy': To Arouse the North Against Slavery," *Mid-American: An Historical Review* 42 (1966): 46.

114. Barnes and Dumond, *Letters*, 814.

115. Dumond, *Crusade for Freedom*, 191.

116. Gerda Lerner, *The Grimke Sisters from South Carolina: Rebels Against Slavery* (New York: Houghton Mifflin, 1967), 226.

117. Yacovone, 60.

118. Zinn, 120.

119. Perry and Fellman, *Antislavery Reconsidered*, 245.

120. Aileen S. Kraditor, *Means and Ends in American Abolitionism: Garrison and His Critics on Strategy and Tactics, 1834–1850* (New York: Random House, 1967), 40.

121. Ibid., 60.

122. Weld's correspondence to the Grimke sisters on this issue can be found in Barnes and Dumond, *Letters,* vol. 1, 425–436.

123. See Barnes and Dumond, *Letters*, vol. 1.

124. Barnes, *Antislavery Impulse*, 157–158; Lerner, *Grimke Sisters*, 203–204.

125. Ceplair, 350–351.

126. Barnes, *Antislavery Impulse*, 159.

127. Abby Kelley was a New England abolitionist who helped William Lloyd Garrison establish the New England Non-Resistance Society in 1838. During the course of her public lectures, she endured ridicule and hostility. She maintained an underground hideout at her residence. In 1845 she married prominent abolitionist Stephen S. Foster. Kelly often compared the servility of slaves to their owners to the submissiveness of wives to their husbands. "In striving to strike his [slaves'] irons off," Kelly said, "we found most surely that we were manacled ourselves."

128. Stewart, 95.

129. Dumond, *Crusade for Freedom*, 286.

130. Kraditor, 8.

131. Ibid., 9.

132. Barnes, *Antislavery Impulse*, 171–174.

133. Duberman, 143–145.

134. Benjamin Quarles, *Black Abolitionists* (New York: Oxford University Press, 1969), 224–225.

135. R. J. M. Blackett, *Building an Antislavery Wall: Black Americans in the Atlantic Abolitionist Movement, 1830–1860* (Ithaca, NY: Cornell University Press, 1983), 195.

136. Dumond, *Crusade for Freedom*, 131–133.

137. Perry and Fellman, *Antislavery Reconsidered*, 83.

138. McKivigan and Harrold, 94.

139. Merton L. Dillon, "The Failure of the American Abolitionists," *The Journal of Southern History* 25, no. 2 (May 1959): 221.

140. McKivigan and Harrold, 96.

141. Dumond, *Antislavery Origins*, 64.

142. Dillon, "Failure," 174.

143. Stewart, *Abolitionist Politics and the Coming of the Civil War*, 222–223.

144. Owen W. Muelder, *The Underground Railroad in Western Illinois* (Jefferson, NC: McFarland, 2008), chap. 2–9.

145. Magdol, *Antislavery Rank and File*, 7.

Chapter 2

1. Robert H. Abzug, *Passionate Liberator: Theodore Dwight Weld and the Dilemma of Reform* (New York: Oxford University Press, 1980), 150–153; Barnes, *Antislavery Impulse*, 105–108.

2. Myers, "Organization of 'The Seventy,'" 42; Dumond, *Crusade for Freedom*, 185.

3. Lane Seminary was established in 1829, and its founders decided to adopt a manual labor school model after a Lane faculty member visited George Washington Gale's Oneida Institute in New York. When Weld arrived at the school, he had already persuaded Arthur Tappan to donate desperately needed funds to help sustain the educational enterprise. Tappan agreed, with the condition that the seminary would appoint Lyman Beecher as its president.

4. H. L. Hammond, "The Gravel Debate: An Anti-Slavery Reminiscence," *Advance Supplement* (Chicago), April 28, 1870; Hiram Foote to Theodore Weld, Sept. 20, 1866, Weld-Grimke papers, Manuscript Division, William L. Clements Library, University of Michigan.

5. Hermann Muelder, 52–56; Barnes, *Antislavery Impulse*, 64–78.

6. Perry and Fellman, *Antislavery Reconsidered*, 71.

7. Ann Hagedorn, *Beyond the River: The Untold Story of the Heroes of the Underground Railroad* (New York: Simon & Schuster, 2002), 70–71.

8. Thomas, 81.

9. Filler, 69–70; Abzug, 123; Robert S. Fletcher, *A History of Oberlin College: From its Foundation through the Civil War*, vol. 1 (Oberlin, OH: R. R. Donnelley & Sons, 1943), 167–190; Kevin C. Julius, *The Abolitionist Decade, 1829–1838: A Year-By-Year History of Early Events in the Antislavery Movement* (Jefferson, NC: McFarland, 2004, 126–128. See Stacey M. Robertson, *Hearts Beating for Liberty* (Chapel Hill: University of North Carolina Press, 2010).

10. Myers, "Agency System," 270.

11. Anthony J. Barker, *Captain Charles Stewart: Anglo-American Abolitionist* (Baton Rouge: Louisiana State University Press, 1986), 89.

12. Richards, 17.

13. Ibid., 15.

14. Ibid., 252–254.

15. Fletcher, 242; Dumond, *Crusade for Freedom*, 184; Hermann Muelder, 60.

16. Barnes, *Antislavery Impulse*, 101–104; Myers, "Organization of 'The Seventy,'" 30.

17. Myers, "Agency System," 397–398; Barnes, *Antislavery Impulse*, 101–102.

18. Myers, "Organization of 'The Seventy,'" 31.

19. Abzug, 150–152; Barnes, *Antislavery Impulse*, 104–105.

20. Lerner, 163; Myers, "Organization of 'The Seventy,'" 41–42.

21. Barnes, *Antislavery Impulse*, 83.

22. Dumond, *Crusade for Freedom*, 185.

23. Myers, "Organization of 'The Seventy,'" 42; Barnes, *Antislavery Impulse*, 107.

24. Barnes and Dumond, *Letters*, vol. 2, 865–866.

25. Myers, "Agency System," 219–225, 272–293; Dumond, *Crusade for Freedom*, 188–189.

26. Myers, "Organization of 'The Seventy,'" 30.

27. John L. Myers, "The Beginnings of Anti-Slavery Agencies in New Hampshire, 1832–1835," *Historical New Hampshire* 25 (Fall 1970): 5.

28. After the AASS split apart, some of Weld's most dedicated former agents settled in Illinois, where they continued to work for the antislavery cause. Among the most active to do so were William T. Allan, who lectured as an agent for the Illinois State Anti-Slavery Society; Jonathan Blanchard, who became seriously involved with the affairs of the Liberty Party and later the Free Soil Party; Ichabod Codding, who delivered abolitionist speeches and was once prevented from speaking by a mob in Peoria; John Cross, who backed the establishment of the Liberty Party in Illinois and openly aided fugitive slaves; and John Miter, who helped put the Illinois State Anti-Slavery Society on its feet and also helped found the Liberty Party in the Prairie State. In addition, Weld's former mentor in upstate New York, George Washington Gale, established Galesburg and Knox College in Western Illinois. The town and college became the most important abolitionist center in downstate Illinois, and Gale was once indicted for supporting the escape of fugitive slaves in Knox County.

29. Bordewich, 164.

30. Barnes, *Antislavery Impulse*, 106–107.

31. Thomas, 125.

32. Hume, 112.

33. John M. Blum, Bruce Catton, Edmund S. Morgan, Arthur M. Schlesinger, Jr., Kenneth M., Stampp, and C. Vann Woodward, *The National Experience* (New York: Harcourt, Brace, & World, 1963), 208.

34. Mandel, 89–90.

35. Ibid., 90.

36. Perry and Fellman, *Antislavery Reconsidered*, 206–207.

37. See Jonathan A. Glickstein's "Poverty Is Not Slavery: American Abolitionists and the Competitive Labor Market," in Perry and Fellman, *Antislavery Reconsidered*, 195–218.

38. Mandel, 88–89.

39. Ibid., 89.

40. Ibid., 72.

41. The investment slaveholders made in slaves, under some circumstances, prohibited them from letting their bondsman be used for extremely dangerous work projects. Between 1831 and 1838 the city of New Orleans constructed the three-mile long New Basin Canal. The project was so hazardous that it took thousands of lives before it was completed. Southerners realized that it was not worth the lost value of slaves to carry out this life-threatening work so they hired Irishmen who contracted yellow fever and cholera while it was built. In many cases these laborers were buried along the Canal route. In Richmond citizens decided that it was cheaper to hire recently arrived immigrants at a very low wage and keep slaves alive for safer work. In Virginia's capital city, both unskilled Irishmen and free Blacks were hired to build levies and work on drainage projects. By the 1850s, as the price of slaves spiraled higher, several Southern businessmen started to hire Irish and German immigrants to do jobs for little pay and not purchase slaves who they would otherwise have to feed and house. A Southern planter, who hired Irishmen for a hazardous job, remarked, "It's dangerous work, and a negro's life is too valuable to be risked at it. If the negro dies, it's a considerable loss, you know." Even the unloading of cotton bales sometimes affected work assignments. Slaves worked on deck but Irishmen were used to stop bales from sliding onto wharfs. "The [slaves] are worth too much to be risked here; if Paddies are knocked overboard, or get their backs broke, nobody loses anything" (see Mandel, *Labor Free and Slaves*, 35). Free blacks were also hired to carry out dangerous unskilled tasks when railroads were constructed across the South.

42. Slave traders prepared slaves to look as good as possible prior to putting them on the block for sale. They shaved men's beards, dyed their hair, and greased their skin with oil in order to give them a healthy appearance. Slaves were often well fed several days before a public sale to literally fatten them up, and they were dressed in better clothing to give a neater appearance. Potential buyers gradually grew leery of these deceptive practices.

43. The Mississippi River became the primary inland channel used by slave traders. A steady stream of slaves was transported from the conjunction of the Ohio and Mississippi Rivers northward to St. Louis and south to Memphis, Natchez, and New Orleans.

44. Peter Kolchin, *American Slavery, 1619–1877* (New York: Hill & Wang, 1993), 96.

45. An infant also tended to cost more money because slave traders and owners expected them to live longer. The time of year also affected the price of slaves. In September, when plantation owners were busy overseeing the harvest of crops, slave traders often reduced their sales by 10 to 20 percent.

46. Sterling, *We Are Your Sisters*, 27.

47. Barnes, *Antislavery Impulse*, 103.

48. Abzug, 127–128; Dumond, *Crusade for Freedom*, 34; Filler, 140.

49. Dumond, *Crusade for Freedom*, 142, 263.

50. Abzug, 150; Barnes, *Antislavery Impulse*, 107.

51. Barker, 109.

52. Richards, 5.

53. Abzug, 150.

54. Goodheart, 66.

55. Jane H. Pease and William H. Pease, *Bound with Them in Chains: A Biographical History of the Antislavery Movement* (Westport, CT: Greenwood Press, 1972), 226.

56. Stewart, 79–81.

57. Wood, 531.

58. Alexis de Tocqueville, *Letters from America* (New Haven, CT: Yale University Press, 2010), 249.

59. Russel B. Nye, *The Cultural Life of the New Nation, 1776–1830* (New York: Harpers and Brothers, 1960), 115–116.

60. John L. Myers, "The Major Efforts of Anti-Slavery Agents in Vermont, 1836–1838," *Vermont Historical Society* 36, no. 4 (Fall 1968): 227.

61. Myers, "Organization of 'The Seventy,'" 185.

62. Dumond, *Crusade for Freedom*, 185.

63. Myers, "Agency System," 410

64. Myers, "New York State, 1836–1837," 163; Myers, "Organization of 'The Seventy,'" 45.

65. Tappan, 247–248.

66. Barnes and Dumond, *Letters*, 298–302.

67. Myers, "Organization of 'The Seventy,'" 43.

68. Ibid., 32

69. Dwight L. Dumond, ed., *Letters of James Gillespie Birney, 1831–1857*, vol. 1 (New York: D. Appleton-Century, 1938), 357.

70. Barnes and Dumond, *Letters*, 154 (see also footnote 23, 274–275).

71. Barnes, *Antislavery Impulse*, 154; Dumond, *James Gillespie Birney*, vol. 1, 357; also see Lerner, *Grimke Sisters*.

72. Dumond, *Crusade for Freedom*, 185.

73. Ceplair, 85.

74. Myers, "Organization of 'The Seventy,'" 39.

75. Myers, "Agency System," 104.

76. *Third Annual Report of the American Anti-Slavery Society.*

77. Lydia Maria Francis was a brilliant writer and editor who joined the abolitionist movement in the early 1830s. She married lawyer David Child, whose interests in various ventures left him impoverished and consequently drew down her earnings. In Boston she gave strong support to William Lloyd Garrison's antislavery efforts, and she closely allied herself to Unitarian abolitionists like Wendell Phillips. In 1833, she published "An Appeal in Favor of that Class of Americans Called Africans." Child was the editor of the *National Anti-Slavery Standard* from 1841 to 1843, and following John Brown's raid on Harper's Ferry, she wrote Brown a letter praising his courage. Child is best remembered today for writing the Thanksgiving poem, "Over the River and Through the Woods."

78. Barnes, *Antislavery Impulse*, 153.

79. Myers, "Organization of 'The Seventy,'" 38.

80. Julie Roy Jeffrey, *The Great Silent Army of Abolitionism: Ordinary Women in the Antislavery Movement* (Chapel Hill: University of North Carolina Press, 1998), 153–154.

81. Abzug, 30–31; Barnes and Dumond, *Letters*, vol. 1, xxi; Milton C. Sernett, *North Star Country: Upstate New York and the Crusade for African American Freedom* (Syracuse, NY: Syracuse University Press, 2002), 28–32.

82. Thomas, 16–17.

83. Barnes, *Antislavery Impulse*, 14–15.

84. Thomas, 14–16. Gale's conversion of Finney can also be found in Finney's memoirs.

85. Hermann Muelder, 7–9.

86. Barker, 33.

87. Henry B. Stanton, *Random Reflections*, 3rd ed. (New York: 1887), 40–42.

88. Dillon, *Dissenting Minority*, 29.

89. Russel B. Nye, *William Lloyd Garrison and the Humanitarian Reformers* Boston: Little, Brown and Co., 1955), 38–39; Dumond, *Crusade for Freedom*, 158.

90. Dumond, *Crusade for Freedom*, 159; Hermann Muelder, 35.
91. Barnes and Dumond, *Letters*, vol. 1, xxi.
92. Hermann Muelder, 28
93. Thomas, 26; Abzug, 70–71.
94. Hermann Muelder, 50.
95. Ibid., 59; Fletcher, 184.
96. Dumond, *Crusade for Freedom*, 183–185.
97. Unidentified newspaper, no date, obituary. "Theodore Dwight Weld Dead — One of the Early Abolitionists — Dies at Hyde Park at the Great Age of 91," Weld Family Papers, Ron August, Jr., Wilmington, DE.
98. Barnes and Dumond, *Letters*, vol. 1, 205–208.
99. Ibid., 226–227.
100. Dumond, *Crusade for Freedom*, 253.
101. John L. Myers, "The Early Anti-Slavery Agency System in Pennsylvania, 1833–1837," *Pennsylvania History* 21 (January 1964): 203–204.
102. Barnes and Dumond, *Letters*, xxiii.
103. Barker, 122.
104. Bordewich, 159.
105. Myers, "Agency System," 166.
106. Ibid., 166.
107. Wendell Phillips graduated from Harvard's law school and opened his law office in 1834. He joined the abolitionist movement after listening to a speech of Garrison's in 1835. Phillips was an outstanding orator who some called abolition's Golden Trumpet. He was put into the limelight after delivering a powerful speech protesting the murder of Illinois abolitionist Elijah P. Lovejoy. "The gun which aimed at the breast of Lovejoy," Phillip said, "brought me to my feet." Phillips frequently contributed articles to the *Liberator*. He broke with Garrison in 1865 when Garrison suggested that the AASS had served its purpose and should be dissolved. Thereafter Phillips became the president of the national society.
108. Myers, "Agency System," 165.
109. Tappan, 176–177.
110. Myers, "Agency System," 272.
111. Duberman, 409.
112. Ibid., 284.
113. Abzug, 151.
114. Thomas, 113.
115. Myers, "Organization of 'The Seventy,'" 33.
116. Wyatt-Brown, 171.
117. Abzug, 151.
118. Ibid., 156–157.
119. Myers, "Organization of 'The Seventy,'" 41.
120. Myers, "Agency System," 402.
121. Ceplair, 23.
122. Lewis Perry, *Radical Abolitionism: Anarchy and the Government of God in Antislavery Thought* (1973; Repr., Knoxville: University of Tennessee Press, 1995), 51–52.
123. Myers, "Organization of 'The Seventy,'" 29–46, 43.
124. *The Liberator*, December 17, 1836.
125. Thomas, 122.
126. Myers, "Organization of 'The Seventy,'" 29–46, 45.
127. Richards, 32.
128. Perry and Fellman, *Antislavery Reconsidered*, 105.
129. Macy, 80.
130. Dumond, *Crusade for Freedom*, 237.
131. Barnes, *Antislavery Impulse*, 126–127, 134.
132. Barnes and Dumond, *Letters*, 403–405.
133. Bordewich, 162.
134. Barnes and Dumond, *Letters*, xiii.
135. Sylvester Graham was a Presbyterian minister who advocated a vegetable and fruit diet to control intemperance. He believed people should eat coarsely ground whole-grain flour made into bread and crackers. Graham thought the healthiest life could be achieved by avoiding stimulants,

taking cold baths daily and one warm bath per week, wearing loose fitting clothes, sleeping with bedroom windows open, maintaining a vigorous routine of exercise, and practicing sexual restraint.

136. Barnes and Dumond, *Letters*, 400.
137. Simms, *Emotions at High Tide*, 16–17.
138. Barnes and Dumond, 231.
139. Fogel, 278.
140. McKivigan and Harrold, 183.
141. Barnes and Dumond, *Letters*, vol. 1, xxv.
142. Abzug, 221.
143. Ibid., 259.
144. Ibid., 286.
145. Dillon, "Failure," 266.
146. After the Civil War, the Grimke sisters discovered that their brother Henry had two sons by his black mistress. Thereafter the Grimkes helped their two nephews complete their educations. In later life Archibald E. Grimke was selected as vice-president of the NAACP and Francis Grimke became a distinguished Presbyterian minister in Washington, D.C.
147. Dillon, "Failure," 287–290.
148. Memorial service upon 74th birthday of Wendell Phillips, held at the residence of William Summer Crosby, no. 517 Broadway, South Boston, Published November 29, 1885, 22.
149. Barnes and Dumond, *Letters*, 966–967.
150. Wyatt-Brown, 249.
151. Ibid., 1005.
152. Stewart, 113–114.

Chapter 3

1. See Barnes and Dumond, *Letters*, 347.
2. See Dumond, *James Gillespie Birney*, vols. 1–2; Hermann Muelder, *Fighters for Freedom*; Fletcher, *History of Oberlin College*; Myers, "New York State, 1836–1837."
3. See Myers, "Vermont, 1836–1838"; Dumond, *James Gillespie Birney*, vols. 1–2; Dumond, *Crusade for Freedom*.
4. See Myers, "Pennsylvania, 1833–1837"; Myers, "Organization of 'The Seventy'"; John L. Myers, "Anti-Slavery Agents in Rhode Island, 1832–1835," *Rhode Island History* 29 (August 1970); John L. Myers, "Anti-Slavery Agents in Rhode Island, 1835–1837," *Rhode Island History* 30 (February 1971).
5. See Dumond, *James Gillespie Birney*, vols. 1–2; Filler, *Crusade Against Slavery*; Myers, "Organization of 'The Seventy'"; Hagedorn, *Beyond the River*.
6. See Myers, "Rhode Island, 1832–1835"; Myers, "Rhode Island, 1835–1837"; Myers, "New York State, 1836–1837"; Fletcher, *History of Oberlin College*.
7. See Hermann Muelder, *Fighters for Freedom*; Myers, "Pennsylvania, 1833–1837"; Dumond, *James Gillespie Birney*, vols. 1–2.
8. See Myers, "New York State, 1836–1837"; Filler, *Crusade Against Slavery*.
9. See Barnes and Dumond, *Letters*; Myers, "Organization of 'The Seventy.'"
10. Ibid.
11. See Bordewich, *Bound for Canaan*; Myers, "New York State, 1836–1837"; Dumond, *James Gillespie Birney*, vols. 1–2; Myers, "Rhode Island, 1832–1835"; Myers, "Rhode Island, 1835–1837."
12. See Myers, "Vermont, 1836–1838"; Barnes and Dumond, *Letters*; Owen Muelder, *Underground Railroad*.
13. See Myers, "New York State, 1836–1837"; Myers, "Vermont, 1832–1836"; Barnes and Dumond, *Letters*.
14. See Fletcher, *History of Oberlin College*; Barnes and Dumond, *Letters*; Myers, "Organization of 'The Seventy.'"
15. See Owen Muelder, *Underground Railroad*; Hermann Muelder, *Fighters for Freedom*; Myers, "New York State, 1836–1837"; Myers, "Pennsylvania, 1833–1837."
16. See Barnes and Dumond, *Letters*; Filler, *Crusade Against Slavery*; Myers, "Organization of 'The Seventy'"; Dumond, *Crusade for Freedom*.
17. See Dumond, *Crusade for Freedom*; Myers, "Pennsylvania, 1833–1837."

18. See Barnes and Dumond, *Letters*; Dumond, *Crusade for Freedom*; Hermann Muelder, *Fighters for Freedom*; Hammond, "The Gravel Debate."
19. See Barnes and Dumond, *Letters*; Myers, "Pennsylvania, 1833–1837."
20. See Abzug, *Passionate Liberator*; Thomas, *Theodore Weld*; Lerner, *Grimke Sisters*; Myers, "Organization of 'The Seventy'"; Dumond, *Crusade for Freedom*.
21. See Barnes and Dumond, *Letters*; Lerner, *Grimke Sisters*; Dumond, *Crusade for Freedom*.
22. See Dumond, *Crusade for Freedom*; Barnes and Dumond, *Letters*; Myers, "Organization of 'The Seventy.'"
23. See Myers, "Agency System"; Barnes and Dumond, *Letters*; Myers "Organization of 'The Seventy'"; Robertson, *Hearts Beating*.
24. See Nye, *William Lloyd Garrison*; Filler, *Crusade Against Slavery*; Myers, "Agency System."
25. See Thomas, *Theodore Weld*; Barnes and Dumond, *Letters*; Barnes, *Antislavery Impulse*.
26. See Myers, "Organization of 'The Seventy'"; Myers, "Vermont, 1836–1838."
27. See Dumond, *Crusade for Freedom*; Myers, "Organization of 'The Seventy'"; Myers, "Pennsylvania, 1833–1837."
28. See Myers, "Vermont, 1836–1838"; Myers, "Organization of 'The Seventy.'"
29. See Thomas, *Theodore Weld*; Barnes and Dumond, *Letters*; Hermann Muelder, *Fighters for Freedom*; Owen Muelder, *Underground Railroad*; Myers, "Pennsylvania, 1833–1837"; John L. Myers, "American Anti-Slavery Society Agents and the Free Negro, 1833–1838," *The Journal of Negro History* 52 (July 1967).
30. See Dumond, *James Gillespie Birney*, vols. 1–2; Myers, "Organization of 'The Seventy.'"
31. See Myers, "Agency System"; Myers "Organization of 'The Seventy.'"
32. See Barnes and Dumond, *Letters*; Fletcher, *History of Oberlin College*; Myers "Organization of 'The Seventy.'"
33. See Myers, "Agency System"; Barnes and Dumond, *Letters*; Myers "Organization of 'The Seventy.'"
34. See Myers, "New York State, 1836–1837"; Myers, "Pennsylvania, 1833–1837"; Myers, "Agency System."
35. See Barnes and Dumond, *Letters*; Myers "Organization of 'The Seventy'"; Myers, "Agency System."
36. See Hagedorn, *Beyond the River*; Dumond, *James Gillespie Birney*, vols. 1–2; Myers, "Organization of 'The Seventy.'"
37. See Hagedorn, *Beyond the River*; Dumond, *James Gillespie Birney*, vols. 1–2; Myers, "Organization of 'The Seventy'"; Barnes and Dumond, *Letters*.
38. See Thomas, *Theodore Weld*; Dumond, *James Gillespie Birney*, vols. 1–2; Hermann Muelder, *Fighters for Freedom*; Myers, "New York State, 1836–1837."
39. See Myers, "Agency System"; Myers, "Organization of 'The Seventy.'"
40. See Barnes, *Antislavery Impulse*; Barnes and Dumond, *Letters*; Dumond, *James Gillespie Birney*, vols. 1–2; Dumond, *Crusade for Freedom*.
41. See Dumond, *James Gillespie Birney*, vols. 1–2; Myers, "Organization of 'The Seventy'"; Myers, "Vermont, 1832–1836."
42. See Dumond, *James Gillespie Birney*, vols. 1–2; Myers, "Organization of 'The Seventy'"; Myers, "New York State, 1836–1837"; Myers, "Agency System."
43. See Barnes, *Antislavery Impulse*; Myers, "Vermont, 1832–1836"; Myers, "Vermont, 1836–1838."
44. See Barnes and Dumond, *Letters*; Barnes, *Antislavery Impulse*; Dumond, *Crusade for Freedom*; Myers, "Organization of 'The Seventy.'"
45. See Myers, "Organization of 'The Seventy'"; Myers, "New York State, 1836–1837"; Barnes and Dumond, *Letters*.
46. See Myers, "Rhode Island, 1835–1837"; Barnes and Dumond, *Letters*; Myers, "Organization of 'The Seventy.'"
47. See Stanton, *Random Reflections*; Myers, "Rhode Island, 1835–1837"; Barnes, *Antislavery Impulse*; Barnes and Dumond, *Letters*; Dillon, *Dissenting Minority*.
48. See Myers, "Vermont, 1832–1836"; Barnes, *Antislavery Impulse*; Dumond, *Crusade for Freedom*; Barnes and Dumond, *Letters*; Myers, "Agency System."
49. See Abzug, *Passionate*; Barnes, *Antislavery Impulse*; Myers, "New York State, 1836–1837"; Dumond, *Crusade for Freedom*; Barnes and Dumond, *Letters*.
50. See Myers, "Organization of 'The Seventy'"; Myers, "Agency System."

51. See Dumond, *James Gillespie Birney*, vols. 1–2; Dumond, *Crusade for Freedom*; Barnes, *Antislavery Impulse*; Myers, "Organization of 'The Seventy.'"

52. See Myers, "New York State, 1836–1837"; Myers, "Pennsylvania, 1833–1837"; Myers, "Organization of 'The Seventy.'"

53. See Barnes and Dumond, *Letters*; Myers, "Organization of 'The Seventy'"; Myers, "Agency System."

54. See Fletcher, *History of Oberlin College*; Myers, "Organization of 'The Seventy'"; Myers, "Agency System."

55. See Myers, "Agency System"; Myers, "Organization of 'The Seventy.'"

56. See Myers, "New York State, 1836–1837"; Myers, "Organization of 'The Seventy.'"

57. See Abzug, *Passionate Liberator*; Filler, *Crusade Against Slavery*; Myers, "Pennsylvania, 1833–1837"; Barnes and Dumond, *Letters*.

58. See Dumond, *James Gillespie Birney*, vols. 1–2; Dumond, *Crusade for Freedom*; Myers, "Organization of 'The Seventy'"; Dumond, *Antislavery Origins*.

59. See Bordewich, *Bound for Canaan*; Myers, "New York State, 1836–1837"; Myers, "Organization of 'The Seventy.'"

60. See Myers, "New York State, 1836–1837"; Myers, "Organization of 'The Seventy.'"

61. See Barnes and Dumond, *Letters*; Dumond, *Crusade for Freedom*; Myers, "Agency System."

62. See Myers, "Agency System"; Myers, "Organization of 'The Seventy.'"

63. See Myers, "Vermont, 1832–1836"; Myers, "Vermont, 1836–1838"; Myers, "Organization of 'The Seventy.'"

64. See Myers, "Pennsylvania, 1833–1837"; Myers, "Organization of 'The Seventy.'"

65. See Dumond, *James Gillespie Birney*, vols. 1–2; Barnes and Dumond, *Letters*; Myers, "Organization of 'The Seventy.'"

66. See Filler, *Crusade Against Slavery*; Barnes and Dumond, *Letters*; Dumond, *James Gillespie Birney*, vols. 1–2; Myers, "Organization of 'The Seventy.'"

67. See Myers, "Free Negro, 1833–1838"; Myers, "Organization of 'The Seventy.'"

68. Myers, "Agency System," 677.

69. See Dumond, *Crusade for Freedom*; Dumond, *James Gillespie Birney*, vols. 1–2.

70. See Barnes and Dumond, *Letters*; Barnes, *Antislavery Impulse*.

71. See Barnes and Dumond, *Letters*; Dumond, *Crusade for Freedom*.

72. See Barnes and Dumond, *Letters*.

73. See Myers, "Agency System."

74. See Barnes, *Antislavery Impulse*.

75. See Barnes and Dumond, *Letters*.

76. See Dumond, *Crusade for Freedom*.

77. Ibid.

78. See Barnes and Dumond, *Letters*.

79. Ibid.

80. Ibid.

81. See Dumond, *James Gillespie Birney*, vols. 1–2.

82. See Barnes and Dumond, *Letters*.

83. Ibid.

Chapter 4

1. Theodore D. Weld, *American Slavery As It Is: Testimony of a Thousand Witnesses* (New York: American Anti-Slavery Society, 1839).

2. *American Anti-Slavery Almanac* (1938): 13.

3. Weld, *American Slavery As It Is*.

4. See Jonathan Blanchard and Nathan Lewis Rice, *A Debate on Slavery: Held in the City of Cincinnati on the First, Second, Third, and Sixth Days of October, 1845, upon the Question: Is Slavery in Itself Sinful, and the Relation between Master and Slave, a Sinful Relation?* (Cincinnati, OH: Wm. H. Moore, 1846; New York: Negro University Press, 1969).

5. "A Tribute to James G. Birney," 1863. Samuel J. May Anti-Slavery Collection. http://dlxs2.library.cornell.edu/cgi/t/text/pageviewer-idx?c=mayantislavery&cc=mayantislavery&idno=16855302&frm=frameset&view=image&seq=3 (accessed December 2, 2010).

6. Edward Magdol, *Owen Lovejoy: Abolitionist in Congress* (New Brunswick, NJ: Rutgers University Press, 1967), 28.
7. See "Tribute to James G. Birney."

Chapter 5

1. Hermann Muelder, 132.
2. Ibid., 96.
3. N. Dwight Harris, *The History of Negro Servitude in Illinois and of the Slavery Agitation in that State, 1719–1864* (Chicago: A. C. McClurg, 1904), 136–137.
4. Owen Muelder, chap. 7–9.
5. See Ibid., 82.
6. *Geneseo Reporter*, July 18, 1913.
7. Emma Chapin letter to Wilbur Siebert, June 11, 1896.
8. Mull, 71.
9. *Signal of Liberty*, May 12, 1841.
10. Mull, 117.
11. Chas. C. Chapman, *History of Knox County, Illinois* (Chicago: Blakely, Brown & March, 1878), 208–209.
12. Knoxville *Republican*, Nov. 30, 1859
13. See Hermann Muelder, *Fighters for Freedom*, chaps. 13, 19.
14. Mary Kay Ricks, *Escape on the Pearl* (New York: Harper Collins, 2007), 31.
15. Bordewich, 295–303.
16. Sernett, 130.
17. Ricks, 219.
18. Sernett, 3n310.
19. Ricks, 230.
20. Mull, 55.
21. Ibid., 56.
22. Hermann Muelder, 213.
23. Ibid., 214–216.
24. Ibid., 216–217.
25. Inez A. Kennedy, *Reflections of the Pioneers of Lee County* (Dixon, IL: Inez A. Kennedy, 1893), 108–109.
26. See "Lighting Freedom's Road," North Country Underground Railroad Historical Association, Plattsburg, New York.
27. See Ibid.
28. Sarah H. Bradford, *Harriet, The Moses of Her People* (Chapel Hill: University of North Carolina Press, 1995), 8.
29. Randolph A. Roth, "The First Radical Abolitionists: The Reverend James Milligan and the Reformed Presbyterians of Vermont," *The New England Quarterly* 55, no. 4 (December 1982): 540–563.
30. Rev. J. S. T. Milligan letter to Wilbur Siebert (no date).
31. Wilbur Henry Siebert, *The Mysteries of Ohio's Underground Railroad* (Columbus, OH: Long's College Book Co., 1951), 71–72.
32. Hagedorn, 275–276.
33. J. Blaine Hudson, *Encyclopedia of the Underground Railroad* (Jefferson, NC: McFarland, 2006), 232–233.
34. Barnes and Dumond, *Letters*, vol. 2, 793–795.
35. Mull, 40.
36. Wilbur H. Siebert, *The Underground Railroad from Slavery to Freedom* (New York: Macmillan, 1898), 107.
37. Barker, 26.
38. John H. Ryan, "A Chapter of the History of the Underground Railroad in Illinois," *Journal of the Illinois Historical Society* 8, no. 1 (April 1915): 25.
39. Magdol, *Owen Lovejoy*, 46–47.
40. Washington, 230.

41. See Siebert, *Slavery to Freedom*; R. C. Smedley, *History of the Underground Railroad in Chester and the Neighboring Counties in Pennsylvania* (Lancaster, PA: Office of the Journal, 1883).

Appendix A

1. Horace E. Scudder, *The Complete Poetical Works of John Greenleaf Whittier* (Boston: Houghton Mifflin, 1894), xxi.
2. Ibid., 270.
3. Ibid., 270–271.
4. Ibid., 278–279.

Appendix B

1. See Myers, "Agency System."
2. See Barnes and Dumond, *Letters*.
3. Ibid.
4. Ibid.

Appendix C

1. Abzug, 90.
2. Hammond, "The Gravel Debate."
3. *Third Annual Report of the American Anti-Slavery Society*, 94.
4. H. L. Hammond was born in Smyrna, New York, in 1815. He attended the Oneida Institute and then transferred to Oberlin College, graduating in 1838. Hammond studied at Union Theological Seminary and Andover Theological Seminary before he was ordained in 1841. He was a clergyman at churches in New York and Michigan and served as the editor of *The Congregational Herald* in Chicago from 1847 to 1861. Hammond was an acting pastor in Princeton, Illinois, from 1861 to 1862 and was the treasurer and General Agent of the Chicago Theological Seminary from 1962 until 1872. Three of his wives died before he married widow Elizabeth L. Wiswall in 1864, who was the niece of martyred abolitionist newspaperman Elijah P. Lovejoy and Illinois antislavery congressman Owen Lovejoy. (See Oberlin College Archives, Alumni Records, Oberlin, Ohio.)
5. Hammond, "The Gravel Debate."
6. University of Southern Mississippi, Library Archives, Hattiesburg.
7. Hiram Foote was born in Burlington, New York, in 1808. He studied at the Oneida Institute, continued his education at the Lane Seminary where he joined the Lane Rebels, and resumed his education at Oberlin, graduating from the school's theological seminary in 1838. He was an agent for the American Anti-Slavery Society in Ohio, serving as one of Weld's Seventy. Foote moved to the Middle West in the late 1830s and was a Congregationalist minister in communities in Illinois and Wisconsin. He was also superintendent of schools in Janesville, Wisconsin, and a trustee of the Wisconsin Institute for the Blind and the Rockford Female Seminary. In addition he worked for the American Tract Society and the American Sunday School Union. One of Foote's sons, Horatio, a soldier in the Civil War, died in a Southern prison. Hiram Foote died at the age of eighty in Rockford, Illinois, in 1889. (See Oberlin College Archives, Alumni Records, Oberlin, Ohio.)
8. Hiram Foote to Theodore Weld.
9. Fletcher, 54.
10. Ibid., 55.
11. Dumond, *Antislavery Origins*, 24–25.
12. Smedley, 264–265, 287.
13. Richards, 96.
14. See Stanton, *Random Reflections*.
15. See George M. Ramsdell, *History of Milford, 1838–1901* (Concord, NH: Rumford Press, 1901).

16. Ibid.
17. Ibid.
18. Ibid.
19. R. J. Ellis, *Harriet Wilson's Our Nig* (New York: Rodopi, 2003), 89.
20. John G. Whittier, "'The Anti-slavery Convention of 1833,' 1874," The Abolitionist, http://afgen.com/slavery5.html (accessed May 24, 2010).

Appendix D

1. Tappan, 424–427.
2. See John Greenleaf Whittier, *Old Portraits, Modern Sketches, Personal Sketches and Tributes Complete*, vol. 6, *The Works of Whittier, 1807–1892* (Project Gutenberg, 2005). http://www.gutenberg.org/catalog/world/readfile?fk_files=1823495.
3. See "Tribute to James G. Birney."

Appendix F

1. "Officers of the American Anti-Slavery Society, 1833–1840," American Abolitionism, http://americanabolitionist.liberalarts.iupui.edu/officers%20of%20the%20american%20anti%20slavery%20society%201833%2040.htm (accessed May 24, 2010).

Bibliography

Books

Abzug, Robert H. *Passionate Liberator: Theodore Dwight Weld and the Dilemma of Reform.* New York: Oxford University Press, 1980.

Andrews, Wayne, ed. *Concise Dictionary of American History.* New York: Charles Scribner's Sons, 1962.

Aptheker, Herbert. *Abolitionism: A Revolutionary Movement.* Boston: Twayne Press, 1989.

Armistead, Wilson. *Five Hundred Strokes for Freedom: A Series of Anti-Slavery Tracts, of Which Half a Million Are Now First Issued by the Friends of the Negro.* New York: Negro Universities Press, 1900. Originally published in 1853 by Leeds Anti-Slavery Society.

Bancroft, Frederic. *Calhoun and the South Carolina Nullification Movement.* Baltimore: John Hopkins Press, 1928.

_____. *Slave-Trading in the Old South.* Baltimore: John Hopkins Press, 1931.

Barker, Anthony J. *Captain Charles Stewart: Anglo-American Abolitionist.* Baton Rouge: Louisiana State University Press, 1986.

Barnes, Gilbert H. *The Antislavery Impulse, 1830–1844.* New York: D. Appleton-Century, 1933.

_____, and Dwight L. Dumond, eds. *Letters of Theodore Dwight Weld, Angelina Grimke Weld, and Sarah Grimke, 1822–1844.* 2 vols. New York: D. Appleton-Century, 1934.

Benfey, Christopher. *A Summer of Hummingbirds: Love, Art, and Scandal in the Intersecting Worlds of Emily Dickinson, Mark Twain, Harriet Beecher Stowe, and Martin Johnson Heade.* New York: Penguin, 2008.

Bennett, Whitman. *Whittier: Bard of Freedom.* Chapel Hill: University of North Carolina Press, 1941.

Berlin, Ira. *The Making of African America.* New York: Viking Penguin, 2010.

_____. *Slaves Without Masters: The Free Negro in the Antebellum South.* New York: Oxford University Press, 1974.

Blackett, R. J. M. *Building an Antislavery Wall: Black Americans in the Atlantic Abolitionist Movement, 1830–1860.* Ithaca, NY: Cornell University Press, 1983.

Blanchard, Jonathan, and Nathan Lewis Rice. *A Debate on Slavery: Held in the City of Cincinnati on the First, Second, Third, and Sixth Days of October, 1845, upon the Question: Is Slavery in Itself Sinful, and the Relation Between Master and Slave, a Sinful Relation?* Cincinnati, OH: Wm. H. Moore, 1846. Reprint New York: Negro University Press, 1969.

Blassingame, John W. *The Slave Community: Plantation Life in the Antebellum South.* New York: Oxford University Press, 1979.

Blum, John M., Bruce Catton, Edmund S. Morgan, Arthur M. Schlesinger, Jr., Kenneth M., Stampp, and C. Vann Woodward. *The National Experience.* New York: Harcourt, Brace, & World, 1963.

Bordewich, Fergus M. *Bound for Canaan: The Underground Railroad and the War for the Soul of America*. New York: HarperCollins, 2005.

Bormann, Ernest. *Forerunners of Black Power*. Englewood Cliffs, NJ: Prentice Hall, 1971.

Bradford, Sarah H. *Harriet, The Moses of Her People*. Chapel Hill: University of North Carolina Press, 1995.

Calarco, Tom. *The Underground Railroad in the Adirondack Region*. Jefferson, NC: McFarland, 2004.

Ceplair, Larry. *The Public Years of Sarah and Angelina Grimke: Selected Writings, 1835–1839*. New York: Columbia University Press, 1989.

Chapman, Chas. C. *History of Knox County, Illinois*. Chicago: Blakely, Brown & March, 1878.

Cunningham, Noble E., Jr. *The Presidency of James Monroe*. Lawrence: University Press of Kansas, 1996.

de Tocqueville, Alexis. *Letters from America*. New Haven, CT: Yale University Press, 2010.

Dillon, Merton L. *The Abolitionists: The Growth of a Dissenting Minority*. DeKalb: Northern Illinois University Press, 1974.

Dodd, William E. *The Cotton Kingdom*. New Haven, CT: Yale University Press, 1920.

Donald, David Herbert. *Lincoln Reconsidered: Essays on the Civil War Era*. New York: Random House, 2001.

Duberman, Martin. *The Antislavery Vanguard: New Essays on the Abolitionists*. Princeton, NJ: Princeton University Press, 1965.

Dumond, Dwight L. *Antislavery: The Crusade for Freedom in America*. Ann Arbor: University of Michigan Press, 1961.

_____. *Antislavery Origins of the Civil War in the United States*. Ann Arbor: University of Michigan Press, 1959.

_____, ed. *Letters of James Gillespie Birney, 1831–1857*. 2 vols. New York: D. Appleton-Century, 1938.

Elkins, Stanley. *Slavery: A Problem of American Institutional and Intellectual Life*. Chicago: University of Chicago Press, 1959.

Ellis, R. J. *Harriet Wilson's Our Nig*. New York: Rodopi, 2003.

Farrow, Anne, Joel Lang, and Jenifer Frank. *Complicity: How the North Promoted and Profited from Slavery*. New York: Hartford Courant, 2005.

Filler, Louis. *The Crusade Against Slavery, 1830–1860*. New York: Harper & Row, 1960.

Finney, Charles Grandison. *Memoirs of Charles Finney*. New York: Harper & Brothers, 1887.

Fletcher, Robert S. *A History of Oberlin College: From Its Foundation through the Civil War*. Vol. 1. Oberlin, OH: R. R. Donnelley & Sons, 1943.

Fogel, Robert William. *Without Consent or Contract: The Rise and Fall of American Slavery*. New York: W. W. Norton, 1989.

Fogel, Robert, and Stanley Engerman. *Time on the Cross: The Economics of American Negro Slavery*. Boston: Little, Brown, and Co., 1974.

Foner, Philip S. *History of Black Americans: From Africa to the Emergence of the Cotton Kingdom*. Westport, CT: Greenwood, 1975.

Ford, Lacy K. *Deliver Us from Evil: The Slavery Question in the Old South*. New York: Oxford University Press, 2009.

Frederickson, George M. *William Lloyd Garrison*. Englewood Cliffs, NJ: Prentice-Hall, 1968.

Ginzberg, Lori D. *Elizabeth Cady Stanton*. New York: Hill & Wang, 2009.

Goodheart, Lawrence B. *Abolitionist, Actuary, Atheist: Elizur Wright and the Reform Impulse*. Kent, OH: Kent State University Press, 1990.

Goodman, Paul. *Of One Blood: Abolitionism and the Origins of Racial Equality*. Berkeley: University of California Press, 1998.

Hagedorn, Ann. *Beyond the River: The Untold Story of the Heroes of the Underground Railroad*. New York: Simon & Schuster, 2002.

Harris, N. Dwight. *The History of Negro Servitude in Illinois and of the Slavery Agitation in that State, 1719–1864*. Chicago: A. C. McClurg, 1904.

Hicks, Mary K. *Escape on the Pearl*. New York: HarperCollins, 2007.

Hochschild, Adam. *Bury the Chains, Prophets and Rebels in the Fight to Free an Empire's Slaves.* New York: First Mariner, 2005.

Horton, James Oliver, and Lois E. Horton. *Slavery and the Making of America.* New York: Oxford University Press, 2005.

Howe, Daniel Walker. *What Hath God Wrought: The Transformation of America 1815–1840.* New York: Oxford University Press, 2004.

Hudson, J. Blaine. *Encyclopedia of the Underground Railroad.* Jefferson, NC: McFarland, 2006.

Hume, John F. *Abolitionists.* New York: G. P. Putnam's Sons, 1905.

Jeffrey, Julie Roy. *The Great Silent Army of Abolitionism: Ordinary Women in the Antislavery Movement.* Chapel Hill: University of North Carolina Press, 1998.

Julius, Kevin C. *The Abolitionist Decade, 1829–1838: A Year-By-Year History of Early Events in the Antislavery Movement.* Jefferson, NC: McFarland, 2004.

Kennedy, Inez A. *Reflections of the Pioneers of Lee County.* Dixon, IL: Inez A. Kennedy, 1893.

Kolchin, Peter. *American Slavery, 1619–1877.* New York: Hill & Wang, 1993.

Kraditor, Aileen S. *Means and Ends in American Abolitionism: Garrison and His Critics on Strategy and Tactics, 1834–1850.* New York: Random House, 1967.

Kuhns, Frederick I. *The American Home Missionary Society in Relation to the Antislavery Controversy in the Old Northwest.* Ann Arbor, MI: Edwards Brothers, 1959.

Lader, Lawrence. *The Bold Brahmins: New England's War Against Slavery, 1831–1863.* Westport, CT: Greenwood Press, 1973.

Laurie, Bruce. *Beyond Garrison: Antislavery and Social Reform.* New York: Cambridge University Press, 2005.

Lerner, Gerda. *The Grimke Sisters from South Carolina: Rebels against Slavery.* Boston: Houghton Mifflin, 1967.

Lesick, Lawrence T. *The Lane Rebels: Evangelicalism and Antislavery in Antebellum America.* Metuchen, NJ: Scarecrow Press, 1980.

Lumpkin, Katharine, D. *The Emancipation of Angelina Grimke.* Chapel Hill: University of North Carolina Press, 1974.

Macy, Jesse. *The Anti-Slavery Crusade.* New Haven, CT: Yale University Press, 1920.

Magdol, Edward. *The Antislavery Rank and File: A Social Profile of the Abolitionists' Constituency.* Westport, CT: Greenwood Press, 1986.

_____. *Owen Lovejoy: Abolitionist in Congress.* New Brunswick, NJ: Rutgers University Press, 1967.

Mandel, Bernard. *Labor: Free and Slave, Workingmen and the Anti-Slavery Movement in the United States.* New York: Associated Authors, 1955.

Marryat, Frederick. *A Diary in America: With Remarks on Its Institutions.* NewYork: Alfred. A. Knopf, 1962.

Mayer, Henry. *All on Fire: William Lloyd Garrison and the Abolition of Slavery.* New York: St. Martin's Press, 1998.

McKivigan, John R. *The War against Proslavery Religion: Abolitionism and the Northern Churches, 1830–1865.* Ithaca, NY: Cornell University Press, 1984.

McKivigan, John R., and Stanley Harrold, eds. *Antislavery Violence: Sectional, Racial, and Cultural Conflict in Antebellum America.* Knoxville: University of Tennessee Press, 1999.

McPherson, James M. *Battle Cry of Freedom.* New York: Oxford University Press, 1988.

Miller, William Lee. *Arguing about Slavery.* New York: Alfred A. Knopf, 1996.

Morgan, Kenneth. *Slavery in America: A Reader and Guide.* Athens: University of Georgia Press, 2005.

Morison, Samuel Eliot. *The Oxford History of the American People.* New York: Oxford University Press, 1965.

Muelder, Hermann R. *Fighters for Freedom: A History of Anti-Slavery Activities of Men and Women Associated with Knox College.* New York: Columbia University Press, 1959.

Muelder, Owen W. *The Underground Railroad in Western Illinois.* Jefferson, NC: McFarland, 2008.

Mull, Carol E. *The Underground Railroad in Michigan.* Jefferson, NC: McFarland, 2010.

Nash, Gary B. *Forging Freedom, The Formation of Philadelphia's Black Community, 1720–1840*. Cambridge, MA: Harvard University Press, 1988.

Nye, Russel B. *The Cultural Life of the New Nation, 1776–1830*. New York: Harper, 1960.

_____. *William Lloyd Garrison and the Humanitarian Reformers*. Boston: Little, Brown and Co., 1955.

Oakes, James. *Slavery and Freedom: An Interpretation of the Old South*. New York: Alfred A. Knopf, 1990.

Okrent, Daniel. *Last Call: The Rise and Fall of Prohibition*. New York: Scribner, 2010.

Pease, Jane H., and William H. Pease. *Bound with Them in Chains: A Biographical History of the Antislavery Movement*. Westport, CT: Greenwood, 1972.

Perry, Lewis. *Radical Abolitionism: Anarchy and the Government of God in Antislavery Thought*. 1973. Reprint, Knoxville: University of Tennessee Press, 1995.

_____, and Michael Fellman, eds. *Antislavery Reconsidered: New Perspectives on the Abolitionists*. Baton Rouge: Louisiana State University Press, 1979.

Phillips, Ulrich B. *American Negro Slavery*. New York: D. Appleton and Co., 1928.

Pickard, Samuel T. *Life and Letters of John Greenleaf Whittier*. Vols. 1 and 2. Boston: Houghton Mifflin, 1907.

Pollard, John A. *John Greenleaf Whittier: Friend of Man*. Boston: Houghton Mifflin, 1969.

Quarles, Benjamin. *Black Abolitionists*. New York: Oxford University Press, 1969.

Ramsdell, George M. *History of Milford, 1838–1901*. Concord, NH: Rumford Press, 1901.

Randall, J. G. *The Civil War and Reconstruction*. 1937. Reprint Boston: D. C. Heath, 1953.

Richards, Leonard L. *"Gentlemen of Property and Standing": Anti-Abolition Mobs in Jacksonian America*. New York: Oxford University Press, 1970.

Ricks, Mary Kay. *Escape on the Pearl*. New York: Harper Collins, 2007.

Robertson, Stacey M. *Hearts Beating for Liberty*. Chapel Hill: University of North Carolina Press, 2010.

_____. *Parker Pillsbury: Radical Abolitionist, Male Feminist*. Ithaca, NY: Cornell University Press, 2000.

Ruchames, Louis. *The Abolitionists: A Collection of their Writings*. New York: G. P. Putnam's Sons, 1963.

Rutkoff, Peter, and William B. Scott. *Fly Away: The Great African American Cultural Migrations*. Baltimore: John Hopkins Press, 2010.

Salerno, Beth. *Sister Societies: Women's Antislavery Organizations in Antebellum America*. DeKalb: Northern Illinois University Press, 2005.

Schneider, Dorothy, and Carl J. Schneider. *Slavery in America from Colonial Times to the Civil War*. New York: Facts on File, 2000

Scudder, Horace E. *The Complete Poetical Works of John Greenleaf Whittier*. Boston: Houghton Mifflin, 1894.

Sernett, Milton C. *North Star Country: Upstate New York and the Crusade for African American Freedom*. Syracuse, NY: Syracuse University Press, 2002.

Siebert, Wilbur Henry. *The Mysteries of Ohio's Underground Railroad*. Columbus, OH: Long's College Book Co., 1951.

_____. *The Underground Railroad from Slavery to Freedom*. New York: Macmillan, 1898.

Simms, Henry H. *Emotions at High Tide: Abolition as a Controversial Factor, 1830–1845*. Richmond: William Bird Press, 1960.

Smedley, R. C. *History of the Underground Railroad in Chester and the Neighboring Counties in Pennsylvania*. Lancaster, PA: Office of the Journal, 1883.

Spears, John R. *The American Slave Trade*. New York: Charles Scribner's Sons, 1900.

Stanton, Henry B. *Random Reflections*. New York: 1887.

Stephenson, Nathaniel W. *Texas and the Mexican War: A Chronicle of the Winning of the Southwest*. New Haven, CT: Yale University Press, 1921.

Sterling, Dorothy. *Ahead of Her Time: Abby Kelley and the Politics of Antislavery*. New York: W. W. Norton, 1991.

_____. *Turning the World Upside Down: The Anti-Slavery Convention of American Women, Held in New York, May 9–12, 1837.* New York: The Feminist Press at the City University of New York, 1987.

_____. *We Are Your Sisters: Black Women in the Nineteenth Century.* New York: W. W. Norton, 1984.

Stewart, James Brewer. *Abolitionist Politics and the Coming of the Civil War.* Amherst: University of Massachusetts Press, 2008.

_____. *Holy Warriors: The Abolitionists and American Slavery.* New York: Hill & Wang, 1976.

Tannenbaum, Frank. *Slave and Citizen: The Negro in the Americas.* New York: Random House, 1963.

Tappan, Lewis. *The Life of Arthur Tappan.* Cambridge: Hurd and Houghton, 1871. Reprint, New York: Arno, 1970.

Thomas, Benjamin P. *Theodore Weld: Crusader for Freedom.* New Brunswick, NJ: Rutgers University Press, 1950.

Thompson, C. Bradley, ed. *Antislavery Political Writing, 1833–1860.* Armonk, NY: M. E. Sharpe, 2004.

Todd, Lewis P., and Merle Curti. *Rise of the American Nation.* New York: Harcourt, Brace, & World, 1964.

Walker, Peter F. *Moral Choices: Memory, Desire, and Imagination in Nineteenth Century American Abolition.* Baton Rouge: Louisiana State University Press, 1978.

Walters, Ronald G. *The Antislavery Appeal: American Abolitionism After 1830.* Baltimore: John Hopkins University Press, 1976.

Washington, Margaret. *Sojourner Truth's America.* Urbana: University of Illinois Press, 2009.

Weld, Theodore D. *American Slavery As It Is: Testimony of a Thousand Witnesses.* New York: American Anti-Slavery Society, 1839.

Wellman, Judith. *Grass Roots Reform in the Burned-Over District of Upstate New York.* New York: Garland, 2000.

Whittier, John Greenleaf. *Old Portraits, Modern Sketches, Personal Sketches and Tributes Complete.* Vol. 6, *The Works of Whittier, 1807–1892.* Project Gutenberg, 2005. http://www.gutenberg.org/catalog/world/readfile?fk_files=1823495.

Wolf, Hazel C. *On Freedom's Altar: The Martyr Complex in the Abolition Movement.* Madison: University of Wisconsin Press, 1952.

Wood, Betty. *The Origins of American Slavery: Freedom and Bondage in the English Colonies.* New York: Hill & Wang, 1997.

Wood, Gordon S. *Empire of Liberty: A History of the Early Republic, 1789–1815.* New York: Oxford University Press, 2009.

Wyatt-Brown, Bertram. *Lewis Tappan and His Evangelical War Against Slavery.* Cleveland, OH: Press of Case Western Reserve University, 1969.

Yacovone, Donald. *Samuel Joseph May and the Dilemmas of the Liberal Persuasion, 1797–1871.* Philadelphia: Temple University Press, 1991.

Zinn, Howard. *A People's History of the United States 1492–Present.* New York: Harper Perennial, 1995.

Scholarly Journals and Newpaper Articles

American Anti-Slavery Society. *The Anti-Slavery Examiner* 1–6 (1836–1838). Collection later published in 1970 Negro University Press.

Dillon, Merton L. "The Failure of the American Abolitionists." *The Journal of Southern History* 25, no. 2 (May 1959).

Hammond, H. L. "The Gravel Debate: An Anti-Slavery Reminiscence." *Advance Supplement* (Chicago), April 28, 1870.

Myers, John L. "American Anti-Slavery Society Agents and the Free Negro, 1833–1838." *The Journal of Negro History* 52 (July 1967): 200–219.

_____. "Anti-Slavery Activities of Five Lane Seminary Boys in 1835–1836." *Historical and Philosophical Society of Ohio Bulletin* 21 (April 1963): 95–111.

_____. "Anti-Slavery Agents in Rhode Island, 1832–1835." *Rhode Island History* 29 (August 1970): 82–93.

_____. "Anti-Slavery Agents in Rhode Island, 1835–1837." *Rhode Island History* 30 (February 1971): 21–31.

_____. "The Beginning of Anti-Slavery Agencies in Vermont, 1832–1836." *Vermont Historical Society* 36, no. 3 (Summer 1968): 126–141.

_____. "The Beginnings of Anti-Slavery Agencies in New Hampshire, 1832–1835." *Historical New Hampshire* 25 (Fall 1970): 3–25.

_____. "The Early Anti-Slavery Agency System in Pennsylvania, 1833–1837." *Pennsylvania History* 21 (January 1964): 62–204.

_____. "The Major Effects of Anti-Slavery Agencies in New Hampshire, 1835–1837." *Historical New Hampshire* 26 (Fall 1971): 3–27.

_____. "The Major Effort of National Anti-Slavery Agents in New York State, 1836–1837." *New York History: Quarterly Journal of the New York State Historical Association* 46 (April 1965): 162–186.

_____. "The Major Efforts of Anti-Slavery Agents in Vermont, 1836–1838." *Vermont Historical Society* 36, no. 4 (Fall 1968): 214–229.

_____. "Organization of 'The Seventy': To Arouse the North Against Slavery." *Mid-American: An Historical Review* 42 (1966): 29–46.

Roth, Randolph A. "The First Radical Abolitionists: The Reverend James Milligan and the Reformed Presbyterians of Vermont." *The New England Quarterly* 55, no. 4 (December 1982): 540–563.

Ryan, John H. "A Chapter of the History of the Underground Railroad in Illinois." *Journal of the Illinois Historical Society* 8, no. 1 (April 1915): 23–27.

Skotheim, Robert Allen. "A Note on Historical Method: David Donald's 'Toward a Reconsideration of Abolitionists.'" *The Journal of Southern History* 25, no. 3 (August 1959): 356–365.

Snyder, Terri L. "Suicide, Slavery, and Memory in North America." *The Journal of American History* 97, no. 1: 39–62.

Anti-Slavery Society Reports

First Annual Report of the American Anti-Slavery Society: With Speeches Delivered at the Anniversary Meeting, Held in Chatham-Street Chapel in the city of New-York, on the Sixth of May, 1834, and the Minutes of the Meetings of the Society for Business. New York: Door and Butterfield, 1834.

Second Annual Report of the American Anti-Slavery Society: With the Speeches Delivered at the Anniversary Meeting, Held in the City of New-York on the 12th May, 1835, and the Minutes of the Meetings of the Society for Business. New York: William S. Door, 1835.

Third Annual Report of the American Anti-Slavery Society: With the Speeches Delivered at the Anniversary Meeting, Held in the City of New-York on the 10th May, 1835, and the Minutes of the Meetings of the Society for Business. New York: William S. Door, 1836.

Fourth Annual Report of the American Anti-Slavery Society: Held in the City of New York on the 9th May, 1837M, and the Minutes of the Meetings of the Society for Business. New York: William S. Door, 1837.

Fifth Annual Report of the Executive Committee of the American Anti-Slavery Society: With the Minutes of the Meetings of the Society for Business, and the Speeches Delivered at the Anniversary Meeting on the 8th May, 1838. New York: William S. Door, 1838.

Sixth Annual Report of the Executive Committee of the American Anti-Slavery Society: With the Speeches Delivered at the Anniversary Meeting Held in the City of New-York, on the 7th of May, 1839, and the Minutes of the Meetings of the Society for Business. New York: William S. Door, 1839.

Seventh Annual Report of the American Anti-Slavery Society, May 1840, and the Minutes of the Meetings of the Society for Business. New York: American Anti-Slavery Society, 1840.

Letters

Emma Chapin to Wilbur Siebert, June 11, 1896, Siebert Collection in UGRR Ohio Historical Society.

Rev. J. S. T. Milligan to Wilbur Siebert (n.d.), Siebert Collection in UGRR Ohio Historical Society.

Hiram Foote to Theodore Weld, Sept. 20, 1866. Weld-Grimke papers, Manuscript Division, William L. Clements Library, University of Michigan.

Newspapers

Emancipator, December 15, 1836.
Friend of Man, December 22, 1836.
Friend of Man, December 29, 1836.
Friend of Man, January 5, 1837.
Friend of Man, January 19, 1837.
Friend of Man, May 24, 1837.
Friend of Man, May 31, 1837.
Geneseo Reporter, July 18, 1913.
The Liberator, January 1, 1831.
The Liberator, August 13, 1836.
The Liberator, December 17, 1836.
Knoxville *Republican,* Nov. 30, 1859.
Signal of Liberty, May 12, 1841.

Doctoral Dissertations

Myers, John L. "The Agency System of the Anti-Slavery Movement, 1832–1837, and its Antecedents in Other Benevolent and Reform Societies." PhD diss., University of Michigan, 1961.

Internet Sources

John G. Whittier. "'The Anti-slavery Convention of 1833,' 1874." The Abolitionist. http://afgen.com/slavery5.html.

"Officers of the American Anti-Slavery Society, 1833–1840." American Abolitionism. http://americanabolitionist.liberalarts.iupui.edu/officers%20of%20the%20american%20anti%20slavery%20society%201833%2040.htm.

"A Tribute to James G. Birney," 1863. Samuel J. May Anti-Slavery Collection. http://dlxs2.library.cornell.edu/cgi/t/text/pageviewer-idx?c=mayantislavery&cc=mayantislavery&idno=16855302&frm=frameset&view=image&seq=3.

Miscellaneous Documents

North Country Underground Railroad Historical Association, Plattsburg, New York.
Unidentified newspaper, no date, obituary. "Theodore Dwight Weld Dead — One of the Early

Abolitionists — Dies at Hyde Park at the Great Age of 91." Weld Family Papers, Ron August, Jr., Wilmington, DE.

Speeches

Memorial service upon 74th birthday of Wendell Phillips, held at the residence of William Summer Crosby, no. 517 Broadway, South Boston, November 29, 1885.

Songs

Chapman, Maria Weston. *Songs of the Free and Hymns of Christian Freedom.* Boston: I. Knapp, 1836.

Index

abolitionism: theological basis for 10–11, 13, 23, 41, 122, 123–25, 139, 168; women in 17–18, 28–31, 74, 75, 91, 96, 148, 151, 157

abolitionists 42–43; advocating violence 33, 84, 97; black 8, 17, 19, 32, 33, 77, 169; and churches 12–13, 71, 80, 81, 87–88, 167–68; conservative vs. radical 31–32, 44–45; pacifism of 16, 33, 73, 76, 91, 97, 144, 166; and politics 22–23, 33–34, 48, 70, 71, 79; and temperance 14, 70, 72, 73, 74, 75, 77, 81, 82, 94, 97, 99, 133, 167; violent attacks against 5, 6, 10, 16, 17, 18, 19, 21–22, 23, 38, 45–46, 65–66, 71, 72, 75, 76, 78, 82, 86, 87, 90, 94, 123, 146

Adams, John Quincy 25, 33, 62, 65, 75, 120, 166

African American Presbyterian Church 33

Allan, James 71, 128

Allan, William T. 60, 69–70, 71, 85, 127–32; account of slavery 100–102

Allen, George 98

Alvord, J. W. 60

American and Foreign Anti-Slavery Society 31, 33, 66, 70, 91, 92

American Anti-Slavery Almanac 19, 88

American Anti-Slavery Examiner 19

American Anti-Slavery Society 5, 7, 8, 23; agents' convention 39, 60–62, 68–69, 76, 78; blacks in 8, 19, 32, 33, 169; constitution 184–88; Declaration of Sentiments 9, 20, 157, 170, 180–84; decline of 27, 31–32, 35, 47–48; fundraising 17, 19, 20, 27, 32, 41, 61, 77, 94, 98, 157, 173; nonviolent principles 9; publications 18–19, 22, 23, 32, 41; rural strategy 45, 46–47; seventy agents 36, 47–52, 58, 59, 61; tactics 21, 27, 38–39, 41, 145, 157; and Underground Railroad 25–26; women in 31, 85, 148; and youth 18–19, 71, 97

American Anti-Slavery Society local auxiliaries 10, 23–24, 27, 41, 45, 94, 146, 157; Canada 90, 95; Connecticut 73, 75, 87, 92; Illinois 41, 69, 74, 76, 77, 81, 127; Indiana 84, 93, 95; Iowa 76; Kentucky 71; Maine 74, 85, 87, 91; Massachusetts 73, 75, 76, 79, 84, 88, 92, 96, 97, 151; Michigan 70, 75, 94, 95; New Hampshire 79, 84, 85, 86, 87, 89, 96; New Jersey 82; New York 20, 71, 72, 73, 75, 76, 82, 83, 84, 85, 87, 88, 89–90, 91, 93, 94, 97, 161; Ohio 57–58, 76, 77, 82, 83, 84, 85, 86, 91, 93, 95, 98; Pennsylvania 72, 73, 75, 76, 77, 80, 81, 83, 87, 96, 97, 164–65; Rhode Island 70, 71, 73, 76, 77, 80, 83, 87, 88, 89, 97; Vermont 74, 80, 81, 87, 95–96; Wisconsin 74, 82

American Colonization Society 15, 16, 61, 72, 173, 176

American Freedman's Union Commission 81

American Home Missionary Society 11–12, 70, 82

American Missionary Society 87, 91

American Slavery As It Is 64, 95, 100–25, 159–60

Amistad incident 32–33

Anti-Slavery Bugle 79, 86

Anti-Slavery Mission Institute 33

anti-slavery petitions 18, 62–63, 72

Anti-Slavery Reporter 157

anti-slavery societies 3–4, 7, 16; blacks in 8, 17, 19, 32, 33, 169; women in 17–18, 31, 85, 148, 151, 157; *see also* names of specific societies

Anti-Slavery Standard 81

Avery, Courtland 98